Teishinkōki

Suzaku Avenue and the Suzaku Gate of the Heian Palace Precincts

Teishinkōki

The Year 939 in the Journal of
Regent Fujiwara no Tadahira

Edited by

Joan R. Piggott

and

Yoshida Sanae

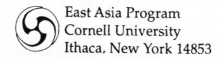

East Asia Program
Cornell University
Ithaca, New York 14853

The Cornell East Asia Series is published by the Cornell University East Asia Program (distinct from Cornell University Press). We publish affordably priced books on a variety of scholarly topics relating to East Asia as a service to the academic community and the general public. Standing orders, which provide for automatic notification and invoicing of each title in the series upon publication, are accepted.

If after review by internal and external readers a manuscript is accepted for publication, it is published on the basis of camera-ready copy provided by the volume author. Each author is thus responsible for any necessary copy-editing and for manuscript formatting. Address submission inquiries to CEAS Editorial Board, East Asia Program, Cornell University, Ithaca, New York 14853-7601.

Number 140 in the Cornell East Asia Series
Copyright © 2008 by Joan R. Piggott and Yoshida Sanae. All rights reserved
ISSN 1050-2955
ISBN: 978-1-933947-10-5 hc
ISBN: 978-1-933947-40-2 pb
Library of Congress Control Number: 2008926176
Printed in the United States of America
24 23 22 21 20 19 18 17 16 15 14 13 12 11 10 09 08   9 8 7 6 5 4 3 2 1

⊚ The paper in this book meets the requirements for permanence of ISO 9706:1994.

Contents

Maps and Figures

FOREWORD
Joan R. Piggott

In Summer 2000, ten members of the fourth Cornell Kanbun Workshop met for 28 days in the East Asia Program Seminar Room at Cornell University to read Heian-period courtier journals under the co-leadership of myself and Professor Yoshida Sanae of the University of Tokyo's Historiographical Institute (Shiryō hensanjo).

Wiebke Denecke	Harvard University	Literature
Aileen Gatten	University of Michigan	Literature
Edward Kamens	Yale University	Literature
Robert Khan	University of Texas	Literature
Christina Laffin	Columbia University	Literature
Thomas Nelson	Cambridge University	History
David Quinter	Stanford University	Religious Studies
Takeshi Watanabe	Yale University	Literature

I had known Professor Yoshida for some years, and had occasionally participated in her *Chūyūki* seminar at the Shiryō hensanjo. I invited her to lead the fourth workshop with me because I had always dreamed that more Westerners interested in the Heian Period could have an opportunity to learn to read, translate, and annotate such courtier journals. I also hoped that readers outside Japan—including those who could never invest in the ten-plus years of language and historical training required for reading such texts in the original—could read translations and learn more about what Heian courtiers like Prince Genji and Tōnochūjō in *The Tale of Genji* might actually have done with their days besides courting ladies, writing morning-after poems, playing musical instruments, and dancing for royal banquets. Reading even a few selections from extant Heian courtier journals leaves no doubt whatever that court leaders certainly did much more.

As the workshop proceeded through the late days of July, Professor Yoshida skillfully and patiently introduced all of us to the new world these journals open up. She began with selections from the Year 939 in the *Teishinkōki*, the journal of the early regent, Fujiwara no Tadahira (880-949). Its entries cover the years from 907 to 948, although some years are now missing from our text, which is actually a digest of Tadahira's original. Known as the *Teishinkōkishō*, this digest was likely made for the personal use of Tadahira's son and heir, Fujiwara no Saneyori (900-970).

Originally Professor Yoshida intended to have the group read selections from *Teishinkōki*, which she chose as our introduction for its early date and the relative spareness of its entries. We were then to move on to selections from later journals, including Fujiwara no Sanesuke's *Shōyūki* and Fujiwara no Munetada's *Chūyūki*. The latter is a text of special interest to Professor Yoshida, since she is editing and annotating its publication in multiple volumes in the *Dai Nihon kokiroku* series of courtier journals published by the Shiryō hensanjo. She knows it very well indeed.

As we slowly made our way through Tadahira's early entries in the year 939, and came thereby to understand something of how this court leader spent his days and nights, we found it difficult to move on. Before we finally began reading Munetada's *Chūyūki*, we had read eight months of entries and gained a multitude of insights into Tadahira's role as regent for the young, but by then adult Suzaku Tennō (923-952, r. 930-946). We also had gained a much better sense of the operation of the tenth-century court and its bureaucracy, and understood the centrality of its annual calendar of rites (*nenjūgyōji*). We had a better appreciation of Buddhist practice both at court and in the lives of nobles like Tadahira, and how religious prohibitions—some would call them superstitions—were potent influences in noble lives of the time. We got to know the geography of Tadahira's capital and its environs as Tadahira moved around them. Finally, while most of us had read the *Shōmonki*, a chronicle that describes the rebellion of the warrior Taira no Masakado (?-940) against Kyoto's provincial administration in eastern Japan during the late 930s, Tadahira's record provided us with a Kyōto-based perspective on the violence. It provides clues as to why in the end the court chose to use local warriors, rather than an expeditionary force from the capital, to defeat Masakado.

When the time came to move on to other journals, at our communal lunch one day a plan began—whose idea was it first, I wonder?—to finish reading, translating, and annotating the rest of the months of Year 939, in hopes that it could be published. We foresaw that the resulting volume would serve the interests of multiple audiences: those who want to know something about Fujiwara no Tadahira as regent, as well as his courtly world; those who want to know more about the form and character of a Heian courtier journal; those who want to expand their *kanbun* reading skills to include such texts; and those who want to practice reading a hand-written (rather than printed) text, with the aid of a printed text. As the plan took more mature form, we anticipated that historians, literature specialists, historians of religion, linguists, and art historians all would find the volume useful. Since then, scholars in Japan too have become more interested in the project, as they have come to comprehend the value of the translation process itself—finding *le mot juste* for a translation demands a very good understanding of what is being translated. Our group has experienced some wonderful times working together on this project, in such varied venues as Ithaca, New Haven, New York, Chicago, Tokyo, and Kyoto. But there have been some rousing debates as well, as specialists from different scholarly fields have struggled to turn Tadahira's cryptic entries into readable and informative English with adequate contextualization. We look forward to the glossary in this volume being added to the super-glossary of the Japan Memory Project, accessible through the website of the Historiographical Institute. It will greatly expand the coverage of their Online Database, which is readily accessible to researchers around the globe.

Following the end of that workshop in 2000, during 2001 a smaller group of participants residing on the east coast met several times at Columbia University in New York City to finish the translation (Kamens, Laffin, Piggott, Watanabe). Then, during 2002 we met again at the national meeting of the Association for Asian Studies to rethink difficult sections and to begin the editing process. And finally in the summer of 2002 the Council for East Asian Studies at Yale University hosted a group of us (Gatten, Kamens, Nelson, Piggott, Quinter), including Professor Yoshida, at Yale in New Haven for a full week, during which we more or less finished editing our translation. Still there was more to be done: the annotation was checked and expanded; the transcription (*kakikudashi*) was completed; maps, charts, glossaries, and indices were made. It was also decided that the two editors would write contextualizing essays for the volume.

Since 2002 major career moves that have included the fashioning of a new graduate program and library collection at the University of Southern California have intervened in my life. Additional Kanbun Workshops, four of them at USC, have come and gone. Now it is plum-viewing season once again, on the verge of spring in 2008. I am delighted at last to be able to complete this manuscript, and to thank the participants, universities, libraries, and foundations whose help made this project possible. And I am very glad to send this manuscript back to press at the very university where the hard work began.

Meanwhile, the team that completed the project is scattered across the globe, but many of us are anticipating another Heian Journals Workshop. I'm ready. . . .

* * * * *

To the Reader, How To Use This Book

Different readers will pick up this volume with different objectives. Some will want to begin with the contextualizing essays in the front of the volume. Others will go straight to the translation. Our translation group imagined that some readers would start with the *Dai Nihon kokiroku* Sino-Japanese text of the Year 939 in the *Teishinkōki* itself, using the notes, maps, figures, classical Japanese transcription, and glossaries. Following the annotated English translation are materials such as a reproduction of the *Tenri toshokan zenpon sōsho* text of the *Teishinkōkishō*, included here for those readers who want to see the hand-brushed manuscript in facsimile. Following that, interested readers will find a chronology of Tadahira's life, two glossaries (one specifically for names), an index of names and terms found in specific entries of the Year 939 in the *Teishinkōki*, and a general bibliography of works cited in the book.

PREFACE

Edward Kamens

There is much to be learned by reading a Heian-period courtier's journal such as Teishinkōkishō, and there is much to be learned in the process of learning *how* to read such a journal. That was my assumption when I made plans to participate in the fourth "Kanbun Workshop" at Cornell University in the summer of 2000. Professor Joan Piggott, now of the University of Southern California, had been organizing, hosting, and participating in these workshops since 1997, and many graduate students and other scholars had already benefited from these opportunities to practice close reading of pre-modern texts and documents in "kanbun" (or, as some would prefer to call it, "Sino-Japanese" or "court Chinese," or just "Chinese") with the guidance of outstanding scholars visiting from the Historiographical Institute of the University of Tokyo and other institutions. The summer 2000 workshop would focus on texts of a period of particular interest to me—the tenth and eleventh centuries—and, specifically, two especially important journals, Fujiwara no Tadahira's Teishinkōkishō and Fujiwara no Munetada's Chūyūki. So I was confident that a month devoted to their study would be more than worthwhile. It certainly proved to be so.

The workshop's visiting expert instructor that year was Professor Yoshida Sanae of the Historiographical Institute, the leader of the team preparing the authoritative edition of Chūyūki in the Dai Nihon kokiroku series. The participants were Wiebke Denecke, Aileen Gatten, Christina Laffin, Robert Khan, Thomas Nelson, David Quinter, Takeshi Watanabe and myself. About mid-way through that session, we began to discuss the idea of publishing a polished version of some part of the work that we had accomplished together, as a way of demonstrating the challenges and rewards of reading, and learning to read, such texts as those to which we were devoting our full attention on those summer days and nights. The workshops themselves were initiated by Joan Piggott to address the paucity of opportunities for American graduate students to learn and practice *kanbun* reading anywhere other than in Japan. (Workshops of this kind have since taken place at Yale University, the University of

Chicago, Stanford University, the University of British Columbia, and the University of Southern California.) Likewise, it was our idea that such a publication would create a tangible record of what we had gleaned from our labors and provide substantive demonstration that such work can throw new light on a variety of materials. It would also open insights of real interest to scholars in many fields of study, including history, literature, religion, and history of art. Indeed we have found that such team-work is especially fruitful when specialists from these diverse disciplines work together, as we did then and in several later post-workshop gatherings of sub-sets of the original group, as we continued through the stages of revision and editing that have led to the appearance of this book. All along the way, the sustained interest and vision of book designer Arnie Olds has helped to keep us moving toward the realization of our vision for this volume.

Until relatively recently, the study of journals such as Fujiwara no Tadahira's *Teishinkōki* was almost exclusively the domain of scholars of history. But especially during the time that this publication of our annotated reading of a year's entries from this journal has been in preparation, the relationship of such journals, which were written in a special, localized style of Chinese, to other kinds of journal and diary writings of the times—many of which are more familiar and accessible, and which have long been treated as exemplars of Heian literary culture—has come under increased scrutiny. This book is but one of several that will appear at around the same time that should provide scholars and students interested in examining this relationship with some new perspectives. It will also join a number of recent and forthcoming publications that open windows onto many aspects of the political, social, and cultural practices of Heian Japan.

That world was, among other things, a world of many different kinds of written texts, created by many different hands for a variety of audiences. A good number of the so-called poetic diaries and other kinds of journals written by women in what we think of as "classical" or "vernacular" Japanese—such as *Kagerō nikki* (The Gossamer Journal, ca. 974), *Izumi Shikibu nikki* (The Diary of Izumi Shikibu, ca. 1007), *Murasaki shikibu nikki* (The Diary of Murasaki Shikibu, ca. 1010), and *Sarashina nikki* (The Sarashina Diary, ca. 1060)—have long been available in modern editions and in English translation. Another acknowledged "classic," *Makura no sōshi* (The Pillow Book of Sei Shōnagon, ca. 1004-12), has many journal-like entries that provide good reason to associate it with these texts as well. Recently, Joshua S. Mostow has published a volume of translations of earlier Heian-period journals by male writers who used and developed this same "vernacular" mode (see his *At the House of Gathered Leaves*). But little if any of the rich corpus of Heian "*kanbun* journals" has been available in translation or in a format accessible to those at the beginning stages of such study, with the exception of Francine Hérail's magisterial French translations of two important *kanbun* journals of this period, *Midō kanpakuki* (*Notes journalières de Fujiwara no Michinaga*) and *Shunki* (*Notes journalières de Fujiwara no Sukefusa*). This publication of a portion of *Teishinkōki* is a small step in that challenging direction.

For me, the study of this and other similar journals is most rewarding as an encounter with yet another of the languages and forms of Heian text, one adapted in particular ways for the purpose of preserving memories. For others, as Joan Piggott's essay herein shows, it offers rich data for understanding the institutional, ritual, and even some of the personal dimensions of the workings of the court aristocracy in very immediate ways. Though it is not a complete translation of Tadahira's journal, the team that has created this book hopes that this representative excerpt (of what is itself a book of excerpts or abstracts, as Yoshida Sanae explains in her essay herein) will be a valuable addition to a growing library of resources in English that lead the way toward deeper and broader exploration of *kanbun* courtier journals and many other related texts. The glossed readings, notes, glossaries, and other apparatus included in the book are meant to show the paths we followed as we worked with the text. But they also demonstrate that many more such paths are there to be traced out by those who would make the effort. We who have worked on this portion of *Teishinkōkishō* in this way have found that effort, and our experience of working in such a team, especially rewarding. We hope that others with similar interests will strike out further along these paths that we have only begun to explore.

ARISTOCRATIC JOURNALS AND THE COURTLY CALENDAR:

The Context of Fujiwara no Tadahira's Teishinkōki

YOSHIDA SANAE

In the early Heian Period (794-1185) many sorts of daily records were kept by officials or travellers, and there are fragments of personal daily records from the eighth century in the Shōsōin archives. But it was in the ninth and tenth centuries, when regents (sesshō) and chiefs-of-staff (kanpaku) from the Northern Fujiwara family led the court, that monarchs (tennō) and leading aristocrats began keeping personal journals and passing them down to their progeny.

There are several reasons why the practice of keeping a journal came to be increasingly esteemed from the tenth century onward. As the ritsuryō system changed and matured, there was a widening gulf between ritsuryō ideals and actual social conditions, and it became increasingly difficult to ignore real problems. In matters both political and ritual there was need for individual judgments according to specific circumstances. As a result, rather than looking to rules spelled out in the ritsuryō codes or supplementary legislation (kyaku), aristocrats responsible for carrying out governance contemplated precedents that might be applied to a given case at hand. At such moments detailed records of past behavior, both ceremonial and administrative, became critical reference material.

Furthermore, development of what might be called an "inner court"—focused on the tennō as a person rather than as an institution—advanced from the ninth century onward. Activities of governance became more and more centered around the throne itself, and ceremonial and administration merged. This trend is represented by the emergence of rule by the regent or the chief-of-staff. They served as representatives or aides to the tennō in all matters and their offices were actually based outside the Council of State (Daijōkan). At the same time, ceremonies that had been imported from the Chinese court to become rites of the Japanese court were reorganized into an annual ritual calendar (nenjūgyōji), and participation therein was limited to holders of the highest ranks.

Among the important political changes that took place during the period between the move to Heiankyō and the establishment of regency government in the mid-ninth century was the progressive narrowing of court leadership, excluding for the most part all but members of the Northern branch of the Fujiwara family and the royally derived Minamoto. These aristocrats were divided into lineages (*ie*) that competed to ensure their hold on court leadership. In an environment where increasingly elaborate ceremonial and protocol were becoming ever more basic to courtly life, reference to precedent became increasingly valuable to them.

These changes took place so rapidly and extensively that the compilation of public records could not catch up. Production of official records ended with the compilation of the Ritual Protocols of the Engi Era (*Engi gishiki*) in the early tenth century. Thereafter, official compilations were replaced by individually authored handbooks for use by the author and his heirs. The same tendency can be seen in the production of official histories. After the completion of the Records of Three Royal Reigns (*Sandai jitsuroku*) in 901, no further official histories were completed.

The appearance of daily journals written by individual courtier aristocrats was one result of this turn away from official record keeping. Necessarily, the nature of record keeping changed. Whereas public records maintained a broad perspective, privately authored records concerning ceremonies (*gishiki*) and administrative processes (*seimu*) focused on specific details of individual conduct, and on appropriate or inappropriate acts or disposition given the author's particular role. The objective of such individual record keeping was to provide reference for the future, such that the writer and his heirs would be informed of the appropriate thing to do given their specific role in the organization of the court.

A second element that nurtured individual journal writing in Heian times was the spread of *kanji* culture—writing in Chinese characters (*kanji*). Chinese characters and writing in Chinese (*kanbun*) came to Japan from China as one of the skills needed by officials to conduct foreign affairs, politics, and administration. In earlier times Chinese characters were used to express Japanese

Figure 1. The *Nenjūgyōji misōjimon* in the Residential Palace

The text of Fujiwara no Mototsune's *Nenjūgyōji no misōji* was posted in front of the entrance of the Royal Intimates' Hall in the Seiryōden, where intimates of the monarch saw it frequently. Mototsune was Tadahira's father, and like his father, Tadahira took a deep and abiding interest in annual rites and protocol at court.

The figure is based on the rendering of the *Nenjūgyōji misōjimon* in the late Heian-period illustrated scroll, *Shigisan engi emaki*.

sounds and meaning, as *man'yōgana*. But by Heian times, in addition to the use of Chinese characters to write poetry in Chinese, texts written in Chinese characters formed the basis of aristocratic education. And as Chinese characters came to be used on an everyday basis, changes were made in pure Chinese-style *kanbun*. Furthermore, while much of the vocabulary was actually Chinese, daily journals were written by Japanese courtiers in a word order closer to actual Japanese called *kirokutai*.

As for the annual ceremonial calendar that played such a key role in the lives of Heian-period aristocrats, it included ceremonies that were performed every year. There are such yearly activities in any cultural setting, especially in agricultural societies which depend so heavily on the changing seasons for their productive activities. The Chinese ceremonial system was imported almost entirely in its mature form, based on continental agricultural practices, but the archipelago had its own yearly celebrations as well.

Specifically, the Chinese calendar (*reki*) featured certain basic customs that gave it structure. To those were added various ceremonies and events associated with the *ritsuryō* codes that articulated and confirmed the authority of the *tennō*-centered state, including religious activities associated both with *kami*-worship and Buddhism. Ceremonies were further refined following Tang fashion during the ninth-century reign of Saga Tennō (r. 809-823). At the same time, events that had originally concerned the *tennō* personally were merged with ceremonies of state, and the annual cycle of courtly events came to be seen as the substance of the royal house itself. Key events such as royal banquets (*sechie*) were moved from the Halls of State (*Chōdōin*), the most important locus for state ceremonies in the eighth century, to the Shishinden or the Seiryōden in the Residential Palace.

These changes became increasingly clear during the era when Fujiwara no Mototsune (836-891) served as prime minister (*daijōdaijin*). Mototsune was the adopted son of the first regent, Fujiwara no Yoshifusa (804-872). Because of the trust of Kōkō Tennō (r. 884-887), Yoshifusa became that ruler's chief-of-staff. And under Uda Tennō (r. 887-897), Yoshifusa continued in that office. Then in 885, Yoshifusa's heir and successor as court leader, Prime Minister Mototsune, authored his Notes on the Annual Court Calendar (*Nenjūgyōji no misōji*). He had the Notes written on a screen—with the day and name of each event, beginning with the first day of the first month—and the inscribed screen, known as the *Nenjūgyōji misōjimon*, was presented to the throne (see Figure 1). Research has shown that the annual cycle of court events of Mototsune's day contained significantly more ceremonies than had the earlier court calendar recorded in the early ninth-century Palace Protocols (*Dairishiki*). Since Mototsune's Notes were posted in front of the entranceway of the Tenjōnoma in the Seiryōden, royal intimates (*tenjōbito*) who served the monarch were constantly made conscious of the importance of the ritual calendar in their courtly lives. Besides wanting to organize court ritual, Mototsune surely drew up the *Nenjūgyōji no misōji* as one means of strengthening his own relations with the throne, while making those bonds quite visible to all. Since Mototsune was Tadahira's father, it was Mototsune's vision of court ritual that was transmitted to Tadahira, author of the *Teishinkōki*.

It is clear from the historical record that the events constituting the annual cycle varied to some extent, but later copies of the 885 list made in the late Heian and early Kamakura periods confirm that today's *Nenjūgyōji misōjimon* faithfully preserves the contents of Mototsune's original gift to the throne. Furthermore, later compendia such as the tenth-century *Saikyūki* and eleventh-century *Hokuzanshō* rely on the *Notes* as their basis. It is true that during the high point of court leadership by the Northern Fujiwara in the eleventh century, and into the epoch when retired monarchs presided over the court in the twelfth century, some ceremonies came to be performed either by the Regent's Lineage (*Sekkanke*) or in the household of the retired monarch (*in*). For instance, originally senior nobles (*kugyō*), royal intimates (*tenjōbito*), and officials (*kanjin*) all paid obeisance to the *tennō* in the Lesser Salutation (*Kochōhai*) ceremony on the first day of the first month. Out of that practice developed the *Hairei* ceremony, in which those same officials reported to the residence of the regent and the retired *tennō*. But wherever performed, participation in events of the annual ceremonial calendar was considered every aristocrat's official duty. Even prayers to the deities and buddhas, which might seem at first glance to have no relationship with politics, were seen to assure the *tennō*'s health, the good fortune of the royal family, and prosperity for the realm.

The annual cycle of ceremonies compiled in Mototsune's *Nenjūgyōji no misōji* thus provided a structure for court events from Mototsune's day onward.

It is possible to categorize annual ceremonies according to their origins, character, or the time when they were performed. There were grand banquets where the leading officials of state gathered around the monarch such as the New Year's Banquet (*Ganjitsu no sechie*), the White Horse Banquet (*Aouma no sechie*), the Song and Dance Banquet (*Tōka no sechie*), and the Archery Competition (*Jarai*). There were events associated with government such as the Rank Appointment Ceremony (*Joi*) in the first month, the Post Appointment Ceremony (*Jimoku*) in the spring and autumn, the annual Initiation of Governance on a propitious day in the first month (*Matsurigoto hajime*), and the Inspection of Lower Rankers (*Rekken*). And there were rites for the deities such as the Kasuga and Kamo festivals, as well as the First Fruits Festival (*Niinamesai*), repasts with the deity (*Jinkonjiki*), major purifications (*Ōharae*), and the presenting of offerings to royal tombs (*Nosaki*). There were Buddhist activities such as the *Misaie* in the first month, the Buddha's Birthday Assembly (*Kanbutsue*) of the fourth month, the Benevolent King Assembly (*Ninnōe*) in the spring and fall, and the Litany of the Buddhas' Names (*Butsumyōe*) of the twelfth month. And there were court entertainments that included wrestling bouts (known as the *Sumai*) in the seventh month.

We can also categorize annual ceremonies according to the way they were scheduled or the frequency of their performance. Some events were always held on a given day in a given month, like the New Year's Banquet, which occurred on the first day of the first month. Others were to be held in a given month on a given day determined according to the sixty-day stem-and-branch cycle. For instance, the Kasuga Festival was held twice yearly on the first monkey (*saru*) day in both the second and eleventh months. Still other events, such as the appointment of non-capital-based officials (*gekan*) in the Agatameshi Jimoku, which occurred sometime during the first month, were held generally about the same time annually. And in terms of frequency, some activities were performed annually, some were performed semiannually, and others were performed seasonally. Still others were performed monthly.

Besides ceremonies held in the residential palaces of the *tennō* and the retired *tennō*, there were also ceremonies held at the homes of aristocrats. The latter spent the year living according to ceremonial calendars that were both official and unofficial. As seen in both the *Tale of Genji* (*Genji monogatari*) and the *Pillow Book* (*Makura no sōshi*), consciousness of the seasons was not limited to the world of literature. Aristocratic society itself was permeated by such consciousness that was further articulated through ceremonial events.

As mentioned earlier, one purpose for writing a journal was that it could serve as an aid to its author's memory. One could perform appropriately at a given ceremony or administrative function if one could refer to previous records of the event. In those days, administration (*gyōsei*) and ceremonial activities (*gishiki*) were interwoven. According to one's role and status, one had to carry out the various phases of all sorts of extraordinary rites such as royal retirements (*jōi*) and accessions (*sokui*) as well as regular events such as sutra readings (*midokyō*), shrine offerings (*hōbei*), and the other occasions of the annual calendar. Those who had to perform such rites were not only the *tennō* but also higher and lesser aristocrats. Even administrative matters required research into precedents.

Records in courtier journals thus made it possible for aristocrats to recall what had happened in the past. Consider for instance the Kujō Lord's Testament (*Kujōdono no yuikai*), written by Tadahira's second son, Fujiwara no Morosuke (908-960), for his sons and grandsons. There he wrote, "Get up, wash your face, pray to the gods, and write down in your journal what happened on the previous day." "But," he cautioned, "on those days when there is much to write, it is probably better not to wait until the following day." Elsewhere he added, "After getting up, look at the calendar to see whether the day is lucky or not, and to ascertain the day's appointed events. And for later reference, write down yesterday's official affairs or important matters of a personal nature. Affairs of governance and ceremonies as well as those concerning the ruler or one's own father should be recorded for future need."

As noted in Morosuke's *Testament*, journals of his day were generally written on official calendars, the *guchūreki*. These generally required two or four rolls of paper and were prepared in the Yinyang Bureau (Onmyōryō). They included notations of such useful information as the season (there were 24 seasonal phases in the solar calendar of the time), whether a day was lucky or not, and annual events scheduled on a given day. Officials of the Yinyang Bureau presented the calendar to the *tennō*, who then distributed copies to each agency or office. High ranking aristocrats could order copies for personal use. After the column devoted to each day, two or three additional columns were generally left blank, and it was there a courtier could write his daily notes. When the author wanted to write at greater length, he could continue writing on the back of the calendar—such entries were called "writings on the reverse side" (*uragaki*). In other cases, courtiers might write notes on a separate piece of paper as a *bekki*—this method was used when a particular ceremony required a more extensive record.

Editing and abstracting were fairly common processes through which a courtier's journal passed. For instance, when a journal covered a lengthy period of time, the author himself might reorganize it or make corrections. And there were times when a particular part of the journal— the section devoted to a particular ceremony or event, for instance—might be conveniently extracted in a specialized record called a *buruiki*. As for the contents of a courtier journal, there are tremendous variations according to the author. Although the objective was to make notes concerning ritual and administrative processes, even highly educated courtiers did not always exhibit significant talent or reflection in composing their journals. There are courtier journals that reveal personal opinions or emotion while others articulate the processes and protocols of both governance and ritual in rich detail. Still others express criticism or dissatisfaction with colleagues or social conditions.

The oldest extant journal written in the author's own hand is the Journal of the Midō Chief-of-staff (*Midō kanpakuki*), by Fujiwara no Michinaga (966-1027). Many days therein have quite short entries, and there are whole series of days that lack any entry at all. But there are also detailed entries that resemble modern journals in which events of the day are jotted down. The *Shōyūki*, authored by Minister of the Right Fujiwara no Sanesuke (957-1046), also contains detailed notes on administrative matters—his entries were written with keen concentration to serve his need for future reference. Sanesuke was the grandson and adopted son of Fujiwara no Saneyori (900-970), who was Fujiwara no Tadahira's son and heir. Sanesuke thus considered himself a direct descendent of Tadahira, and his objective was to transmit his own knowledge of ceremonial protocols and administration as it had been transmitted to him from Tadahira's day. Sanesuke is well known as a particularly talented official, and there are cases in which he actually cites sections from the journals of earlier aristocrats. Since his work was particularly valued among journal writers, the *Shōyūki* is often cited in later courtier journals.

The style of writing used in courtier journals is not pure Chinese. Rather, it is what specialists call *kirokutai*, a style of writing that is reasonably close to Japanese. The education of leading Heian aristocrats was not the product of schools—most aristocrats studied in their own homes with their own tutors. Even if they read the same texts from China in addition to the Japanese classics, the way they learned those texts was quite varied. Furthermore, authors intended their journals to be read by only a limited in-group. When the writing style of journals is compared to that of public documents and records, there is significant variation. Authors followed the style and used the vocabulary that they learned from their fathers and grandfathers. As a result, courtier journals are more difficult to read and comprehend than are other types of written materials from the same era.

Since many journals are extant only in fragmentary form, it is not always certain when a given author began or ceased writing his journal. Later cases suggest, however, that a journal was often begun after the individual's coming-of-age ceremony (*genpuku*). Many aristocrats initiated their journals when they began serving as officials at court. And more than half of the journals that we have extant today end at a time of sickness or death. In the case of Fujiwara no Munetada's *Chūyūki*, entries end when Munetada (1062-1141) "left the world" (*shukke*) to take Buddhist vows. Also, as mentioned earlier, some authors revised or reorganized their journals. They edited certain entries, added to those they found inadequate, and even erased those that were considered infelicitous for one reason or another.

Contrary to common wisdom, journals were not kept simply to be passed down and copied by heirs. Rather, they were highly prized for their contemporary usefulness by the author himself and by his contemporaries. Occasionally the journal writer received a request to send out a particular section of his journal; sometimes an extract was borrowed or viewed; and sometimes a journal was copied and quoted in others' journals, with the result that sections survived down to our time even when other parts were lost. In some cases, the entire journal was copied. Each artistocratic lineage (*ie*) had journals that were particularly valued as sources of information. These became one pillar of a lineage's sense of self and status. While there was a natural desire to obtain and read journals from other lineages, it was quite difficult to do so. In many cases only the heir (*chakushi*) could view his sire's journal. There were occasions, however, when the family head might give permission to an outsider to consult an important journal. High ranking courtiers also used various means, including cliental relationships, factional bonds, and marital ties to get hold of the most important journals. Although a journal was considered the property of a given lineage, when the *tennō*, regent, chief-of-staff, or other high ranker asked to view a journal, it was difficult to refuse. So were the royal family and the regents' line able to accumulate many courtiers' journals over the generations.

Early in its history the contents of a given journal were considered extremely important and were thus frequently cited. But over time, reference became less frequent. Important sections were extracted or abstracted in *buruiki*. By the eleventh and twelfth centuries, as the houses of the aristocracy segmented, journals came to be regarded as treasures passed down from earlier ages and as sources of both continuity and legitimacy. Houses with such journals came to be called "houses with journals," *nikki no ie*. But when heirs eventually faced loss of influence and penury, even in such distinguished lineages, the usefulness of journals decreased and they were sold. That is why we have but fragments of many journals extant today.

The *Teishinkōki*, for which the extant abstracted entries from the year 939 are translated in this volume, was the journal of the early regent and chief-of-staff Fujiwara no Tadahira (880-949). It was not common for someone keeping a journal to give it a name. Rather, the title of Tadahira's journal derives from Tadahira's posthumous name, Teishinkō, "the sagacious and trustworthy lord." We have no extant original manuscript written by Tadahira's own hand, nor do we have a copy of the original

18

journal. We have only the abstract known as the *Teishinkōkishō,* "the abstracted *Teishinkōki.*" There are, however, additional fragments from Tadahira's journal cited in various ceremonial handbooks (*gishikisho*) and in other courtiers' journals. We do not know when Tadahira actually began or stopped writing the journal. The *Teishinkōkishō* includes entries from 907, when the author was 28 years old, until 948, when he was 69. It is possible that the author of the abstract included only those entries needed for his own reference, which did not include the early years of Tadahira's career when he held relatively low rank and post. It is entirely possible that Tadahira began to write journal entries before 907. Since Tadahira became ill in 949, it seems likely that he continued writing entries up to the time when his physical condition deteriorated.

The best extant text of the abstract comprises ten volumes and has been archived in the library of Tenri University since 1955. Bearing the title *Teishinkō gokishō,* it is thought to have been copied in the early Kamakura Period (1185-1333). Subsequently it was passed down by heirs of the Northern Fujiwara Kujō lineage, one of the five houses of the Regents' Line. It contains entries dating from 907 to 948. In addition there is a later copy from the Edo Period (1600-1868) in the library at Kyoto University, known as the "Manuscript from the Old Cellar of the Hiramatsu House" (Hiramatsuke kyūzōbon). It includes entries from 932 to 933 that are missing from the older copy. While this Edo-period copy lacks numbered scrolls, the Kamakura-period copy bears markers with scroll numbers, indicating that the original abstract comprised twenty scrolls. Entries from the years 908 to 910 (Engi 7 to 10) were contained in the first scroll, and those for 948 and 949 (Tenryaku 2 and 3) were in the twentieth. Together these two manuscripts constitute our extant abstract of Tadahira's *Teishinkōki* journal.

As for when the abstract was originally copied out and by whom, an answer was proposed by the editor of the *Dai Nihon kokiroku* edition. The abstract contains occasional notes to the effect that, "My comment is" (*Shiki ni iwaku*). There are also refences to "my father" here and there. These suggest that it was Tadahira's eldest son, Fujiwara no Saneyori, who was also called Ononomiyadono, that made the abstract. There is also a reference to "the Late Minister of the Right" (*ko'ujōshō*), indicating that the abstract was made after the death of Saneyori's younger brother, Morosuke, in 960. Since Saneyori himself died in 970, the abstract must have been being made between 960 and 970.

Entries in the abstracted journal are relatively short. The first scroll contains very brief entries for the first four years. However, as the journal advances, entries become longer and more detailed—those from the latter half, when Tadahira was regent or chief-of-staff, are noticeably richer in content. But when entries from the abstract are compared with citations in various ritual handbooks, it is clear that the abstract preserves only portions of the original. Indeed, when Saneyori made the abstract, he was minister of the left and either regent or chief-of-staff. He had little reason for interest in the early entries, when Tadahira's rank and post had been modest. Nonetheless, what we have extant from Tadahira's entries is still quite detailed compared with records kept by other courtiers.

As for the actual content of entries in the abstracted journal, a day's record generally notes ceremonial activities (*gyōji*) together with the names of persons who were responsible for or participated in them. Particular protocols or the order of ceremonial events (*gishiki shidai*), together with breaches of same, are also noted. A royal illness or other indisposition, unusual events including omens, and court responses thereto are all recorded. Thereafter come orders issued by Tadahira as court leader, whether as *sesshō* or *kanpaku*. And finally, there are occasional brief notes concerning Tadahira's personal affairs such as Buddhist ceremonies he sponsored, various shrine affairs, and reports on his health. The journal does not, however, shed much light on his personal or family life.

Many extant fragments of Tadahira's journal are archived in the ritual handbook compiled by Minamoto no Takaakira (914-982) and entitled Notes from the Western Palace (*Saikyūki*). Takaakira was a prince of Daigo Tennō (r. 897-930) who rose to the high court post of minister of the left. But rivals trumped up charges against him in the so-called Anna Coup of 969, and they were successful in getting Takaakira exiled to the Dazaifu in Kyūshū for several years.

Takaakira was an expert in court ceremonial and administration, interests that Tadahira had had before him. Moreover, Takaakira had as consorts two daughters of Fujiwara no Morosuke, Tadahira's second son, who was himself deeply interested in these same matters. Takaakira regarded Tadahira's diary as an exemplary text, full of information to be carefully studied and committed to memory. According to the editor's introduction in the *Dai Nihon kokiroku* edition of *Teishinkōki*, fully half of our extant fragments of *Teishinkōki* are found in Takaakira's *Notes*, but those found in the latter are generally less detailed than those found elsewhere. It is therefore suspected that the manuscript of *Teishinkōki* used by Takaakira was Saneyori's abstract rather than Tadahira's original. Given that Tadahira's two sons, Saneyori and Morosuke, competed over the posts of regent and chief-of-staff; and that they disagreed about what their father had taught them concerning ceremonial protocols (which disagreements they passed on to their sons and grandsons), Takaakira's use of Saneyori's manuscript represents a noteworthy clue to Takaakira's relations with the Regents' Line at the time of compilation.

There are also citations from the *Teishinkōki* in the early eleventh-century *Hokuzanshō* by Fujiwara no Kintō (966-1041). While a few of those can be traced to Saneyori's *Teishinkōkishō*, others are more detailed. Therefore we can suspect that either because of his father, or because of his cousin, Sanesuke—who was Saneyori's grandson, adopted son, and heir—Kintō had access to Tadahira's original *Teishinkōki* manuscript. Kintō, who was the son of Fujiwara no Yoritada (924-989), is famed not only for his grasp of court protocol passed down by his grandfather but also as a scholar with substantial literary and musical talents. An outstanding member of the aristocracy of his day, he compiled a series of specialized ceremonial notes and extracts (*buruiki*) based on Saneyori's own journal.

The purpose of the *Dai Nihon kokiroku* series of courtier journals, including the volume that contains the *Teishinkōkishō* on which our translation is based, is to publish all of the major courtier journals dating from Heian through Edo times. The editors are faculty members at the Historiographical Institute of Tokyo University. Publication of the series began in 1957 and it includes the best possible textual readings and annotation for each journal. Therefore the series is widely trusted by the scholarly world. The *Teishinkōkishō* edition printed therein is based on the early archival manuscript owned by the Tenri University Library.

In the *Dai Nihon kokiroku* edition, unreadable characters or suspected mistakes in the text are marked with square brackets. Our English translation of the entries from 939, the second year of the Tengyō era during the reign of Suzaku Tennō (930-946), is faithfully based on that publication. In the translation we have marked with curly brackets personal and geographical names added for completeness.

Courtier journals developed as a response to changes in government and social organization in the Heian Period. Even as the pace of change continued at court, the journals remained valuable. But as courtier society waned politically and economically, and as warrior government emerged in the late twelfth century, fortunately the journals we have extant today were long preserved as the jewels of particular aristocratic lineages.

Map 1. Tadahira's Heiankyō

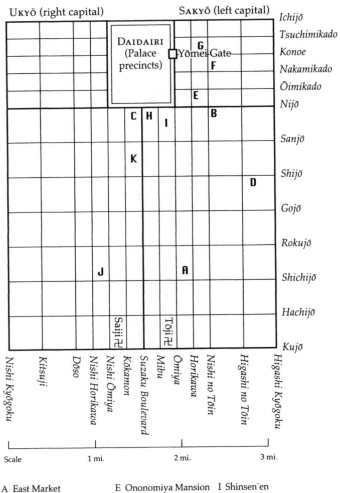

UKYŌ (right capital) SAKYŌ (left capital)

DAIDAIRI (Palace precincts)

Yōmei Gate

Ichijō
Tsuchimikado
Konoe
Nakamikado
Ōimikado
Nijō
Sanjō
Shijō
Gojō
Rokujō
Shichijō
Hachijō
Kujō

Saiji 卍 Tōji 卍

Nishi Kyōgoku
Kitsuji
Dōso
Nishi Horikawa
Nishi Ōmiya
Kōkamon
Suzaku Boulevard
Mibu
Ōmiya
Horikawa
Nishi no Tōin
Higashi no Tōin
Higashi Kyōgoku

Scale 1 mi. 2 mi. 3 mi.

A East Market
B Higashi Sanjō Mansion
C Kokusōin
D Gojō Mansion
E Ononomiya Mansion
F Repairs Agency
G Royal Police
H Royal University
I Shinsen'en
J West Market
K Suzakuin

What Did a Regent Do?

Fujiwara no Tadahira in the 930s

Joan R. Piggott

In this essay I will introduce the early Heian regent Fujiwara no Tadahira (880-949) through entries from his *Teishinkōki* journal during the 930s. I am particularly interested in how journal entries illuminate Tadahira's regental leadership at Suzaku Tennō's court between 931 and 939. Entries from 939 have, of course, been translated later in this volume. Furthermore, given that there is broad agreement that the structures and protocols utilized by later Northern Fujiwara regents were being set in Tadahira's day, insights from this formative era provide an excellent foundation for understanding his successors' work as regents.

Little has been written in English about how Northern Fujiwara regents led the court, including their relations with the child *tennō*, ministers of the Council of State (Daijōkan), royal wives and female officials in the Back Palace, retired monarchs, and various units of officialdom.[1] The term "court" itself remains fuzzy—we need to know more about the composition and operation of that body that ruled over capital and provinces in mid-Heian times. In the English historiography, the regent's authority has been explained by his matrilineal ties to the child monarch—so, we are told, did high ranking courtier patriarchs engage in "marriage politics" to marry their daughters to future monarchs and thus assure close personal influence over the throne. Moreover, because of the frequent accession of child *tennō* from Seiwa (850-880, r. 858-876) onward—frequently following manipulative power plays or outright coups—regents from Yoshifusa's lineage of the Northern Fujiwara (Hokke Fujiwara) were able to assert their dominance by the mid-ninth century.[2]

There are, however, other important perspectives on the regency to be considered, including the regent's authority and prerogatives, actual venues of policy making and execution, and the degree of continuity with the earlier *tennō*-centered court.

As for the template from which the regent's mandate derived, Takeuchi Rizō (1907-1997) and others have argued that the supreme minister's (*daijōdaijin*) post provided a model for

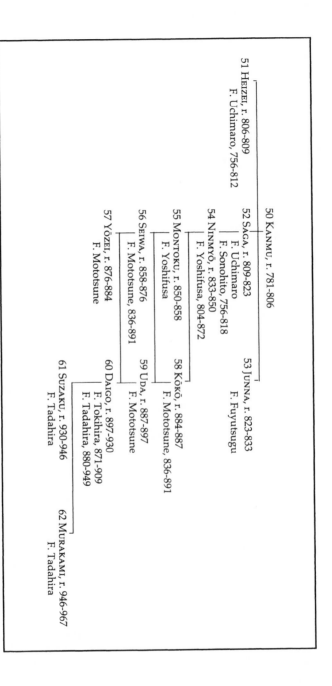

Figure 2. Early Heian *Tennō* and Northern Fujiwara Lead Ministers, Regents, and Chiefs-of-staff

the regency. According to the Law on Personnel (*Shikiinryō*) of the *ritsuryō* codes, the supreme minister was to aid and guide the monarch by means of his exemplary learning and counsel.[3] Yoshikawa Shinji has also pointed to similarities between the prerogatives of seventh- and eighth-century inner palace ministers (*naidaijin*)—such as Fujiwara no Kamatari (614-669), his son Fuhito (659-720), and his grandson Nakamaro (706-764)—and those of Heian regents.[4] In addition, use of an "affinal strategy" —recruiting ministerial inlaws to support the ruler—dates back to the pre-*ritsuryō* Yamato monarchy.

Concerning the venue where policy was decided and promulgated in mid-Heian times, Kuroita Katsumi (1874-1946) proposed early in the twentieth century that the regent led court and realm by means of his household chancellery (*mandokoro*).[5] But Tsuchida Naoshige and Hashimoto Yoshihiko have argued since the 1960s that the monarch's residential palace (*dairi*) remained the center of government during the regents' age. They see the two pillars of *ritsuryō* government—*tennō* and Council of State—continuing to play significant roles.[6] Hashimoto has pointed out too that the regent exercised leadership at court not simply through his matrilineal relationship with the young monarch but also through his prerogatives as a senior noble of the Council of State. While individual monarchs and regents sometimes had divergent ideas and interests, institutionally the regency served to link the powers of throne and Council to provide greater stability and legitimacy for the monarchy.

On the other hand, Satō Sōjun sees more change than continuity. In his comparison of the courts of *ritsuryō* and later regency times, he points out that the social organization and politics of court society had changed substantially by Tadahira's day. By then a new aristocracy of mostly Northern Fujiwara and Minamoto princely scions had taken charge, and its members and their followers were fine-tuning processes to maximize their status, wealth, and power.[7] Ihara Masao, Kon Masahide, and Ōtsu Tōru also emphasize change. They see the Northern Fujiwara regency as one component of an increasingly routinized monarchy that gained support from multiple centers of authority including the retired monarch and powerful aristocratic households. Among the latter, the Regents' Line (Sekkanke) was preeminent.[8] Ōtsu too sees the regent as leader and arbiter of an

Figure 3. A Mid-ninth-century Noble's Residence

What might the residence of a Heian noble of Tadahira's day have looked like? To what extent had *shinden* aristocratic architecture developed? In the late 1960s, the architectural specialist Ōta Seiroku argued that the early decades of the tenth century witnessed the full development of *shinden* architecture, represented by the Suzakuin retirement palace used by Uda, Suzaku, and Murakami. In a photograph of the model of Heiankyō made for the celebration of Kyoto's 1200th anniversary, we see a reconstruction of an upper-class residential compound excavated in the Sixth Ward of the Right Capital. Thought to date from the mid-ninth century, the compound included a spacious main hall, the *shinden*, which looked out over a garden— just as did the monarch's own formal reception hall, the Southern Hall, sketched below. In the noble's compound, there was another hall to the back, and additional halls to the east and west, that were all linked to the main *shinden* by roofed corridors. In other words, the basics of *shinden* style had already emerged before Tadahira's lifetime. A variety of utility buildings, garden plots, and a well were located to the rear of the property, and the entire compound was surrounded by a fence.

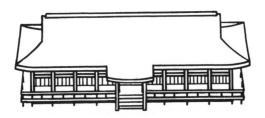

aristocratic alliance (*jōryū rengō taisei*).[9] Along these same lines Tamai Chikara has argued that a "stake-holder kingship" presiding over various centers of power took form after the breakup of the earlier *tennō*-led *ritsuryō* officialdom, and that the regent represented the interests of the nobility therein.[10]

From Kon's perspective, on the other hand, structural changes such as the return to stem-line royal succession in the mid-ninth century together with courtiers' desire to avoid clashes between retired and sitting monarchs, led to the empowering of ministerial regents like Yoshifusa, Mototsune, and Tadahira. They served as proxies for the child monarchs who inherited their fathers' thrones.[11] Similarly Furuse Natsuko and Kuramoto Kazuhiro stress the bilineal (*miuchiteki*) rather than matrilineal basis of regency-era monarchy: while the queen's family advised the throne, so did the paternal retired monarch.[12]

There is also an ongoing debate as to how to periodize Tadahira's regency within the longer trajectory of regental development. Yoshikawa Shinji calls Tadahira's era "the early regency," which he terms "*ritsuryō*-like" since it relied on *ritsuryō* structures such as the Council and prebendal tax units (*fuko*) for its fiscal base. Later in the tenth century, however, Yoshikawa shows how regents moved away from such codal practices.[13] Other researchers paint Tadahira's era, and that of his sons Saneyori and Morosuke, as a transitional time when the new aristocracy was solidifying its hold over capital and provinces. Routinization and specialization of court offices proceeded, as did clientalism in the form of status-ordered vertical factions. Nonetheless the new aristocracy was deeply conservative, and it valued the *ritsuryō* codes that had spawned it. They particularly prized the Chinese ideal of stemline patrilineal succession, even if their own kinship and marital practices remained more bilineal than patrilineal. As a result, in the sphere of family organization and succession there were tensions. The stake-holder monarchy was therefore subject to frequent disputes from within and without, making it an unstable entity.

As we undertake a close reading of Tadahira's Journal of the Wise & Loyal Lord, named for Tadahira's posthumous sobriquet Teishinkō, in addition to learning what Regent Tadahira did, I also want to consider his role in this stake-holder kingship of the early tenth century.

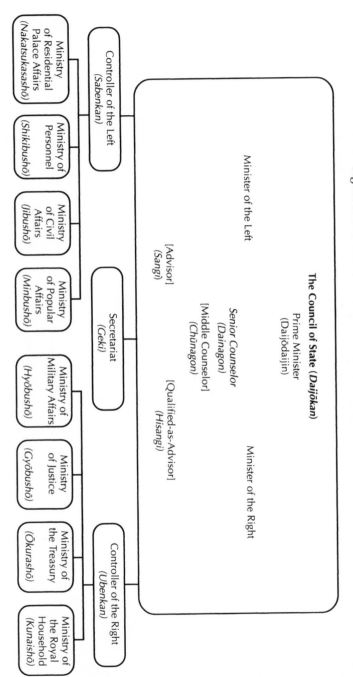

Figure 4. The Council of State—The Senior Nobles and their Staff

The Council of State (Daijōkan)

Prime Minister
(Daijōdaijin)

Minister of the Left

Minister of the Right

Senior Counselor
(Dainagon)

[Middle Counselor]
(Chūnagon)

[Advisor]
(Sangi)

[Qualified-as-Advisor]
(Hisangi)

Controller of the Left
(Sabenkan)

Secretariat
(Geki)

Controller of the Right
(Ubenkan)

Ministry
of Residential
Palace Affairs
(Nakatsukasashō)

Ministry of
Personnel
(Shikibushō)

Ministry
of Civil
Affairs
(Jibushō)

Ministry
of Popular
Affairs
(Minbushō)

Ministry of
Military Affairs
(Hyōbushō)

Ministry
of Justice
(Gyōbushō)

Ministry of
the Treasury
(Ōkurashō)

Ministry of
the Royal
Household
(Kunaishō)

Extant sections of the journal record Tadahira's daily activities and concerns from 907—long before he became regent in 930—up to the year of his death in 949. Despite the fact that our extant text contains only extracts probably copied out by Tadahira's son and heir Fujiwara no Saneyori (900-970), it nonetheless provides a wealth of information concerning the organization and procedures of the court as well as Tadahira's own activities and thoughts. And while no official court annals cover Tadahira's tenure as regent—the last of the six official annals, the *Nihon sandai jitsuroku*, ends in 887, with the reign of Kōkō Tennō from 884 to 887—other sources can aid contextualization and interpretation of journal entries. Heian-era compilations such as the *Nihon kiryaku, Honchō seiki, Ruijū fusenshō, Seiji yōryaku,* and *Honchō monzui*, as well as individual records in the modern *Heian ibun* compiled by Takeuchi Rizō, are particularly useful.[14] We can also refer to the sources compiled in the modern annal, *Dai Nihon shiryō* (Sources of Japan), by researchers at the University of Tokyo Historiographical Institute.[15] Finally there are also the journals kept by Tadahira's second son, Morosuke (908-960), and his son-in-law, Prince Shigeakira (906-954).[16]

My focal point in this study is the 930s, when Tadahira first served as regent (*sesshō*) for the young Suzaku Tennō (923-952; r. 930-946). I will spotlight entries from 931, the first full year of Tadahira's regency, in contrast with those of 939, that are translated in this volume. By 939 Tadahira had been regent for nearly a decade. And although Suzaku Tennō had celebrated his coming-of-age ceremony in 937, the sickly monarch refused to accept his regent's resignation.[17]

It will become clear in the analysis that follows, and from the translation later in the volume, that the regental post required Tadahira's daily efforts to coordinate the work of his ministerial colleagues on the Council, as well as that of a staff of busy controllers, Council secretaries, royal secretaries, and other specialists. We will also see how throne and Council remained actively involved in government to an extent unappreciated in the English historiography to date. New posts, processes, and practices had come into being, and they linked throne and council as well as capital and provinces in new ways. The particulars of Tadahira's regency seen through entries from *Teishinkōki* for the

930s thus provide us with significant new insights into Heian monarchy, regency, and court government.

EARLY YEARS

Before we turn to Regent Tadahira's activities, some attention to his early life and preparation for court leadership is helpful. Fujiwara no Tadahira was born the fourth son of Fujiwara no Mototsune (836-891), the adopted heir (and nephew) of Fujiwara no Yoshifusa (804-872). The latter served as the first ministerial regent for the first Heian-period child *tennō*, Seiwa; and subsequently Mototsune served as regent to another child *tennō*, Yōzei (868-949, r. 877-884). Tadahira's birth in Mototsune's lineage (see Figure 2) meant that his forebears' status and experiences provided important precedents for his own career at court.

Tadahira's life at court began in 895, with his coming-of-age ceremony at the age of sixteen. It was followed by appointment as a senior-fifth-rank chamberlain (*jijū*) for the then reigning Uda Tennō (867-931, r. 887-897). Monarch and chamberlain got on well, and six years later Tadahira was chosen by Uda, then retired, to marry his foster daughter, Minamoto no Nobuko, who was also related to Uda's esteemed advisor, the scholar-minister Sugawara no Michizane (845-903).[18] Marriages between royals and commoners were not generally permitted, but the custom of marriage between a high ranking Northern Fujiwara and a royal woman had precedent in Saga Tennō's (786-842; r. 809-823) day—one of the latter's daughters married Yoshifusa. Tadahira was promoted to right senior controller (*udaiben*) in 900, and in that office he would have consulted closely on all sorts of governmental business with officials in Daigo Tennō's residential palace as well as with senior nobles (*kugyō*) in the Council of State.[19] By 903 he had achieved the junior fourth rank. Tadahira's residence during these years was the mansion in the Fifth Ward, Gojō, that had once belonged to Mototsune (see Figure 3 and Map 1).[20]

At the turn of the tenth century Tadahira's elder brother Tokihira had already advanced to the pinnacle of the court hierarchy. While he never held the title of regent, Tokihira was Mototsune's first son and heir. As a result, from 899 until he convinced the monarch Daigo Tennō (885-930, r. 897-930) to exile

Minister of the Right Michizane in 901, Tokihira and Michizane conjointly led the Council of State (see Figure 4), whose members were usually called senior nobles.[21]

The Council remained important at the tenth-century court. Formal memorials from its members to the throne called *kansō* were still considered significant, and its proposals that the throne approved were transformed into royal orders.[22] After sealing—the monarch would brush "permitted" (*yurusu*) on those he accepted, and add the date—the orders were returned to the Council, whose secretaries (*geki*) prepared directives (*kanpu*) to promulgate them (see Figure 5). The Council also participated in important deliberative activities called *Gekisei* and *Jin no sadame*. For *Gekisei* the senior nobles assembled in the office of Council secretaries, the Gekichō, east of the Kenshun Gate. Senior nobles who joined those discussions included the grand ministers of the left and the right as well as lesser Council members including counselors and advisors. Council secretaries served nearby.[23] In contrast, *Jin no sadame* were special discussions by the senior nobles to determine possible responses to crisis situations. After such meetings, each member's opinions were sent on to the throne for consideration.[24]

Tadahira's post as a controller and his close personal connections with Uda, Tokihira, and Daigo's consort, Fujiwara no Yasuko—she was full sister to both Tokihira and Tadahira—made Tadahira a key liaison between the *tennō's* residential palace, the Council, and the retired monarch. But after Michizane's exile in 901, to which Uda was strongly opposed, there would have been distance between the brothers (and their households), the royals (and their households), and their associates and clients. Such was an effect of the segmentary nature of the stake-holder monarchy.[25]

Nonetheless Tadahira's promotion to the junior fourth rank in 903 suggests warmer relations, and in 908 Tadahira was promoted to a seat on the Council as an advisor (*sangi*). He was also made head of the Crown Prince's Household and commander of both the Left Palace Guards and the Royal Police (*Kebiishichō*).[26] Since such appointments put him in charge of security, provisioning, and operations at Daigo's residential palace, the greater palace precincts, and the capital itself, Tokihira and Daigo were clearly relying heavily on Tadahira. Notably it is from this time, beginning in 907, that we have entries from Tadahira's *Teishinkōki* journal.[27]

Figure 5.
Structures and Processes of Ninth- and Tenth-Century Government

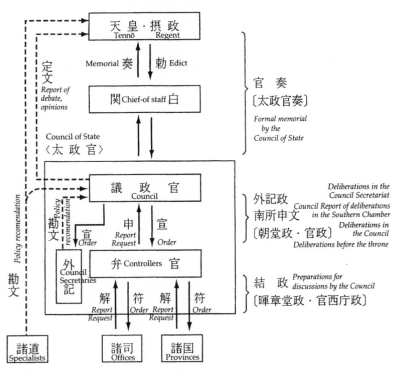

After Yoshikawa Shinji, *Heiankyō* (Tokyo: Yoshikawa kōbunkan, 2002), 63

When Tokihira died suddenly in the fourth month of 909—the consensus at court was that the angry shade (goryō) of Michizane was to blame—Tadahira was promoted to director of the Royal Secretariat (Kurōdo) and commander of the Right Inner Palace Guards.[28] Since Tadahira had been close to Michizane, perhaps it was thought that he could calm the specter's wrath. In the following year, he was named a middle counselor, in which post he became eligible to serve as a noble-in-charge (shōkei) with full voting privileges in Council discussions.[29] Middle counselors could also directly advise the throne.[30] About this same time, Tadahira was compiling the Engi shiki, a massive compendium of procedures and protocols that was only finished in 927. Work on that project would have given him an overview of the entire organization of court government. In 911 Tadahira advanced to senior counselor, and in 914 he became minister of the right.[31] Given that there was no minister of the left at the time, Tadahira thus became the ranking senior noble. The appointment would likely have worried Tokihira's son and heir, Yasutada (890-936), who saw his own inheritance of his father's court leadership slipping away.

After 914, however, Tadahira's advance slowed. Although his daughter entered the crown prince's palace as a consort in 918 and his royal consort sister lived at his Gojō residence for awhile in 920, it was in 924 that Tadahira became minister of the left. That promotion came bundled with other decisions by Daigo Tennō concerning royal succession. Specifically, Tadahira's sister Yasuko was named Daigo's queen-consort (chūgū) in 923, and her two-year-old son—Tadahira's nephew born at his own Gojō home—was named crown prince in 925.

In addition to leading court and Council as ranking minister, Tadahira also acted as the Fujiwara family head (chōja). One of his responsibilities was to oversee affairs at the family temple, Kōfukuji, in Nara; and at the adjacent family shrine, Kasugasha. He also managed the Kangakuin dormitory for Fujiwara studying at the royal university, as well as several estates (shōen) in various provinces. While entries in the journal suggest that Tadahira never ventured far from the capital, he travelled frequently to Fukakusa in the Fushimi vicinity during the 920s (see Map 2). In 925, perhaps in thanksgiving for his recent promotion, Tadahira had a new chapel constructed there, at Hosshōji.[32] It was nearby the tomb of Nimmyō Tennō, as well as the Kajōji and Jōganji temples built by Yoshifusa and Mototsune. When he visited Fukukusa, perhaps Tadahira occasionally continued on to Kōfukuji in Nara (see Figure 6). His ancestor Fujiwara no Fuyutsugu (775-826)—whose close relations with Saga Tennō (786-842, r. 809-823) gained the Northern Fujiwara house much of its political capital in early Heian times—had constructed the Nan'endō there in 813.[33]

A tragedy in 930 changed circumstances at court instantaneously. A lightening bolt struck the residential palace, killing a royal intimate and leaving Daigo blinded. Rumors again attributed the mishap to Michizane's shade. The independent-minded monarch took little time in deciding to pass his throne to the eight-year-old crown prince, and he dubbed the fifty-one-year-old Tadahira regent.[34] Tokihira's son reportedly cowered, given this proof of the continuing rage of Michizane's spirit.[35]

TADAHIRA BECOMES REGENT, 930

The order appointing Tadahira regent would have articulated Tadahira's mandate as regent but unfortunately it is not extant. A fragment of it, however, is preserved in the late Heian-period annal, the *Nihon kiryaku*, in its entry for 930 09/22:

> The *tennō* retired from the throne, passing it to Crown Prince Hiroaki. There was a royal order: "Minister of the Left Sir Fujiwara no Tadahira shall protect and help the young lord, and take charge (*setsugyō*) of governmental matters (*matsurigoto*)."[36]

An additional fragment is quoted in a missive written by Tadahira and requesting permission to refuse the appointment. It reads:

> While he is not yet familiar with the plenipotentiary powers of rulership (*banki*), protect and aid the sacred person and take charge of governmental affairs.[37]

A key term in this royal order is *setsu*, meaning "to grasp or steer." Another important term is *banki*, which denotes the plenary powers of the monarch. The presence of the two terms together recalls an incident from the *Nihon shoki*, a court chronicle compiled in the eighth century, which describes how the famed Prince Umayado (alt. Prince Shōtoku) aided the monarch Suiko at the turn of the seventh century by "overseeing (*sōsetsu*) all the plenary powers of the throne."[38] Later, other senior princes of the late seventh century such as Prince Naka (626-671, r. as Great King Tenji, 668-671) and Prince Kusakabe (662-689) received this same mandate.

Meanwhile the verb *setsugyō*, meaning "to carry out," appears in later royal orders issued to ministerial regents in 866 and 876. The first (dated 866 08/19) empowered Seiwa Tennō's maternal grandfather, Yoshifusa, as supreme minister, "to oversee governance of all under Heaven"—"*Tenka no matsurigoto wo setsugyō seshimeyo*"—in the wake of the alleged Ōtenmon Coup of that year.[39] This order of 866 has long been seen by historians as the earliest articulation of Yoshifusa's regental powers. The second order (dated 876 11/29) was issued by Seiwa Tennō when he passed the throne to his heir, Yōzei. It directed that Yoshifusa's heir, Minister of the Right Mototsune

> take up decision-making within and without the palace, and serve day and night without cease. As the monarch's uncle, look after and protect him, and let the young lord depend on your advice. As long as he remains unprepared for the throne's plenary powers, carry them out and serve nearby as the faithful and just minister (*chūnin no kō*).[40]

In this description of the ministerial regent's role, we hear an echo of the codal mandate for a supreme minister: to educate the monarch and provide guidance for all within the four seas. He was to accomplish his role while making straight the Way of Heaven, enabled by his unparalleled comprehension of nature's way.[41] His regental mandate thus fused the powers of the throne with the responsibilities of a supreme minister. In this respect Tadahira's regency was founded on precedents dating back to the hoary past of the seventh century, and to a more recent past in the eighth and ninth centuries, when Tadahira's ancestors wrote the *ritsuryō* codes and then established the ministerial regency.

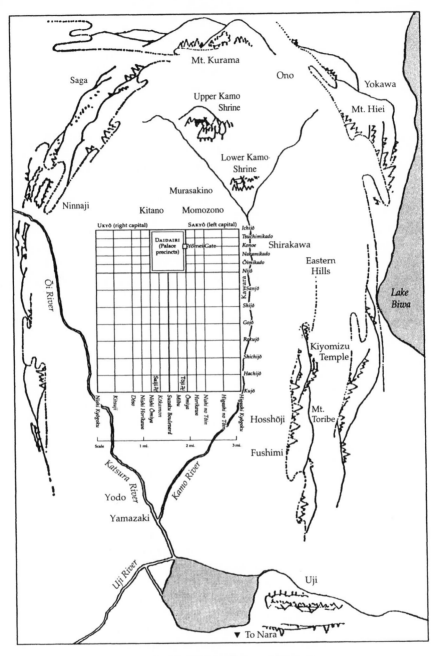

Map 2. Heian Capital and Vicinity

We also need to consider the sorts of prerogatives and perquisites that were actually included in Tadahira's mandate to "protect and help the young lord, and take charge of governmental affairs." In the sections that follow I will describe four categories of tasks that we see filling Regent Tadahira's days in the 930s. To begin, he served as the *tennō's* proxy and aide close to the throne, usually in the residential palace. Second, he oversaw performance of events that comprised the annual ritual calendar. Third, he supervised governance of the realm by provincial governors, who were none other than His Majesty's emissaries to the provinces. And fourth, as court leader he stepped into the breach whenever crisis management was needed. To accomplish such tasks Regent Tadahira required help from a grand cast of officials at court and beyond, so we need to keep close track of who served in what post each year, and the sorts of responsibilities each official had. Those who served in 939 on the Council as well as in the Controllers' Office, the Council Secretariat, the various Guards' headquarters, the Royal Police, the Royal Secretariat, and the Prelates' Office are all listed in Appendix B at the end of this essay.[42]

It is also important to note the historical context. The 930s was a time when court government faced serious challenges. The historical record shows endemic plague; frequent complaints of drought, banditry, and piracy; occasional earthquakes; violence in the capital, on the Yodo River, on the Inland Sea, and along eastern highways. There were reports of lack of cooperation by provincial governors who neglected to forward full tax payments to the capital, and ongoing rumors of Michizane's haunting the households of Daigo and Fujiwara no Tokihira. The rebellion of Taira no Masakado (?-940) in the Bandō (in today's Tokyo region) and far-flung attacks by the pirate leader Fujiwara no Sumitomo (?-941) in the Inland Sea were the most serious in a long list of challenges to the court's "heavenly" government.[43] Such was the backdrop for successful preaching by the Amidist Kūya (903-972), who urged capital residents to turn to Amida Buddha for salvation in the Latter Days of the Law (*mappō*), a time when humans could no longer save themselves. Oracles and cults—some openly critical of the *tennō's* court—also proliferated

Figure 6. Kōfukuji, the Fujiwara Family Temple
in Early Heian Times

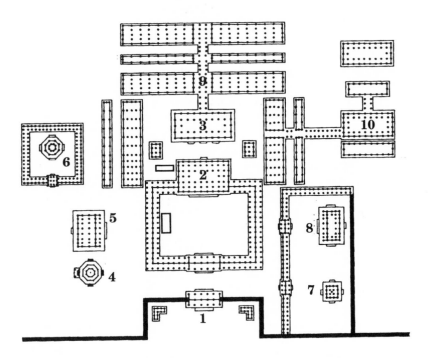

1. South Gate
2. Middle Golden Hall
3. Lecture Hall
4. South Octagonal Hall
5. West Golden Hall
6. Northern Octagonal Hall
7. Five-Story Tower
8. East Golden Hall
9. Monastic Residences
10. Monks' Eating Hall

As regent and also head of the Fujiwara family, Tadahira was deeply in-
volved with Kōfukuji, which was both an official temple (*daiji*) dedicated to
realm protection and the Fujiwara family temple. One of three great official
Buddhist rites was performed there yearly in the tenth month, the Yuimae.
It was dedicated to Tadahira's ancestor, the first Fujiwara, Kamatari (614-
69). His son Fuhito (659-720) built Kōfukuji, and the Northern Fujiwara
Fuyutsugu (775-826) added the South Octagonal Hall in early Heian times.
It enshrined an image of the Fukūkenjaku Kannon. What buildings were
standing at Kōfukuji in Tadahira's day? The Lecture Hall seems to have
been in ruins—images were moved out of it to other halls. In 878 and 925
some of the monastic residence halls burned. Then the record does not show
additional building at Kōfukuji until the Ichijōin cloister was constructed
around 970.

in the provinces.[44] Such were the challenges faced by the court of Regent Tadahira in the 930s.

TENNŌ'S PROXY AND AIDE

Regent Tadahira's primacy over other ministers as the young *tennō's* proxy and aide is visible in terms of his special prerogatives and perquisites, and in various of the responsibilities he discharged.

A conversation between Tadahira and his second son, Morosuke, that was recorded in Morosuke's *Kyūreki* journal shines light on how Morosuke viewed the regent's special status. Tadahira and his son were debating which protocols should be followed at a ministerial banquet to be hosted by Tadahira. While Tadahira opined that his post was not that of the supreme minister, and that therefore protocols for such such should not be utilized, his son responded, "Even though you are not the supreme minister, the regental post is unlike that of all other ministers."[45] As regent, Tadahira occupied an office in the Back Palace itself. In 939 it was located in the same Umetsubo hall where the Queen's Household Agency (*Chūgūshiki*) was located (see Figure 10, p. 154). This would have been a convenient location for Tadahira because that agency served his sister, Queen-consort Yasuko, and the boy monarch who lived with her. Meanwhile Tadahira's own daughter, Takako, worked in the Back Palace as Mistress of the Royal Wardrobe, situated in the Higyōsha.[46]

Making his premier ministerial status clear to all, Tadahira received special attendants and guards, just as had Yoshifusa and Mototsune in the past. Immediately following his regental appointment in 930, a royal order granted Tadahira two inner palace attendants (*udoneri*) as well as an honor guard of eight outriders from the Left and Right Inner Palace Guards. Since Yoshifusa's day, such attendants had become markers of the regent's special status.[47]

As his tenure progressed, Tadahira received more honors. In 932 he was promoted to the junior first rank with the privilege of entering the palace precincts via the Jōtō Gate in an ox-drawn carriage—other ministers were obliged to do so on foot (see Figure 7). He was named supreme minister—an honor which the codes termed extraordinary—in 936. And in 939, he was proclaimed "an equal in status to the three queens" (jusangū), as Yoshifusa had been before him.[48] The new status served to increase his allotment of prebendal tax units as well as his powers of patronage to nominate appointees for office.[49]

As early as 931 the nine-year-old Suzaku began to visit the Southern Hall "to learn the ways of government," but Regent Tadahira nonetheless served as his proxy for him in a wide variety of tasks.[50] For instance during 931, the first full year of his regental tenure, Tadahira recorded how he assembled the female courtiers from the Back Palace and led them outside for snow viewing. He had apparently done the same for male courtiers earlier.[51] Here it seems likely that Tadahira was standing in for the young monarch as the adult leader of the residential palace.

Similarly, while an adult tennō would have personally sent off provincial governors departing for their bailiwicks, in the eighth month of 939 it was Regent Tadahira who dispatched the new governor of Mutsu with gifts and admonitions to rule well for the throne's sake:

I went to the Shirakawa residence and hosted a departure banquet for the governor of Mutsu, Sir [Taira no] Koresuke. We had a bit of playing of flutes and strings. Appropriate rewards were distributed.[52]

As for other tasks the regent took over for the child tennō, at times of drought or famine Tadahira would routinely order alms distributed to the poor and sick in the capital.[53] He oversaw diplomatic affairs, as when he ordered special provisions for an embassy from Paekche in 931.[54] The regent received or denied requests from high rankers to retire from His Majesty's service.[55] And in 931 we read how Tadahira consulted with Left Junior Controller Ōe no Asatsuna (886-957) to select a new era name for Suzaku's reign. "Shōhei," meaning "receiving Heaven's peace," was their choice.[56] And finally Regent Tadahira frequently ordered members of the Council to discuss a specific policy or issue, and then to memorialize recommendations to the throne.[57]

The regental order commanded Tadahira to protect, provide for, and educate his young charge. At a time when there was still great concern about Michizane's shade, we see Tadahira frequently ordering court officials to schedule Buddhist rites, divining sessions, or offerings to be sent to shrines and temples. Two prelates from Enryakuji on Mount Hiei, Son'i and Gikai, were frequent visitors at the residential palace, where they performed protective Buddhist rites.[58] Indeed, their prominence in Tadahira's journal indicates the preeminence of Enryakuji as a realm-protecting Buddhist venue in Tadahira's day. Nonetheless sutra readings were often performed at other official temples as well, as we see in the entry for the tenth day of the seventh month in 939:

> I ordered the Prelates' Office to have the fifteen great
> temples and Enryakuji, along with other state-supported
> temples, perform an abbreviated reading of the Benevolent
> King Sutra for three days, beginning the day after
> tomorrow. This is to pray for rain.

Another document from 938 names eleven of these great temples as Jingoji, Gokurakuji, Zenrinji, Anjōji, Jōjūji, Hosshōji, Kanshūji, Kaiinji, Gangyōji, Ninnaji, and Daigoji.[59] Tōdaiji, Kōfukuji, Tōji, and Saiji likely comprised the remainder.

Regent Tadahira was also responsible for the young monarch's education. He arranged calligraphy sessions, readings of Japanese and Chinese classics, and other training to prepare the monarch for visits to the Southern Pavilion to learn about rulership.[60] He also concerned himself with his charge's filial responsibilities: the deceased Daigo had vowed to construct a new temple southeast of the capital, and Tadahira was much involved in constructing Daigoji during the 930s.[61] In such circumstances Regent Tadahira clearly acted as the young tennō's chief aide and mentor.

Who assisted Tadahira with these tasks? Council ministers whose names appear frequently in entries from 939 include Senior Counselor Taira no Koremochi (881-939), head of the Queen-consort's Household and Tadahira's cousin; and Senior Counselor Fujiwara no Saneyori, Tadahira's first son and heir, who was then serving as the left senior commander of the Inner Palace Guards.

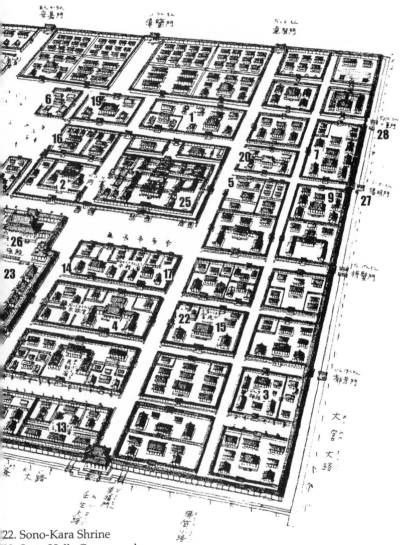

安嘉門　偉鑒門　達智門

6　19　1

16　28

20　1

2　5　9　27

25

園韓神寺

14　中務　11

22　15　4

26　神祇官

23

3

13

大宮大路

壬生門　郁芳門

嘉福門

壬生大路　佛光路

22. Sono-Kara Shrine
23. State Halls Compound
24. Suzaku Gate
25. Tennō's Residential Palace
26. Throne Hall
27. Yōmei Gate
28. Jōtō Gate

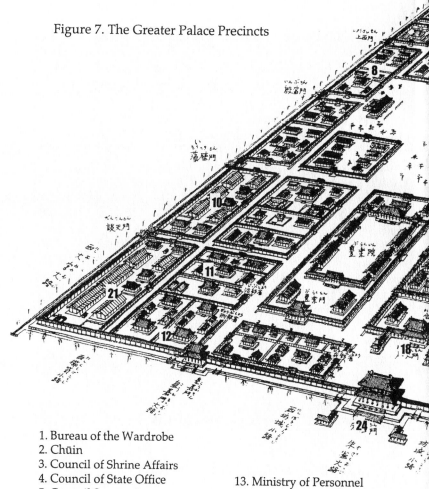

Figure 7. The Greater Palace Precincts

1. Bureau of the Wardrobe
2. Chūin
3. Council of Shrine Affairs
4. Council of State Office
5. Council Secretariat
6. Custodial Office
7. Inner Left Guards' Headquarters
8. Inner Right Guards' Headquarters
9. Left Palace Guards' Headquarters
10. Left Stables
11. Ministry of Civil Affairs
12. Ministry of Justice

13. Ministry of Personnel
14. Ministry of Residential Palace Affa
15. Ministry of the Royal Household
16. Office of the Royal Table
17. Yin-yang Bureau
18. Ōtenmon Gate
19. Palace Provisions Office
20. Queen Consort's Agency
21. Right Stables

From the Controller's Office, Tadahira conferred often with Senior Left Controller Minamoto no Koreshige and Middle Left Controller Minamoto no Sukemoto. Controllers were the workhorses of Tadahira's court, moving from the residential palace to the regent and on to confer with members of the Council.[62] Senior controllers were themselves Council members, while lesser controllers—Sukemoto, for instance—served as a member of the Royal Secretariat. Sukemoto was such a frequent visitor to Tadahira's place that he is generally referred to in the journal with a nickname, Controller Sō.[63]

From the Royal Secretariat in the residential palace the fifth-rank secretary (go'i kurōdo) Fujiwara no Asatada, who was also posted as the left junior commander of the Inner Palace Guards, frequently received Tadahira's commands or notified him of conditions at the residential palace. He and other members of the Royal Secretariat were charged with coordinating provisions, scheduling, staffing, and protection for the monarch's residence. The Secretariat's five to ten appointees included two directors plus several members holding the fifth and sixth ranks. All were normally chosen by the tennō, but during Suzaku's minority they would have been selected by Tadahira in consultation with other stake-holders such as Queen Yasuko and the retired Uda.

Concurrent appointments of the royal secretaries facilitated their work. In 931, for instance, the fifth-rank royal secretary Minamoto no Kintada doubled as right junior controller; and the fifth-rank secretary Fujiwara no Asatada served as a chamberlain in the Residential Palace Ministry, which oversaw the processing of royal orders brought to it by a chamberlain (see Figure 4). He was also an officer in the Right Outer Palace Guards.[64] The latter were frequently posted concurrently as members of the Royal Police Office, which was responsible for performing cleansing rituals (harae) inside and outside the greater palace precincts. Still another secretary was Fujiwara no Arisuke, who was a Secretariat sixth-ranker co-posted to the Left Outer Palace Guards. Royal secretaries frequently served in the Royal Storehouse Bureau (Kuraryō) and the Carpentry Bureau (Mokuryō), whence provisions and repairs for the residential palace came. Communications, defense, and provisioning were well served by such arrangements.

Meanwhile what of relations between Regent Tadahira and the retired Uda Tennō? Until his death in the summer of 931, Uda resided outside the greater palace precincts, as had retired *tennō* since Saga's retirement.[65] Uda was nonetheless Tadahira's longtime patron with whom he kept in touch. When Tadahira was too sick to oversee the appointments process in 931, for instance, he notified Uda of that fact. In 939 we see emissaries from Uda visiting Tadahira from time to time, sometimes to discuss emoluments and perquisites for Uda or his clients. Tadahira's elder brother Nakahira (875-945), a man known more for his interest in poetry than politics, seems to have served frequently as Uda's emissary.[66]

Indeed in the 930s a network of familial relations—blood and affinal bonds—linked the court's leadership. To list a few of the kin relations in which Regent Tadahira was situated in 939, he was the younger brother of the queen-dowager; son-in-law to the royal grandfather who was also retired monarch; brother to the head of the Council, Minister of the Left Nakahira; and cousin and intimate to one senior counselor while being the father of another. All this means that we need to revise the common wisdom that the Northern Fujiwara regents depended on matrilineal ties to the throne. Tadahira was but one member of the bilineal kin network that presided over the court.[67] At the same time, the information and efforts on which that network depended to make its decisions and carry them out required a much broader group of officials, most of them of the fifth rank or higher, of which Regent Tadahira was the hub.

PRODUCER OF THE ANNUAL RITUAL CYCLE

As leader of the court, Regent Tadahira spent a great deal of effort overseeing the court's ritual calendar. Journal entries for the 930s indicate that Tadahira was engaged daily in planning, provisioning, and supervising its events. Appendix A at the end of this essay lists more than forty annual activities that are mentioned in our abstracted entries for 939. If we had Tadahira's complete journal, there would be many more because fragments quoted in other sources refer to additional ritual occasions.

As Appendix A demonstrates, the ritual calendar of Tadahira's day comprised a variety of events, each of which provides insights into the world of tenth-century courtiers. Yoshida Sanae points out in her essay earlier in this volume how Fujiwara no Mototsune, Tadahira's father, had a list of annual events—the *Nenjūgyōji no misōji*—compiled and then displayed in the residential palace in 885.[68] Additional events were added in Uda Tennō's era.[69] Among them were activities that spotlighted the *tennō*, such as the New Year Assembly (*Chōga*), royal banquets (*sechie*), ceremonies for promotions in rank and post (*Jimoku*), and special reports to the throne, like the Derelict Field Surveys Memorial (*Fukandendensō*). Unlike in Nara times, however, such events mostly took place within the *tennō*'s residential palace rather than in the Halls of State (Chōdōin) and its Throne Hall (Daigokuden).[70] The monarch should have participated in these events in 939—he had, by then, passed his coming-of-age ceremony. But Tadahira's entries indicate that Suzaku was frequently sick or under taboo. Never mind, protocols had already developed in the ninth century for holding these events without the *tennō*'s presence.

Another category of events included Buddhist rites, such as regularly scheduled or specially scheduled readings of the Benevolent King Sutra (Ninnōkyō), official assemblies like the Yuimae at Nara's Kōfukuji, and the Buddhist Litany held at the palace. Other events involved offerings, prayers, and celebrations to the deities (*kami*) of heaven and earth as realm protectors. In 939 the Kamo and Ise shrines are seen receiving frequent propitiation, although the Sono and Kara deities within the palace precincts as well as provincial deities at official shrines called *hōbeisha* also received offerings. Still another category included educational activities, such as lectures on the Chinese or Japanese classics including the Classic of Filial Piety (Kōkyō) and the Chronicle of Japan (*Nihon shoki*). These took place in front of the monarch and members of the Council. And there were grand entertainments, such as sumo and archery matches. By the early tenth century, the Heian court had developed a much more varied cycle of rites than in Nara times, and Northern Fujiwara regents had been key to the innovation process.[71] Tadahira was aware of that legacy and serious about living up to it.

Many events lasted for several days, and some days—especially those in the first month—witnessed multiple events. All required extensive planning and provisioning in which Tadahira was frequently involved, although he might assign some tasks to others. He could also order colleagues on the Council or in the Controllers' Office to debate and decide a course of action after research into past precedents. Before plans were set, in any case, Tadahira would receive either oral or written proposals to approve or reject. Results were then sent on to the monarch for his signature.

A few examples will provide insights into how Regent Tadahira produced these events. Consider the example of Suzaku Tennō's Enthronement Rite (Daijōsai) in 931. Such activities were generally planned by a group of officials organized as a project planning team (gyōjisho). It included a senior noble-in-charge from the Council who was assisted by a controller. Whenever difficulties were encountered, however, it was Regent Tadahira who was notified, and it was up to him to decide the next step. On the twenty-eighth of the fifth month in 931, for instance, Tadahira heard reports of a shortage of provisions for the enthronement. Working together with the Capital Affairs Agency, the controllers proposed a solution:

> Left Middle Controller reported that (resources to employ) labor to construct the yuki and suki pavilions (for the Daijōsai) were lacking. But there is a proposal from the Capital Affairs Agency to borrow (the needed rice) resources from (emergency stores in the) Gisō, and to (later) repay it with coin collected from taxes (chōsen).[72]

Tadahira, however, was unpersuaded that this was the best course of action. He sent the matter to the Council of State for further discussion. On the following day, the Council proposed another tack: they wanted to appropriate coin and rice from provincial taxes and interest from official loans. Tadahira accepted their plan.[73]

Regent Tadahira frequently initiated the planning process for major events, as he did in the second month in 939 for a special Benevolent King Assembly (Ninnōe). Specifically he gave the senior counselor Koremochi orders to begin preparations, which involved scheduling and selection of elite monks to read the Benevolent King Sutra. Such sutra readings were regularly held in the spring and autumn, but this was a special event to respond to ominous signs including an earthquake and what was considered an astral warning: "triple alignment" of Jupiter, the sun, and the Guest Star.[74] Tadahira checked later on the planning process, issued further orders, and was informed when the assembly took place—we don't know where, but it was probably held either in the residential palace or at the Throne Hall (see Figure 7).[75] On still other occasions in 939, Tadahira ordered the Council to organize performances of realm-protective rites at the fifteen official temples in the vicinity of the capital.

Tadahira also consulted members of the Yingyang Bureau (Onmyōryō) in dealing with ominous signs. It was their responsibility to determine cause and seriousness, and to propose responses. During the seventh month of 939, for example, Onmyō officials were charged by Tadahira with carrying out rain prayers, including a Five Dragon Festival.[76] According to the journal, they had some success, but not enough. Therefore on Tadahira's explicit orders, their efforts were supplemented by offerings to various shrines and by more reading of the Benevolent King Sutra both at the palace and at Enryakuji on Mount Hiei. The event was presided over by the highest ranking prelate of the realm, the Tendai abbot Son'i.[77]

When officials reported illness or some other impure condition that impeded their participation in court rituals, Regent Tadahira called on his knowledge of precedent and protocol to make alternative plans. Late in 931, for instance, a Council secretary approached Tadahira with news that members of the Council and royal intimates (tenjōbito) were all indisposed and could not attend the annual presentation of the new calendar to the throne. In that case Tadahira ordered that the female director of the Back Palace (Naishi no kami) herself memorialize the calendar before the young tennō.[78] And in 939, when Minister of Civil Affairs Fujiwara no Masamoto was unable to preside at the Sono and Kara deities' service due to advanced age, Tadahira ordered a Council secretary to proceed after consulting precedents for the Ōharano Festival. The latter had occasionally been held without the participation of a Council member.[79] And when colleagues were unavailable, Tadahira would sometimes take the duty himself.[80] He did more of that in the early 930s than he did in 939, when he was suffering from more illness. Sometimes he tried relying on his elder brother, Nakahira, then minister of the left and head of the Council. But in late 939, that proved unsuccessful:

> Because it was an inauspicious day, His Majesty needed to take special care. I sent Controller Sō to Minister of the Left to order him to arrange prayers to the deities. But saying that he was ill, he did not receive him and Sukemoto returned without having carried out his charge. Is this any way for a minister of the throne to act?[81]

Nonetheless, as his full brother Nakahira was clearly an important member of Tadahira's team. Indeed one of Tadahira's several extant poems fetes Nakahira's promotion to minister of the left in 933, and celebrates their shared paternity:

> The flowers of the plum, whether late or early,
> Bloom in the end—who is it that has planted the seed?[82]

On occasion Tadahira even criticized his own son and heir Saneyori, as when the latter bungled the order of events at the Grand Archery Ceremony in the first month of 939:

> I heard that Senior Captain of the Right {Fujiwara no Saneyori} arrived at his seat in the tent in the Great Courtyard {for the Grand Archery Ceremony} but that then there was a summons. When he entered {the residential palace}, he was told His Majesty would not be present {for the proceedings}. It was a blunder.[83]

According to the usual calendar, the Grand Archery Meet (*Jarai*) was held on the seventeenth day of the first month to assure good fortune in the coming year.[84] The Great Courtyard (Ōba) was the open area in front of the residential palace, outside of the Kenrei Gate (see Figure 10, p. 154). It seems that Saneyori had not studied the precedents sufficiently to know the proper order of events: he was not to have gone directly to the Great Courtyard without first determining whether the *tennō* would attend.

Ill omens or a death could result in cancellation of important court rituals. For instance, on the eleventh of the fourth month in 939, the senior nobles decided, at Tadahira's request, that the

Fifth-month Banquet (alternatively known as *Tango no sechie*) should not be held that year, given concerns about Taira no Masakado's violent activities in the east.[85]

When weather or other circumstances led to a need for such adjustments in the ritual calendar, Regent Tadahira was the final authority. The annual Kamo Festival in the fourth month was the occasion of a procession of courtiers bearing offerings to the Kamo Shrine north of the capital (see Map 2), but in 939 flooding prevented the princess-priestess (*saiō*) and her attendants from crossing the river. Throughout the emergency on the fourteenth and the fifteenth days, Tadahira stayed involved:

The fourteenth   Kamo Festival. Rain fell all day. The Kamo Priestess set out, but the river was flooded and I heard that people had trouble crossing. In the evening Middle Controller of the Right hurried over to report that neither the Kamo Priestess nor the others could cross the river and that they were stranded. I ordered that they should await the arrival of messengers tomorrow, and then continue on. But the messengers [from the Inner Palace Guards and other offices] should cross by boat this evening and deliver the votive offerings.

The fifteenth   In the early morning I sent the attendant Zaijō to deliver a message to the Kamo Priestess. Sir Kintada, in charge of events, delivered a message from her that arrived last night. He also said he looked for the messengers to transmit my orders but no one was found. Then this morning they appeared and everyone set out for the shrine.

Tadahira demonstrated his mastery of ritual knowledge when he wrote out notes to instruct the *tennō* on the Seasonal Ceremony (*Shun*) on the first day of the tenth month of 939:

Minister of the Left went to the residential palace and determined today's agenda. In short order he selected and recorded the extra ceremonial chamberlains {to be present for the Seasonal Ceremony} and then submitted the list to His Majesty. I also wrote down the sequence of events for the Seasonal Ceremony to memorialize to His Majesty. His Majesty was present in the Southern Hall. After the lighting of the lamps, the guards and Lesser Counselor presented memorials. In all this I heard that many violations of protocol occurred.[86]

Originally held on the first, eleventh, and twenty-first of each month, the *Shun* brought courtiers before the *tennō* to report on matters of governance in their respective offices.[87] On such occasions the *tennō* also hosted banquets for courtiers. By the tenth century, however, *Shun* was conducted only on the first day of the fourth and tenth months, during the spring and winter seasons. They were thus called "Seasonal Rites." [88]

Given his mandate to oversee all governmental affairs for his young lord, when officials failed to report for their jobs promptly, Regent Tadahira would order reprimands, sanctions, and replacements. For example, in the entry for the fifth day of the sixth month in 939 we find,

> I reprimanded two junior controllers, Asa{tsuna} and Suke{moto}, for absenteeism in the offices of the Council. The two said that they had decided among themselves who would come on the days of required service and on the days before and after. I censured them: "How could you decide about attendance for those days. Mind you, attend every day." But since a man is not made of wood and stone, how can there not be days when there are absences?

As we have seen, controllers were among the busiest officials at the tenth-century court. They were critical links between the regent, Council members, the retired monarch, and the residential palace. Tadahira was distressed to learn that they were limiting their days on duty. But at the same time, he revealed his human side. As a man who suffered illness himself, he understood that no one could work every day. And yet he prided himself on the highest standards for getting His Majesty's government done with propriety and efficacy. That is why at the end of the sixth month Tadahira checked back on matters in the Controllers' Office:

I summoned the controller Genkan. I ordered him to tally up the days that controllers and junior secretaries of the Council of State had reported for work last month in the Council Office and Preparatory Office.[89]

Since there is no entry indicating otherwise, perhaps he was satisfied by the response.

OVERSEER OF THE APPOINTMENT PROCESS

In the court of Tadahira's day the *tennō* was still the apical ordinator—responsibility for all appointments to the fifth rank or higher, and for posts granted to such high rankers, belonged to the Heavenly Sovereign. Nonetheless in the 930s Regent Tadahira oversaw the appointment process as the child monarch's proxy.

In Nara times both rank and post had been important, but by 900, post was most important. To become eligible for posts that conferred both power and livelihood, the fifth rank was necessary. Fifth-rankers could enter the royal presence, and they still received official remuneration.[90] Therefore promotion from the sixth to the fifth rank, a process called *joshaku*, was considered crucial. Council secretaries nominated candidates for *joshaku*: they evaluated the seniority of applicants and passed on their own recommendations (*kanmon*) for discussion by the senior nobles in front of the *tennō* or his regental proxy.[91] Other royals, such as the queen-consort and the retired *tennō* as well as high ranking nobles, could put forth *joshaku* nominations for members of their households and other clients.[92] In 939, for instance, Tadahira recorded that the list of those qualified for promotion in rank was memorialized to the throne on the seventh day of the fourth month, after vetting by controllers and discussions by the Council. Then on the twentieth of the following month those promoted received their certificates of rank (*iki*).[93]

Tadahira's entries for 931 include a series of records for the appointment process that year. Most appointment-related activities for the first half of that year were postponed until the third month since Tadahira was too ill to participate. Late in the first month, Tadahira sent a messenger to the retired Uda to advise him of his illness. Still later, when discussions concerning candidates finally began on 3/11—these meetings were called

"Deliberations concerning Appointments" (*Jimoku no gi*)—they were held in the regent's quarters in the Umetsubo (see Figure 10, p. 154). There the regent, still weak from his illness, remained sequestered behind curtains while two senior nobles led the discussion that continued through the morning of the thirteenth.[94]

> *Jimoku no gi*—it began in the Umetsubo. Since I was ill, deliberations were put off until this point. The senior nobles expressed the view, "To wait until you recuperate—it is hard to know what may happen. However untoward, let it be carried out without your going out to the usual site for such deliberations." I summoned Senior Counselor and Her Majesty's steward before my curtains, and we carried out deliberations.[95]

A key component of these discussions concerned possible appointees to vacant provincial governorships. Back in the first month the process of reviewing governors' service by scrutinizing their resumés (*rōchō*) had begun.[96] But on the last day of deliberations, the trio found that they needed additional evidence, and they called in the head of the Left Gate Guards as well as a Council advisor. After these discussions finally ended the list of recommended appointees was formally memorialized by Minamoto no Kintada, a royal secretary and controller, on the fifteenth. After that, additional appointments and emendations were made in a ceremony called the *Naoshimono* on the eighteenth and the twenty-sixth, and on into the fifth month. It was the middle of the fourth month before certificates of rank for those newly admitted to the fifth rank were prepared by residential palace secretaries (*naiki*) for Tadahira's viewing, after which they were presented to His Majesty, sealed by the royal hand, and then distributed to appointees.[97]

Lower ranking posts were often filled by persons nominated by high ranking courtiers in an event called *Ichibumeshi*. For instance, in 931 nominations were sent in by the retired Uda and subsequently discussed in the Council. Only after such deliberations were the nominations submitted to Tadahira. Tadahira himself received the right to make one such nomination in 939.[98] And in 939 we find that Uda requested a reward for the director of his own royal pasture in Shinano—he had done good work and so should have his tenure extended by two years.[99] Tadahira approved the request and entrusted it to Minamoto no Kintada for action.[100] In 939 the ceremony of appointment for these nominees was held on the fifteenth and sixteenth days of the third month.[101]

Other appointments could be made by royal order without Council deliberation. The Royal Secretariat facilitated these appointments. Seats on the Council, membership in the Royal Secretariat, headships of Secretariat offices called *tokoro*, lay director (*zokubettō*) posts at official temples, heads (*bettō*) of temple construction agencies, and appointments of monk ritualists for official rituals were all made by royal command and transmitted by directive.[102] And on the fifth day of the fourth month in 931, Tadahira passed orders to the royal secretary who also served as right junior controller, Minamoto no Kintada, concerning the appointment of the second-in-charge (*kengyō*) at the Office to Oversee Provincial Governor Performance (Kageyushi). There were also two appointments to the Royal Police.[103] In the third month of that same year, Tadahira approved written drafts of royal orders appointing abbots for Kōfukuji and Kairyūōji, as well as another order naming twenty-one monks to participate in a protective rite for the *tennō*.[104]

And in early 939, we also find references to the semi-annual *Jimoku no gi* on 2/1, and again at year's end, on 12/26 and 12/27. As for appointments by direct royal command, in the eighth month we see:

> I went to the residential palace. The ceremony to name
> senior nobles was held in the presence of His Majesty.
> Minister of the Left and I were present. At its conclusion we
> summoned Senior Captain of the Right and had the formal
> record prepared.[105]

This was a momentous event for Tadahira, for it saw Saneyori, promoted to the Council as an advisor. Circumstances had changed substantially since 931. The *tennō* had already had his coming of age ceremony and was considered an adult monarch, even though he was refusing to accept Tadahira's resignation as regent. Still the *tennō* was now present for the *Jimoku*, and it is likely that the meeting took place in the Back Palace pavilion that was then serving as the royal residence, the Ryōkiden.

Regent Tadahira maintained a certain distance from other Council ministers, perhaps to demonstrate his special relationship with the throne. In 931, for instance, there were only three occasions when Tadahira went to the Inner Guards' guardpost (*jin*) where the senior nobles deliberated: he went twice for Emendation of Appointments discussions, and once when a Council report (*Jin no mōshibumi*) was in preparation.[106] In the latter instance, on the nineteenth of the sixth month of 931, Tadahira may have attended after being alerted to difficulties caused by the absence of the presiding minister:

> Went to the guardpost. There was a Council report (*mōshibumi*). Asked the council secretary whether Preparatory Work in the Council Secretariat (*Gekisei*) was complete. The senior controller replied, "Since the eighth (day), the presiding minister has not appeared." Also, "A royal seal is needed--today the matter of the storehouse should be sealed." Right Senior Captain should memorialize the matter.[107]

Unfortunately we know nothing about why the presiding Minister of the Right Fujiwara no Sadakata had not come to the palace for eleven days. Nonetheless it apparently took Regent Tadahira's participation to get the governing process moving, by ordering his brother, then a senior counselor, to memorialize the throne in place of the absent minister. Strikingly, he himself did not do so.

OVERSEER OF PROVINCIAL GOVERNMENT

Regent Tadahira's role as proxy for the young *tennō* made him responsible for supervising provincial governors who administered the "royal land" (*ōdo*), as the provinces were sometimes called.[108] The wherewithal supporting royal and aristocratic livelihoods came from taxing the provinces, while provincial administration also provided livelihoods to fifth-rankers who worked as provincial governors (*zuryō*). The latter bore responsibility for tax collection and shipping proceeds to the capital. Moreover many senior nobles and other courtiers whose names appear in Appendix B held provincial governorships as sinecures from which they drew income, even if they never went out to the provinces.[109]

Concerns about provincial administration increased in the 930s, given frequent outbreaks of banditry and piracy as well as the tendency for governors to underpay taxes.[110] Under Tadahira's leadership the court developed a stricter system of evaluation for custodial provincial governors, which process was called "Evaluation of Efficacy" (*Kōka sadame*). Staffers in the Controllers' Office and the Office to Oversee Provincial Governor Performance evaluated end-of-term reports submitted by governors themselves. Those records were then discussed by the senior nobles and the results were memorialized to the throne.[111] Only governors who received good marks could expect future appointments as *zuryō*.

Another crucial issue was maximizing taxable fields. From the Engi era (901-923) onward, the court sent agents to each province to consult with governors about derelict fields—uncultivated or unprofitable fields—and how such fields could be brought back into cultivation. By the tenth century, regulations were tightened further and governors were ordered to decrease such fields on an annual basis. Their number was to be reported in the eighth month; and based on the report, a lesser number was allowed. In 938 a new policy of exempting only two-thirds of reported derelict fields was put in place.

According to the *Saikyūki* ritual handbook of the late tenth century, activities at court concerning the *Fukandenden* Memorial were numerous during the ninth month.[112] Given evidence in Tadahira's journal, however, the process had not yet been routinized. Prior to the memorial the senior nobles discussed reports from provincial governors that had been vetted by controllers and Council secretaries. The results were compiled in the memorial, and Regent Tadahira was clearly involved in that process. Tadahira first received information on the number of uncultivated fields in the third month.[113] Then in the fifth month he ordered the right middle controller to prepare directives ordering provincial authorities to meet stipulated quotas.[114] There are few entries concerning the process in 939, but Tadahira did record that the memorial was read before Suzaku Tennō on the second day of the eleventh month.[115]

The Performance Office had been established in 797 to evaluate the service of provincial governors. Later its work was shifted to the controllers. By the tenth century, however, the Office was again evaluating governors, who were required to submit their reports to the director (*bettō*) of the Royal Secretariat. Given this, it seems likely the Office was then operating as a unit of the Secretariat.

Its work was laborious, as reflected by constant complaints about its slow pace and a resulting lack of candidates for reappointment. In an entry from the second of the seventh month in 939, we hear of a case that ended well for one governor, but only after his complaints about the slow process:

> The Governor of Ise, Shigetoki, was promoted to senior fifth rank for service in Higo. He should have been promoted in the first month, but he did not obtain the comprehensive receipt for one year's taxes in kind and labor, and so he was not promoted. However today he was promoted because there were precedents for doing so, and also because he submitted a complaint.[116]

In addition to requiring full payment of regular taxes and special levies, Regent Tadahira tightened up rules mandating prompt departure for provincial posts.[117] When a governor became ill in 931, for instance, he was required to seek permission to remain in the capital to recuperate. His formal request was brought to Tadahira by a controller, to whom Tadahira issued his command to have a royal order of permission drawn up.[118] In 939 Tadahira also ordered that selected provincial governors provide supplies and labor to repair the wall surrounding the greater palace precincts—it had fallen into such disrepair that animals wandered in, and there was also a great fear of bandits. After issuing that order, Tadahira kept close watch on the project, sternly demanding that recalcitrant governors be punished.[119]

From the governors' perspective, tax collection was made more difficult by the ongoing tendency for local elites (*fugō no tomogara*) and capital aristocrats (*ōshinke, kenmon seika*) to ally themselves against the governors' authority.[120] As Karl Friday has noted, the ninth- and tenth-century countryside was a stage for increasingly violent competition between local elites, provincial governors, and the nobility, with members of each group wanting more of its wealth.[121] Governors and their staffs were frequently targets of violence—Abe Takeshi has identified 59 murders of provincial governors between 795 and 1104.[122] Indeed in 939, for instance, express messengers arrived one night at Tadahira's residence to announce that the governor of Owari had been murdered, followed by news that same evening of ongoing violence against the authorities in Dewa:

> News arrived that the governor of Owari, Tomomasa, had been shot and killed by an arrow. An express courier from Dewa {also} arrived. And another express courier from Owari came in the middle of the night.[123]

Investigation proved slow going—three months later Tadahira recorded that no progress had been made in identifying the culprits in Owari.[124] Later that year Tadahira also heard reports that two governors had been kidnapped by pirates as they were returning to the capital from their bailiwicks in western Japan.[125]

Regent Tadahira was also vexed by the difficulty of getting tax proceeds delivered promptly to the capital. In 931, for example, he ordered a controller to investigate remedies for delinquent delivery of silk levies—such silk was to have been purchased with tax proceeds by provincial authorities and then shipped to the capital, but full shipments were not being received. On another occasion, Tadahira directed a controller to ascertain how much polished rice had to be levied on various provinces to meet expected need.[126] After nearly a month, advisor and controller Minamoto no Sukemoto recommended that some 2000 *koku* of rice be ordered polished and remitted by designated provincial governors.[127] Tadahira approved the plan, but someone must have done some further calculations because a few days later the amount was increased to 3000 *koku*.[128] In another instance, there were deliberations as to how much polished rice would be needed from the distant Dazaifu in Kyūshū for gifts at upcoming royal banquets.[129] Securing such shipments from pirate attack would have been a major concern along the Inland Sea. And since provisions had to be brought from distant points, maintenance of the transport infrastructure was a concern. During 931, for instance, Tadahira gave orders to a controller concerning the lumber needed to repair the Yamazaki Bridge, which spanned the Yodo River and was thus a key transit point south of the capital (see Map 2).[130]

Rice and silk are the most frequently mentioned commodities in Tadahira's journal entries. In the tenth month of 931, for instance, Tadahira ordered that a special levy from Yamato tax rice be used to cover shortages in the provisions for that year's realm-protecting Yuima Assembly at Kōfukuji.[131] And in that same year, Tadahira ordered a controller to see that cloth for clothing and rice for the Back Palace, including the Office of Female Musicians and Dancers, was provided.[132] The court also continued to mint coinage in the early tenth century: in the fifth month of 931, for instance, Tadahira ordered a controller to send a directive requisitioning coins from the Minting Office (Juzenshi) in distant Suō Province. Coin was also ordered spent later that year to pay for government expenses.[133]

While it has sometimes been charged that Regent Tadahira and his colleagues were ignorant of and indifferent to the provinces, Tadahira's journal indicates significant involvement in provincial administration. And certainly the Engi shiki that Tadahira helped to assemble gave significant attention to provincial governance—some 29 of its 50 rolls concern such matters. The 930s also saw compilation of Japan's first encyclopedia, the Wamyōruijūshō, by Minamoto no Shitagō (911-983). Shitagō was a third-generation descendent of the throne and tutor for a daughter of Daigo Tennō. On her behalf, Shitagō wrote some 70 rolls containing 3000 articles in 24 categorical chapters that are full of information about not only court and capital but also about places in and products from the provinces. All this indicates that Tadahira and his fellows were deeply interested in the provinces over which they ruled.

CRISIS MANAGER

Teishinkōki entries indicate that Regent Tadahira was frequently called upon to manage crises. In such cases he would typically direct subordinates—controllers or Council members—to research precedents, deliberate, and propose a solution.

A major crisis was the death of the retired Uda Tennō in the seventh month in 931. Uda had been a key figure for a long time, having taken the throne in 887. The death of such an important player at court had the potential for destabilizing the realm. There were immediate discussions as to the need for shutting the three barriers and for palace defense. There were also discussions about funerary arrangements, despite Uda's stated wishes that such activities and their costs be minimized.

On the day after Uda's passing, Tadahira gave orders to Controller Ki no Yoshimitsu and Middle Counselor Fujiwara no Tsunesuke to head up the project team overseeing funerary activities.[134] The problem was, however, that Council members were not coming to court to carry on their deliberative responsibilities, perhaps due to mourning.[135] The journal records Tadahira's disapproval but provides no explanation. Two months later planning for Uda's tomb, and that for the deceased Daigo as well, was still unfinished. Tadahira called Ki in to discuss Council directives then being drafted, including some concerning special provincial levies needed to fund both tomb construction and Suzaku Tennō's Enthronement Rite. Tadahira stressed to Ki that the levies had to be kept separate, to prevent pollution: one had to do with the world of the living and the other concerned that of the dead.[136]

Tadahira also faced the challenge of getting the court back to work. He began his efforts two days after Uda's passing, but only in the tenth month did the court resume normal activities.[137] This may be evidence of how concerns about ritual purity constituted a serious obstacle to getting the court's work done.

Tadahira faced other sorts of emergencies as well. In the second and fourth months of 931, for instance, officials came to Tadahira with alarming reports of cadavers found in palace wells. Tadahira responded by ordering divining by the Bureau of Yinyang to determine the extent of ritual pollution and potential ritual responses.[138] Yet another threat to the ritual purity of the palace came from carcasses of dead dogs, and cattle found roaming within the greater palace precincts. In the latter case, Tadahira ordered that the animals be rounded up and turned over to the Stable Bureau.

Piracy was a worsening threat in the 930s. Readers familiar with Ki no Tsurayuki's *Tosa nikki* will remember Tsurayuki's account of his harrowing return to the capital from Tosa Province in 934. In his journal we see Regent Tadahira transmitting orders to Minamoto no Kintada concerning defense against piracy in 931, three years earlier. Most likely, Kintada then had written orders prepared by the Controllers' staff—enforcers may well have been appointed.[139] And in the twelfth month of the same year, Tadahira ordered advisor and controller Sukemoto to have the Yamashiro provincial governor post guards at the river ports of Yodo and Yamazaki, and at other points in the Kinai, to defend against bandit bands (see Figure 8 and Map 2).[140]

Law and order issues worsened appreciably in 939. In the fifth month Tadahira heard reports of a rebellion by frontier dwellers (Emishi) in Akita District, the site of Akita Stockade in northern Dewa Province (see Maps 3 and 4):

> An express courier came from Dewa. The report stated that rebels arrived at the Akita District office. They broke open storehouses, stole the rice, and burned local cultivators' property. It is even said that they brought demons with them.[141]

Fighting there continued for several months. And two months earlier, the court had evaluated reports about feuding between the provincial elite Taira no Masakado and his relatives in the Bandō provinces of eastern Japan (see Figure 9). Tadahira was deeply involved because in his youth Masakado had once served him. Probably because he remained Tadahira's client, charges against him were dismissed in the third month. But in the sixth month new accusations led Tadahira to direct the Council to discuss sending special investigative and enforcement agents to the Bandō:

> I summoned Sir Kintada and had him transmit the following to Minister of the Left: first, that secret agents to investigate allegations of trouble {in the Kantō} be appointed; second, concerning the above, there is need to decide whether to follow precedent in this matter. I went to my office in the Queen-consort's Quarters and instructed senior nobles to appoint the investigative agents. In the evening Minister of Popular Affairs brought the list of appointees.[142]

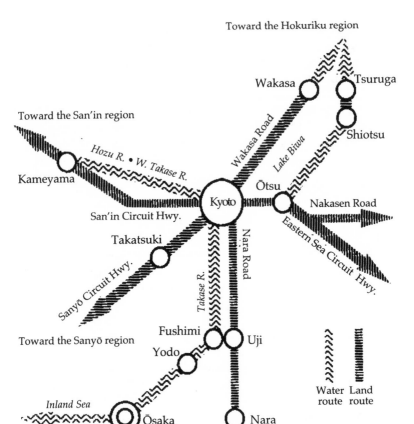

Toward the Hokuriku region

Toward the San'in region

Wakasa

Tsuruga

Shiotsu

Hozu R. • W. Takase R.

Kameyama

Wakasa Road

Lake Biwa

Ōtsu

Kyoto

Nakasen Road

San'in Circuit Hwy.

Eastern Sea Circuit Hwy.

Takatsuki

Nara Road

Sanyō Circuit Hwy.

Takase R.

Toward the Sanyō region

Fushimi

Uji

Yodo

Water   Land
route   route

Inland Sea

Ōsaka

Nara

Toward the west country

After Yamada Kunikazu, *Kara- bukksu Kyōto*, p. 144. Hoikusha, 1993

Figure 8. Transit from Tadahira's Kyoto

Even then, however, Tadahira remained wary of actually posting the agents. Perhaps he was still hoping that some sort of peaceful solution could be found to resolve the violence between Masakado and his kinsmen. Tadahira also doubted the truth of the accusations. As his staff made inquiries, Tadahira ordered the Council and controllers to schedule prayers for peace at official shrines and temples.[143] But one month later Tadahira decided to appoint both investigators and enforcers, even though Masakado's accuser had been jailed for making false allegations:

> Senior Counselor came and showed me Tadaaki's report that the initiator of the allegations {from Musashi Province} should be placed under arrest. In response, I gave him the following instructions: {Minamoto no} Tsunemoto should be detained in the headquarters of the Left Palace Guards; and Morooki and Koreshige should be appointed commanders. However, precedents for appointing persons of the fifth rank for this purpose should be verified. I ordered that a Council directive appointing the investigative agents be drafted immediately.[144]

About this same time news of increasing piracy in the Inland Sea region led by a one-time provincial governor named Fujiwara no Sumitomo also reached the regent's ears. That was in the twelfth month, only a few days before Tadahira heard that Masakado had attacked the provincial headquarters of Shimozuke Province.[145] So as 939 ended, Tadahira and his colleagues at court found themselves facing a two-front battle against violent rebels in both the east and the west. At the very end of the twelfth month Tadahira recorded in his journal:

> I commanded the promulgation of royal orders and directives of the Council of State to the various provinces. Senior Right Captain {of the Inner Palace Guards} officiated.[146]

This officiant was none other than Tadahira's first son and heir, Saneyori, who by then was serving as a senior counselor. Meanwhile Tadahira's second son, Morosuke, was head of the Left Outer Palace Guards as well as director of the Royal Police.

Map 3. The Circuit Highways

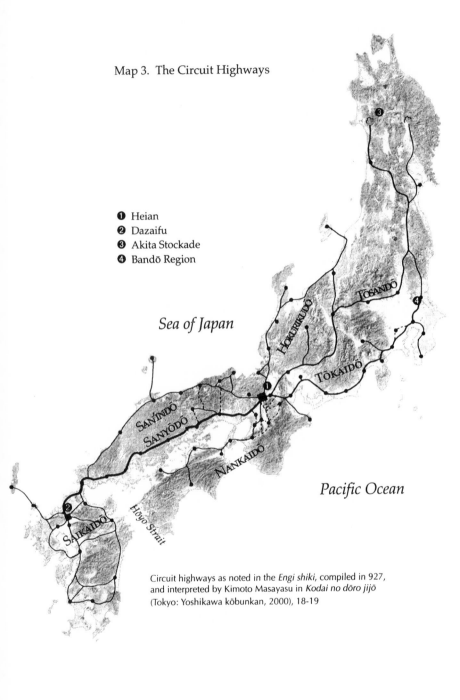

❶ Heian
❷ Dazaifu
❸ Akita Stockade
❹ Bandō Region

Sea of Japan

HOKURIKUDŌ

TŌSANDŌ

TŌKAIDŌ

SANINDŌ

SANYŌDŌ

NANKAIDŌ

Pacific Ocean

Hoyo Strait

SAIKAIDŌ

Circuit highways as noted in the *Engi shiki*, compiled in 927, and interpreted by Kimoto Masayasu in *Kodai no dōro jijō* (Tokyo: Yoshikawa kōbunkan, 2000), 18-19

He was no doubt deeply engaged in organizing military efforts against Masakado and Sumitomo. In the residential palace, Tadahira's sister, Queen-dowager Yasuko, lived with her royal son.

Kin relations thus remained critical to Tadahira's leadership at court in 939. At the same time, surrounding throne and regent were also colleagues and clients who had been personally selected by Tadahira to serve in the Royal Secretariat and on the Council. Some had concurrent postings in the Controllers' Office. Many of them visited Tadahira frequently, coming and going between his venue—whether at home or in the residential palace—and those of various senior nobles. And in the Prelates' Office monks like Abbot Son'i of Enryakuji who were close to Tadahira looked after Buddhist affairs under the Council's watchful eyes. Such were the core members of Tadahira's court in 939, as it faced its darkest hours since the eighth-century rebellions of Fujiwara no Hirotsugu (?-740) and Fujiwara no Nakamaro.[147]

CONCLUSION

What can we conclude from this study of Regent Tadahira's activities as recorded in his *Teishinkōki* journal? First, it is abundantly clear that *ritsuryō* structures including the throne and Council continued to play prominent parts in decision making and policy execution during Tadahira's regency in the 930s. Members of extra-codal structures such as the Royal Secretariat and the Royal Police functioned as links between throne and Council. The primary venue of government in Regent Tadahira's day was not the Halls of State and its Great Throne Hall as in Nara times. Rather it was the residential palace. And while in Nara times Council and throne had functioned as largely parallel structures, by Tadahira's day leadership was clearly being exercised from the throne's side with the regent acting as the monarch's proxy. *Teishinkōki* entries from the 930s indicate that the senior nobles deliberated, memorialized, and executed policy as ordered by Regent Tadahira. Meanwhile the regent worked at the hub of a network whose members, many of whom were his kin, were constantly engaged in consultation. Communications moved

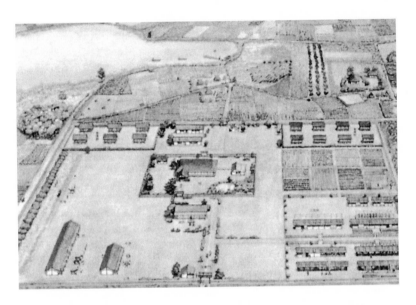

Figure 9. A Provincial Magnate's Residence in the Bandō

The prose work *Utsuho monogatari* (*The Tale of the Hollow Tree*), probably written in the tenth century, describes a wealthy landholder who oversaw cultivation of extensive fields in the Heian countryside. Here is a site reconstruction based on clues from the *Utsuho* narrative and data unearthed by archaeologists in Ibaraki Prefecture. The site has been associated with Taira no Masakado—one of his enemies, Minamoto no Mamoru, who was locally known as "the Great Second-in-command" (*ōsuke*) may have resided at this place, then known as Nomoto. In the *Masakadoki*, Masakado reportedly razed all the houses of Nomoto, Shida, Ōgushi, and Motoki. Masakado would likely have lived in such a residence himself.

We see many storehouses in which the magnate's wealth was stored. There was a smithy for making metal tools, a carpenter's shop, a dye shop, and a place for producing silk cloth. In the vicinity lived dependents who worked for the magnate in various capacities. An adminstrative office (*mandokoro*) was located in front of the residential compound. To the right front were various crafts shops where needed goods were fashioned, including iron tools. Production of such everyday necessities was a great source of power. In the distance are seen the scattered homes of followers (*banrui*) who would have worked the magnate's vast fields, planted with wet rice and other crops. The property at Akahama stretched out over two square *chō*, and the house was surrounded by a defensive embankment and a ditch. There would have been a temple in the neighborhood, and nearby is the best harbor in the vicinity.

Based on a drawing by Nogami Hayao in *Shūkan Asahi hyakka Nihon no rekishi* 59: *Kodai kara chūsei e: Shōhei, Tengyō no ran to miyako*. Asahi shinbunsha, 1987, p. 3-112, 3-113.

between the residential palace, the senior nobles, controllers, other units of officialdom, the retired monarch's palace, and great religious institutions.[148] These were "the stake-holders" of tenth-century court and monarchy.

Among these stake-holders Regent Tadahira was, as his second son Morosuke had once reminded him, "different from other ministers." Following his distinctive regental mandate, Regent Tadahira acted as protector and helper of the young monarch, exercising the full powers of the throne while advising the young lord as his wise and loyal minister. His were the combined powers of throne and Council. But Regent Tadahira belonged more intimately to the residential palace side—he rarely participated in Council deliberations after becoming regent.[149] His role was to call on Council members for deliberation and proposals. Meanwhile controllers, royal secretaries, Council secretaries, and royal intimates, all of whom were Tadahira's relatives and clients by 939, moved between Council and monarch to assure consensus on matters of government as well as the availability of goods and services needed by the members of both.[150]

We have seen that as regent Tadahira oversaw four categories of tasks. He served as Suzaku Tennō's proxy and aide in the residential palace; he oversaw production of events required by the annual ritual calendar; he worked with the Council to oversee provincial administration by His Majesty's emissaries, the provincial governors; and whenever needed, he stepped into the fray to manage crises. He was especially busy with this latter category of tasks in 939.

Among his many responsibilities, overseeing the annual calendar was particularly important to him. Tadahira's notes about such events make up a large percentage of each day's entries. Such rites were the tenth-century court's major *raison d'etre*. In addition to rites that concerned governance itself—the biannual Ceremony for Assigning Posts and the Derelict Field Surveys Memorial are examples—a great many of the court's ceremonies focused on propitiating the gods and buddhas at official shrines and temples, whether in the Kinai or in the provinces. Seen from this perspective, the tenth-century *tennō* remained a sacral monarch who linked Heaven and earth while presiding over a realm that needed protection by *kami* and the

Buddha. The regent educated the young monarch as to these responsibilities, and then supervised and facilitated his fulfillment of them. In every instance, the most important aspects of protocol—who came, who stood where, who did what when, who wore what, who sat on what sort of seat—needed to be recorded for future reference. Such rules were basic to the very order that configured the *tennō*'s court, for which the regent was exemplar and highest arbiter of propriety.

NOTES

[1] . I refer here to the "Northern Fujiwara regents" rather than the "Fujiwara regents" since the descendents of only one line of the larger Fujiwara family dominated the Heian-period regency.

[2] . In 764 Fujiwara no Nakamaro's rebellion had robbed the Southern (Nanke) Fujiwara of much of their leadership capital at court. The so-called Kusuko Coup of 810 essentially removed the Shiki lineage (Shikike) from court leadership. And the Jōwa Coup in 842 strengthened the Northern Fujiwara Yoshifusa's position after the death of the long lived Saga Tennō. In the aftermath of the alleged coup attempt, succession was settled in favor of the future Montoku Tennō, Yoshifusa's nephew. Recent historians view the Jōwa Coup as a plot by Yoshifusa likely backed by Saga's widow, Tachibana no Kachiko, and supporters of the future Montoku. See Endō Keita 2000. On the Ōtenmon Coup of 866 and the regency, see Yoshida Takashi et al. 1995; and Tamai Chikara 2000. An overview of regency history is Yoneda Yūsuke 2002. A compilation of the English historiography is Shively and McCullough 1999, esp. 20-182. In French see Hérail 1995 and Hérail 2006.

[3] . Takeuchi Rizō 1954. I am translating *daijōdaijin* as "supreme minister," in place of the usual "prime minister" to emphasize the extraordinary and preeminent nature of the post, above the (great, grand) ministers (*daijin*) of left and right. For the Law on Personnel (*Shikiinryō*), see Inoue Mitsusada 1976, 159-60.

[4] . Yoshikawa Shinji 1995, esp. 77-91.

[5] . Kuroita's proposition, called "the theory of government by the regental household chancellery" (*Sekkanke mandokoro seijiron*), was first published in 1909. See Yoshioka Masayuki 1993, Tsuchida Naoshige 1992a, and Hashimoto Yoshihiko 1976. Recent discussions include Yoshikawa Shinji 1995, Yoshikawa Shinji 1998, and Ōtsu Tōru 1996. In English see the recently published Morita Tei 2006 and Sasaki Muneo 2005.

[6] .Tsuchida Naoshige 1992a. For Hashimoto's views see Hashimoto Yoshihiko 1976.

[7] . Satō Sōjun 1977.

[8] . Ihara Kesao 1995. Ihara uses the term, "corporate monarchy."

[9] Ōtsu Tōru 1996. For Ōtsu, the tenth-century regency era witnessed "an aristocratic alliance" (*kizoku rengō taisei*) wherein the *tennō* with his regent, the Council (especially through the noble-in-charge *shōkei* system, and its decision-making process resulting in directives), and custodial governors (*zuryō*) cooperated in "mature *ritsuryō* government."

[10] . Tamai Chikara 2000. My own view is that this "stake-holder kingship" was at the center of "the court-centered polity" (*ōchō kokka*). See the translated essays by Morita and Sasaki in Piggott 2006, including the table on page 241. On earlier *ritsuryō* monarchy see Piggott 1997, esp. chapters 6 and 7.

[11] . Kon Masahide 1997. Takinami Sadako also sees precedents for the regency in the authority exercised by senior retired monarchs (*daijōtennō*) in Nara times. See Takinami Sadako 2000.

¹² . See Furuse Natsuko 2001 and Kuramoto Kazuhiro 2000.

¹³ . Yoshikawa Shinji 1998 and Yoshikawa Shinji 1995, esp. 92-111. Yoshikawa emphasizes how the strengthened monarchy (throne plus regent) gained prominence and how, by the late tenth century, the regent "peeled away" from the Council. At the same time clientage relations were increasing, resulting in "the aristocratic overlord (*kenmon*)." The deliberating function of the Council thus declined. Both Yoshikawa and Ōtsu view the mid-tenth century as an epochal moment for regency and polity.

¹⁴ . For an annotated guide to these and other classical sources, see Piggott et al. 2006. For a compendium of Heian documents see Takeuchi Rizō 1973-1978.

¹⁵ .Volumes three through nine of the First Series of the *Dai Nihon shiryō* compiled by the Historiographical Institute (Shiryō hensanjo) at Tokyo University span the years from 901 to 953.

¹⁶. Parts of Morosuke's journal, the *Kyūreki*, have been published in the *Dai Nihon kōkiroku* series of courtier diaries. For Shigeakira's *Rihōōki*, see Yoneda Yūsuke and Yoshioka Masayuki 1974 (*Shiryō sanshū*).

¹⁷ . Tadahira therefore remained regent until 941, when he was named chief-of-staff (*kanpaku*) for the adult *tennō*. In this essay I focus only on Tadahira's regency for Suzaku's reign. I have dealt to some extent with his tenure as Suzaku's *kanpaku* in Piggott 2007.

¹⁸ .Tsunoda Bun'ei 1984, 185; and Tsunoda Bun'ei 1994, vol. 2, 2437. Hotate Michihisa, who stresses the importance of marital relations in court politics, has described Uda's relative autonomy in the 890s, after the death of previous allies who had provided him with consorts. The latter including Mototsune and Tachibana no Hironari. He then sought new allies through affinal ties with such courtiers as Minamoto no Tōru, Michizane, and Tadahira. See Hotate Michihisa 1996, 57-62. Concerning Uda as retired monarch, see Mezaki Tokue 1969.

¹⁹ . Concerning Tadahira's tenure as a controller, see Piggott 2007, 39. On how new relations between the *tennō* and senior nobles on the Council developed in the Heian Period see Hayakawa Shōhachi 1984 and Yoshikawa Shinji 1988. Although Tadahira was appointed an advisor (*sangi*) in 900 (*Kugyō bunin*), he resigned the same year. See Takinami Sadako 1986, esp. 75-76. Sugawara no Michizane was exiled in 901. If Tadahira had his daughter as a consort, that may be why Tadahira resigned his advisor's seat. On Michizane see Tokoro Isao 2002. and, in English, Borgen 1986.

²⁰ . Tsunoda Bun'ei 1984, 185. Concerning Tadahira's Gojō Mansion, see Tsunoda Bun'ei and Kodaigaku kyōkai/Kodaigaku kenkyūjo 1994, 265-66. For a concise description of aristocratic residential architecture in Heian times, see Louis Frédéric 2002, 863-864. Tadahira also had a residence in the Ninth Ward (Kujō) that became the home of his second son, Morosuke. See Tsunoda Bun'ei, 1994, 306-307.

²¹ . The earliest extant reference to *kugyō* dates from 795. It denoted "senior ministers down to advisors," that is, members of the Coujncil of State. See Takinami Sadako 1986, esp. 75-76.

²² . See Sasaki Muneo 1999 and Kamiya Masaaki 1996.

²³ . The Gekichō was also called the Daijōkankōchō or Gekikōchō. An early reference to such discussions is found in a record dated 822 in the *Ruijū fusenshō*, a compendium of official orders compiled in the late eleventh century. See

Kuroita Katsumi 1933 (Shintei zōho Kokushi taikei). In Heian times, as more and more court events took place in the residential palace, a meeting place for the senior nobles was prepared there. It became a customary working place (chokuji) for Council secretaries (geki). Preparation for discussions by the senior noble, called Gekisei, is described in late tenth-century Saikyūki and the eleventh-century Goke shidai. In brief, controllers, lesser counselors, Council secretaries, and varous secretaries and recorders (ex. the ben, shōnagon, geki, and shi) were all to arrive first for Katanashi, to prepare documents for discussion by the kugyō. Senior nobles from the noble-in-charge down would arrive at the Gekichō, and the others would sit down with them. The controller would ask a scribe to read out reports (mōshibumi) submitted by various offices and agencies on which action was needed. Then the noble-in-charge would decide (kessai) about such action. Thereafter would come the shōin ceremony in which various documents were sealed with the gai'in, or Council seal. Then the noble-in-charge would stand up and depart, followed by lower ranking kugyō. They then moved to the Chamberlain's Office (Jijūsho), and a memorial to the throne (Jin no mōshibumi) was prepared. There were then refreshments. According to the ritual handbooks Gekisei was to be held daily save for on the fifth day of the month (a holiday) and on days when court was cancelled (called haimu). Opening time from the third to the seventh month was tatsu no sankoku (around 8 AM) and from the ninth to the first months, inu no ni koku (9:30 AM). In the second and eighth months Gekisei began at inu no ikoku (9 AM).

[24] . Mikawa Kei 1994, 31.

[25] . On the legacy of segmentary monarchy going back to the days of Yamato kingship, see Nitō Atsushi 1996 and Nitō Atsushi 1990.

[26] . On the development of the Royal Police Office, see Yamada Mitsuaki 1996. In English, see Friday 1992, 128-144.

[27] . The scholarly consensus is that earlier entries once existed but that Saneyori did not copy them out.

[28] . The Royal Secretariat was established in 810. It had five to ten members normally selected by the monarch himself. See Tamai Chikara 1973, Kakehi Toshio 1991, and Kon Masahide 1994. According to Tamai, the era between 890 and 920 witnessed its development into a royal household agency. Within the Secretariat, there were 23 subordinate units (tokoro) by Tadahira's day. Their managers were appointed by Royal Secretariat directives (Kurōdo senji) that Tadahira presumably approved in the tennō's place.

[29] . See Tsuchida Naoshige 1992b on the role of the noble-in-charge (shōkei). According to Morita Tei, a protocol from the Kōnin era (810-824) concerning operation of the Council of State mandated, "In general, report affairs to the Council of State. Should a senior minister not be available, relay matters to a middle counselor or someone higher. In the case of very important matters, (the minister should) memorialize the throne for a decision." From this we can assume that a middle counselor or higher member of the Council could act as noble-in-charge. See Morita Tei 2006.

[30] . See Kugyō bunin vol. 1, 163 (Shintei zōho Kokushi taikei). Ōtsū Tōru agrees that only members of the Council with a chūnagon post or higher could participate in making decisions in the Council concerning petitions and reports (mōshibumi); and only they could take reports or petitions to the throne. Middle counselors also

served as directors (*bettō*) of the subordinate offices in the Royal Secretariat. See Ōtsu Tōru 1996, 109-10.

[31]. For a useful chronology of Tadahira's life, see the appendix of the *Teishinkōki* in the *Dai Nihon kokiroku* series. Selected elements appear in the chronology at the back of this book. See also Arakawa Reiko 1996, vol. 1, 19-24.

[32]. Paul Groner notes the importance of Tadahira's Hosshōji as a Tendai center. See Groner 2002, 40.

[33]. Izumiya Yasuo 1997, 14-27.

[34]. According to Hotate Michihisa and others (Satō Sōjun, Tokoro Isao, and Tsunoda Bun'ei), Daigo Tennō was determined to preserve his autonomy as monarch by maintaining independent rule (*shinsei*).

[35]. See Tsunoda Bun'ei 1969, 306 and passim.

[36]. *Nihon kiryaku* 930 9/22. The *Nihon kiryaku* (subsequently cited as NKR) was compiled in late Heian times. It is published in *the Shintei zōho Kokushi taikei*. Also, a convenient compilation of records concerning the regency is the two-volume *Kōshitsu seido shiryō, Sesshō* (Kunaichō shoryobu 1981). For this document, see vol. 1, 22..

[37]. *Honchō monzui* 4, which is an eleventh-century compendium of works in Sino-Japanese, prose and poetry. It is published in *the Shintei zōho Kokushi taikei*. See also *Kōshitsu seido shiryō* vol. 1, 8-9 and 158-59.

[38]. *Kōshitsu seido shiryō*, vol. 1, 4, 16. Concerning Shōtoku's role in Suiko's court see Piggott 1997, 79-83. The term *setsu* also appears in a *Nihon shoki* entry concerning the warrior queen Jingū, when she "grasped governmental affairs" (*sesshō*) after the death of her husband, the monarch Chūai. See Yamada Munemutsu 1992.

[39]. *Kōshitsu seido shiryō*, vol. 1, 4, 46.

[40]. *Sandai jitsuroku* 876 11/29; also, *Kōshitsu seido shiryō* vol. 1, 20-21. The *Sandai jitsuroku* is published in the *Shintei zōho Kokushi taikei*. The epithet, "the faithful and just minister," had been given to Yoshifusa earlier.

[41]. See the *Shikiinryō*, in Inoue Mitsusada 1976, 158.

[42]. Appendix B has been compiled using such appointment registers as *Kugyō bunin, Benkan bunin, Kanshi bunin, Kurōdo bunin, Kebiishi bunin, Geki bunin, Eimonfu bunin, Kon'efu bunin,* and *Sōgō bunin*. All save *Kugyō bunin* (published in *Zōho shintei Kokushi taikei*) and *Sōgō bunin* (Nanjō Bun'yū 1915, 61-288), were published by the now defunct Zokugunshoruijū kanseikai.

[43]. For an account of Masakado's rebellion see the introduction and translation in Rabinovitch 1986. For a recent analysis see Friday 2008.

[44]. On Kūya see Ishii Yoshinaga 2002. A provincial movement was the Shidara cult of 945. See Takatori Masao 1970; Kawane Yoshiyasu 2003; and in English, Piggott 2007, esp. 52.

[45]. See Kawakita Agaru 1979, 445.

[46]. Takako, who was the widow of one of Daigo's earlier crown princes, became director (*bettō*) of the royal wardrobe (Mikushigedono) in the Higyōsha in 932.

[47]. NKR 930 (Enchō 8) 12/04; and in *Kōshitsu seido shiryō* vol. 2, 112-13.

[48]. NKR 939 02/28.

73

[49] . The text we have used for our translations in this volume is that in the *Dai Nihon kokiroku* (subsequently cited as TKK). For this passage, see TKK 939 03/03. We know that Tadahira possessed prebendal units because in 933-934, and again some years later, he gave some units away to support the newly constructed Daigoji. Those he gave away were in the provinces of Shinano and Sanuki. See *Dai Nihon shiryō* First Series, vol. 6, 617 and 626, citing the *Daigoji shinyōroku*.

[50] . TKK 939 03/14.

[51] . TKK 931 01/09.

[52] . TKK 939 8/17. Presumably this refers to the Shirakawain, a mansion owned by the regents and located east of the Kamo River in Shirakawa. According to the *Heian jidaishi jiten*, Yoshifusa and Mototsune both utilized it. On the development of provincial governorship, see Morita Tei 1978. Note: in quotes from the translation, square brackets indicate annotations by the editor of the Dai Nihon kokiroku text. Curly brackets indicate interpolations by our translation group.

[53] . TKK 939 05/23, 12/09.

[54] . TKK 931 01/22.

[55] . TKK 939 03/15.

[56] . TKK 931 04/13.

[57] . Entries in TKK indicate that on average members of the Council and their staff met ten times monthly during Tadahira's era to deal with issues of governance. Ihara argues that Tadahira's court continued the old *ritsuryō* pattern whereby the Council proposed and the *tennō* decided, even if new elements such as the noble-in-charge (*shōkei*) and direct royal orders (*senji*) represented more routinized royal authority. See Ihara Kesao 1995, 192-195.

[58] . On Son'i and Gikai, see Groner 2002, 42-43. Both monks seem to have stradled the Ennin-Enchin factionalism within the Tendai school. They were specialists in both exoteric and esoteric Buddhist knowledge. Groner provides a very useful discussion of Enryakuji and official Buddhism in the early tenth century in his Chapters 3 through 5. And on relations between Tadahira and Ryōgen, see pp. 66-70.

[59] . This list appears in the *Honchō seiki* entry for 938 07/03. It is a record of court activities and proceedings compiled around 1150. It is published in the *Shintei zōho Kokushi taikei*. Also see *Dai Nihon shiryō* Series 1 vol. 7, 227-228.

[60] . TKK 931 04/14 , 12/25; and NKR 931 12/25.

[61] . See TKK 931 3/18 for appointments of staff for a construction agency; and TKK 931 5/20, when Tadahira gave orders regarding lumber needed for the construction project.. See *Dai Nihon shiryō* Series 1 vol. 6, 428. The *Rihōōki*, by Prince Shigeakira, provides substantial information on construction of Daigoji. The Prince, as a member of the royal family and head of the Ministry of Personnel, was deeply involved. See Yoneda Yūsuke and Yoshioka Masayuki 1974, passim.

[62] . According to Ōsumi, the main function of the Controllers' Office was to promulgate orders received from the throne by the Council. See Ōsumi Kiyoharu 1991, 42. Memorials that were approved by the throne were transformed into written commands by middle or lesser controllers and then sent back to the Council for promulgation by means of a Council directive (*kanpu*) or order (*senji*) by a controller (*ben*) or scribe (*shi*).

[63]. A senior noble who was concurrently an advisor and senior controller frequently transmitted Council memorials (kansō) to the throne. Another such transmitter was the tenjō-ben, a royal intimate (tenjōbito) who served as a controller. See Ōsumi Kiyoharu 1991, 20. As for Controller Sō's nickname, his real name was "Sukemoto," and "Sō" is the Chinese reading of the "Suke" character. See, for instance, the TKK entry for 939 02/05.

[64]. There were generally eight chamberlains. They were junior fifth rankers who served near the tennō and did his bidding, including delivering orders to the Residential Palace Ministry (Nakatsukasashō). Residential palace secretaries (naiki) would then write up royal orders in the form of choku and senmyō, working with a noble-in-charge to promulgate the royal will. The head of the Residential Palace Ministry might serve as a chamberlain to facilitate the process. In 931 and 939, there were also members of the Royal Secretariat serving as chamberlains.

[65]. After the so-called Kusuko Coup of 810 (which was really an attempt by the retired Heizei Tennō to take back his throne from his own chosen heir, Saga Tennō), it was recognized that quarrels between the sitting and retired monarchs were dangerous—they split the court. From Saga's time on, it was therefore decided that the tennō was to be head of state while the retired tennō would be considered subordinate. And when Saga Tennō retired, he moved to a detached palace. Ostensibly he refrained from involvement in the decisions of the court. But the sitting tennō was still expected to show personal filiality to a retired "senior monarch" (daijōtennō), and there is no doubt that consultation went on between members of the tennō's court and those around the retired tennō on matters of state. See, for instance, Haruna Hiroaki 1993; Haruna Hiroaki 1991; Takinami Sadako 1982; and Okamura Sachiko 2003. In English, see Hurst 1976, 36-100.

[66]. Notably, Nakahira is said to have had a daughter of Sugawara no Michizane as wife, as did Tadahira. See Yamagiwa 1966, 289, note 375.

[67]. See Kuramoto Kazuhiro 2000, esp. 1-41. Kuramoto's focus is later, during the reign of Ichijō (r. 986-1011), but his argument is apt for Tadahira's regency as well.

[68]. For more details on the Misōjimon see Tokoro Isao 1984 and Kōda Toshio 1976. Mototsune's adoptive father, Yoshifusa, was also involved with compiling the Dairi shiki, an earlier effort to summarize court ritual in 821. See Furuse Natsuko 1998, 248-261.

[69]. Okada Shōji 2004. Also see Kodaigaku kyōkai 1969 for more historical research concerning the Engi and Tenryaku eras.

[70]. Furuse Natsuko 1998, esp. 128-71 and 248-316. The idea of utilizing specialized venues for various types of court functions came from Tang China. Increasing influence of Tang China can be traced back to Kōken-Shōtoku's era in the 750s. See also Piggott 2003.

[71]. Yoshida Takashi 1998, 40.

[72]. TKK 931 05/28. In our translation we have differentiated post names used as appellations, as in this case, by omitting the article.

[73]. TKK 931 05/29.

[74]. TKK 939 02/04, 02/10, 02/12, 02/22. On the "Triple Alignment," see note 23 of the translation later in the volume.

[75] . For instance on 07/15 the sutra was read in the Throne Hall—see TKK 939 07/15. Both the Hall of Ministries (Chōdōin) and Throne Hall (Daigokuden) were still in use, but there are reports of disrepair at these facilities in the 930s. Tadahira was trying to get the wall surrounding the palace precincts rebuilt but he was having a tough time due to lack of resources.

[76] . TKK 939 07/02, 07/08.

[77] . TKK 939 07/08, 07/10, 07/15. Son'i was actually posted as the second-ranking prelate (daisōzu), but since there was no first-ranker (daisōjō), he would have functioned as head of the Prelates' Office (Sōgōsho).

[78] . See TKK 931 11/02. Council secretaries (geki) were responsible for the annual presentation of a new calendar in the eleventh month.

[79] . TKK 939 02/17, 02/18.

[80] . For instance, in the second month of 931, when other senior nobles and royal intimates were unavailable to spend the night with the boy monarch, Tadahira served in their stead: TKK 931 02/19.

[81] . TKK 12/02.

[82] . Yamagiwa 1966, 63. The Kokka taikan database lists 74 poems by Tadahira—my thanks to Ms. Rieko Kamei for this information.

[83] . TKK 939 01/17.

[84] . For a history of the Grand Archery Meet, see Obinata Katsumi 1993.

[85] . Tango no sechie originated in China where it had a strong associations with military activities. But another custom was to place bunches of irises around the eaves of buildings to ward off illness. At the Japanese court the celebration was seen as a way of assuring good health. A useful guide to the history and significance of events in the ritual cycle is Abe Takeshi et al. 2003.

[86] . TKK 939 10/01.

[87] . Shun literally denotes a period of ten days—the month equalled three of them.

[88] . When the tennō did not attend these occasions, the protocol was then for a Shun no hiraza, "Shun without the tennō in attendance." In that case, the senior nobles would attend a separate banquet in the Giyōden (see Figure 10).

[89] . TKK 939 6/29. The Preparatory Office (Katanashidokoro) was the place where controllers and Council secretaries organized materials before discussions of the senior nobles. It was located in the Council Office compound near the Kenshun Gate (see Figure 10).

[90] . Yoshikawa Shinji 1989. By the tenth century only senior nobles, a few royals, and those close to the throne were receiving payments from prebendal units (fuko) or seasonal remunerations. Those of lower ranks and posts had to depend on patrons for their livelihoods. A sixth ranker, for instance, might receive a nomination for promotion to the fifth rank from a high ranking patron, such as the regent, queen, or senior minister.

[91] . See Tamai Chikara 2000.

[92] . Promotions to the fifth rank could also come by nomination (uji no shaku) of the family head (uji no chōja). Nominations by the retired tennō were called inkyū.

[93] . TKK 939 04/07 and 939 05/20.

[94] . Normally, *Jimoku no gi* deliberations were held in front of the *tennō*. The senior nobles were led to the outer east porch (*higashi magobisashi*) of the royal dwelling by a member of the Royal Secretariat.. On the nature of deliberation (*gi*) at the *ritsuryō* court see Kawajiri Akio 2000. Yoshikawa Shinji notes the key role of Council secretaries in assembling the paperwork to determine which officials should be promoted to the fifth rank (Yoshikawa Shinji 1989). Furuse Natsuko argues that as long as Suzaku remained a child, Queen-mother Yasuko likely participated in personnel decisions: Furuse Natsuko 2001, esp. 15. Furuse's evidence postdates Tadahira, but she argues that precedents for later queen-mothers involving themselves in appointments originated in Yasuko's time.

[95] . TKK 931 03/11

[96] . TKK 931 01/29.

[97] . TKK 931 04/15. In 946 as well the *naiki* were directed to prepare certificates of rank. See TKK 946 05/03; and in *Dai Nihon shiryō* Series 1 vol. 8, 653.

[98] . TKK 939 02/21.

[99] . Horses were highly valued at court—they were often presented as gifts, and there were numerous ceremonies at the palace that included presentation of horses from provincial pastures. On horses and pastures in the Nara and early Heian periods, see Yamaguchi Hideo 1995a.

[100] . TKK 931 04/07.

[101] . TKK 939 03/16.

[102] . Yoshida Takashi et al. see these *senji* as a new form of royal command that emerged in the tenth century. See Yoshida Takashi 1998, 34; and Yoshida Takashi et al. 1995. Per Tamai, there is an early *kansenji* dating from 869 that shows how the noble-in-charge received the *tennō's* order and transmitted it to the controller, who gave it to a scribe to draw up the written order, a *kansenji*. See Tamai Chikara 1973.

[103] . TKK 931 04/05.

[104] . See TKK 931 03/15 and 03/20.

[105] . TKK 939 08/27.

[106] . For the entries concerning *Naoshimono*, see TKK 931 04/11 and 05/29. For a report by the senior nobles (*Jin no mōshibumi*), see TKK 931 06/19. On the *Jimoku*, see Tsunoda Bun'ei 1994 vol. 1, 1141-1142.

[107] . TKK 931 06/19.

[108] . See Murai Shōsuke 1995. Murai analyzes an oral decree (*senmyō*) sent to the Chikuzen Munakata Shrine in 870. It included the invocation, "The realm of Japan is a divine domain. With the gods' help, what aggression by soldiers can approach us? The great deity of Ise will also aid us when we are attacked by Sillans. When these pirates land, attack and repulse them. Should there be marauders within the realm, or floods, drought, or pestilence, you deities show your deep love for cultivators and exclude all such misfortunes. Protect us and give us peace within the realm."

[109] . Courtiers who were likely to draw income from sinecures as provincial governors included members of the Royal Secretariat, the second-in-command of the Ministry of Personnel, the second-in-command of the Ministry of Popular Affairs, Council secretaries, their staffers called *shi*, and the Royal Police. See Tamai Chikara 2000.

[110] . On the emergence of custodial provincial governors in the later ninth century, see Tamai Chikara 2000 and Katō Tomoyasu 2002, esp. 55-68. In English see Kiley 1999, Batten 1993, and Piggott 2007. For Tadahira's involvement, see Kimura Shigemitsu 1993.

[111] . Reports of this sort are preserved in the *Hokuzanshō*, a ritual compendium of the early 11th century. It is published in the original *Kojitsu sōsho* series of ritual handbooks. On this method of controlling provincial governors, see Sasaki Muneo's translated article, "The Court-centered Polity," in Piggott 2006, esp. 234-36.

[112] . See the entry on the *Fukandendensō* in Abe Takeshi et al. 2003 and Tsunoda Bun'ei 1994, vol. 2, 2029-2030. Also see the mandate that went out to the Kinai and seven circuit provinces on 931 12/10 in *Seiji yōryaku* (*Shintei zōho Kokushi taikei*, vol. 2, 494-495).

[113] . TKK 931 03/22.

[114] . TKK 931 5/25. According to the ninth-century *Ryōnogige* legal commentary, a royal order should be sent to the provinces together with a Council order (*kanpu*) prepared by Council secretaries or the Controllers' Office.

[115] . TKK 939 11/02.

[116] . TKK 939 07/02.

[117] . Yoshida Takashi et al. 1995, 50-52..

[118] . TKK 931 02/21.

[119] . See TKK 939 02/12, 03/17.

[120] . Yoshida Takashi et al. 1995, 50-52. An increasing wealth of goods was being transported across the realm, and local elites were deeply involved. A readable and short overview is Yamaguchi Hideo 1995b. See too the essay on traffic and transit by Hotate Michihisa in Piggott 2006, 166-208; and Piggott 2007.

[121] . Friday 1992, 72-76.

[122] . Abe Takeshi 1974, 329-332. One is reminded too of events in 865 and 866, when provincial governors in Owari and Mino complained about violence perpetrated against them by district chieftains. See *Nihon sandai jitsuroku* 865 12/27, 866 07/09, 866 07/26 (in the *Shintei zōho Kokushi taikei*). Fifty years later there was also the famous Owari Petition of 988, wherein district chieftains complained in detail about crimes by the provincial governor, including his use of armed enforcers: see the recently published von Verschuer 2007.

[123] . TKK 939 08/11.

[124] . TKK 939 11/12.

[125] . TKK 939 12/26. For more details see Friday 2008, 109-14.

[126] . TKK 931 01/28.

[127] . TKK 931 2/27. A *koku* is traditionally said to be the amount of rice needed to feed a person for one year.

[128] . TKK 931 03/04.

[129] . TKK 931 04/03.

[130] . TKK 931 04/23.

[131] . TKK 931 10/02.

[132] . TKK 931 01/26.

[133] . TKK 931 03/20, 05/07, 05/08, 05/29.

[134] . TKK 931 07/20.

[135]. TKK 931 07/23.

[136]. TKK 931 11/17. Preparations for the *Daijōsai* continued into 932. The *Daijōsai* was normally held within the year of the accession of a new monarch. See Bock 1990.

[137]. See, for instance, TKK 931 07/20, 07/23, 07/24, 07/25, and 07/29.

[138]. See TKK entries for 931 02/06, 02/19, 04/10, 04/11, and 04/12.

[139]. For more details see documentary materials in *Dai Nihon shiryō* Series 1, vol. 6, 414.

[140]. TKK 931 12/02.

[141]. TKK 939 05/06. Akita Stockade had been constructed in Nara times, in 733. Previously, on 04/17, Tadahira had heard that rebels had attacked the stockade. Now they were attacking the district office. Fighting continued because Tadahira continued receiving reports or ordered response on 05/06, 07/15, 07/17, and 08/12. Offerings were made to temples and shrines for pacification in the eighth month: TKK 939 08/18.

[142]. TKK 939 06/07.

[143]. See, for instance, TKK entries for 939 06/07 and 06/09.

[144]. TKK 939 06/09.

[145]. TKK 12/17. Sumitomo first appears in the historical record in the early 930s as a provincial governor. He was pursuing pirates in the Inland Sea region in 936. By the twelfth month of 939, he was himself accused as a pirate leader. On Sumitomo, see Iwai shishi hensan iinkai 1996, esp. 109-167; and Matsubara Hironobu 1999. In English, see Friday 2008, 110-114 and 143-146; and Farris 1992, 131-162.

[146]. TKK 939 12/29.

[147]. On these rebellions see Piggott 1997, 253-254; and Piggott 2003, 58-59.

[148]. Hashimoto Yoshihiko 1976.

[149]. For a discussion of the relationship of early regental authority to the Council of State in English, see Morita Tei 2006.

[150]. Extant entries from the journal refer only rarely to Tadahira's household and its chancellery, confirming that it did not play a routine role in government in Tadahira's day.

Appendix A

Events of the Court Calendar in Tadahira's Journal for 939

DATE	CEREMONY	
1/1	Shihōhai,	Bows to the Four Directions,
	Ganjitsu no sechie	New Year's Royal Banquet
1/4	Daijin daikyō	Senior Minister's Grand Banquet
1/7	Aouma no sechie	White Horse Royal Banquet
1/8	Onna joi	Ceremony for Women's Promotion in Rank
1/16	Onna tōka no sechie	Dance and Song Royal Banquet
1/17	Jarai	Grand Archery Ceremony
1/18	Noriyumi	Archery Matches
1/28->	Jimoku	Ceremony for Assigning Posts
2/13	Naoshimono	Ceremony for Modification of Appointments
2/17	Sonokara kami no matsuri	Sono and Kara Deities' Rite
2/22	Rinji Ninnōe	Extraordinary Benevolent King Assembly
3/10	Nyokankyō	Banquet for Female Officials
3/15	Ki no midokyō	Seasonal Sutra Reading
3/16	Ichibumeshi	Ceremony for Appointing Lowest Ranking Posts
3/29	Kō Nihongi	Reading and Lecture on the *Chronicle of Japan*
4/1	Shun	Seasonal Ceremony
4/14	Kamo no matsuri	Kamo Festival
4/20	Gunji dokusō	Memorial to Appoint District Chieftains
6/8	Kōkyōsho no en	Classics Reading Final Banquet
6/11	Tsukinamisai	Semi-annual Festival for the Ise Deity
6/20	Rinji dokyō	Extraordinary Sutra Reading
7/17	Ki no midokyō	Seasonal Sutra Reading
7/27	Sumai no meshi awase	Wrestling Matches
7/5*	Kojimoku	Lesser Ceremony for Assigning Posts
8/10	Uchi rongi	Residential Palace Debate
8/18	Ki'nenkoku hōbei	Dispatch of Offerings to Official Shrines
9/11	Ise hōbei	Dispatch of Offerings to Ise Shrine
10/1	Shun	Seasonal Ceremony
11/14	Gosho hajime	Reading and Lecture on the Classics
11/24	Niinamesai	First Fruits Rite
11/25	Toyo no akari no sechie	Flushed Faces Royal Banquet
12/1	Kamo no rinji sai	Extraordinary Kamo Festival
12/11	Tsukinamisai (Jinkonjiki)	Semi-annual Festival for the Ise Deity
12/16	Gunji meshi	Appointment of District Chieftains
12/18	Nosaki	Dispatch of Offerings to Royal Mausolea
12/21	Mibutsumyō	Litany of Buddha Names
12/27	Jimoku	Ceremony for Assigning Posts

* Intercalary

APPENDIX B: THE PLAYERS AT COURT, 939

KUGYŌ COUNCIL

SESSHŌ DAIJŌDAIJIN: Fujiwara no Tadahira

SADAIJIN: Fujiwara no Nakahira (SATAISHŌ)

DAINAGON: Taira no Koremochi (MINBUKYŌ, CHŪGŪ TAIFU)
Fujiwara no Saneyori (UTAISHŌ, AZECHI)

CHŪNAGON: Tachibana no Kinyori (DAZAI GONSHI)
(GON) Minamoto no Kiyokage (UEMON KAMI)
(GON) Fujiwara no Morosuke (SAEMON KAMI, KEBIISHI BETTŌ, CHŪGŪ TAIFU)
(GON) Minamoto no Koreshige (->MINBUKYŌ)

SANGI: Fujiwara no Masamoto (JIBUKYŌ)   Ki no Yoshimitsu (UDAIBEN, BIZEN GONKAMI)
Fujiwara no Motokata   Fujiwara no Akitada (GYŌBUKYŌ, ŌMI GONKAMI)
Minamoto no Takaakira Ban no Yasuhira (HARIMA KAMI)
Fujiwara no Tadafumi   Fujiwara no Atsutada (SAKON CHŪJŌ)

BENKANKYOKU

SADAIBEN: Minamoto no Koreshige (SANGI-> CHŪNAGON, ŌMI KAMI)

Ki no Yoshimitsu (SANGI, KUNAIKYŌ, BIZEN GONKAMI)

UDAIBEN: Ki no Yoshimitsu (SANGI) Minamoto no Kiyohara

SACHŪBEN: Fujiwara no Arihira (SHIKIBU SHŌSUKE->DAISUKE)

UCHŪBEN:

SASHŌBEN: Ōe no Asatsuna (MONJO HAKASE, IYO SUKE)

USHŌBEN: Minamoto no Sukemoto (UCHIKURA KAMI)

GEKIKYOKU

DAIGEKI: Sugano no Kiyokata Mimune no Kintada Sakanoue no Takaharu

SHŌGEKI: Abe no Ariharu Ifukube no Yasuchika Mononobe no Sadamochi

SATAISHI: Owari no Genkan

KONOEFU

SATAISHŌ: Fujiwara no Nakahira (SADAIJIN, KURŌDO BETTŌ)

UTAISHŌ: Fujiwara no Saneyori (CHŪNAGON)
Minamoto no Hideaki (IYO GONKAMI)

SACHŪJŌ: Fujiwara no Atsutada (KURŌDO BETTŌ, HARIMA KAMI)

UCHŪJŌ: Minamoto no Masaaki (KII GONKAMI)
Minamoto no Kaneakira

SASHŌSHŌ: Fujiwara no Morouji (ŌMI GONSUKE)
Fujiwara no Asatada (GOI KURŌDO, HARIMA GONSUKE)

USHŌSHŌ: Yoshimine no Yoshikata (GOI KURŌDO)
Ono no Yoshifuru (CHŪGŪ SUKE, BIZEN GONSUKE)

KEBIISHICHŌ

BETTŌ: Fujiwara no Morosuke (GONCHŪNAGON, CHŪGŪ TAIFU, SAEMON GONSUKE)

SAEMON GONSUKE: Taira no Yoritoki

UEMON GONSUKE: Minamoto no Suguru

SAEMON SHŌJŌ: Takashina no Yoshiomi

Teishinkōki
YEAR 939, TENGYŌ 2

Dai Nihon Kokiroku text

忠平本年六十歳、從一位、攝政、太政大臣、

天慶二年（朱雀天皇）（臨本、前行ニ續キ、圈線ヲ以テ改行ヲ示ス）

正月

元日節會

一日、（朱雀天皇）上御南殿、諸司綏忽、左近稱無當色、遲開門、陰陽官人遲參、中務輔乍□不參進、依如此

Teishinkoki
YEAR 939, TENGYŌ 2

Transcription in Classical Japanese
by Christina Laffin

天慶二年正月

一日、上（朱雀天皇）南殿に御す。諸司緩怠す。左近当色無しと称し、開門遅る。陰陽の官人遅参す。中務の輔□乍ら参進せず。此の如きの事に依り刀称遅引す。

春日社鳴動　　二日、春日社鳴如擊鼓、又有鳴鏑聲、

忠平大饗　　　四日、家大饗、自舊年心神乖適、不出簾外、錄事召仰乎（乎伊別）、大納言行之、

敍位　　　　　六日、叙位議、於桂芳坊行之、

靑馬節會　　　七日、依御物忌不御南殿、不卷玉簾、靑馬渡南殿前之後必渡御前者也、而不渡分配所〻、適以所遺七疋、隨仰引渡、但左右助不候、依此可勘責之由仰大納言、

女敍位
敍位　　　　　八日、有女叙位、又男」二人、大納言執筆、（以上、底本、天慶三年目錄ヨリ根ケテ迷書ス、今他ノ部載ニ從ヒテ便宜ニ行ス）

地震　　　　　十一日、地震、

之事刀弥遅引、

（2張）

二日、春日社鳴ずること撃皷の如し。又鳴、鏑の声あり。

四日、家の大饗なり。旧年自り心神適を乖れ、簾外に出でず。録事召仰せの事、大納言（平 伊望）之を行う。

六日、叙位議。桂芳坊に於いて之を行う。

七日、御物忌に依り南殿に御せず。玉簾を巻かず。青馬南殿の前を渡すの後、必ず御前を渡す者なり。而に渡さず所々に分配す。適遺る所の七疋を以て、仰せに随い引き渡す。但し左右の助候わず。此に依り勘責すべきの由大納言に仰す。

八日、女叙位有り。又男二人。大納言執筆なり。

十一日、地震。

86

踏歌節會
夫侍從ヲ補ス

射禮

射遺
賭弓

忠平屬ヲ上ル

外記政始

十六日、節會如例、但大臣・大納言各依病不參、右大將行內辨歟、外辨無納言、次圍從九人皆出、

令大將奏之、

十七日、右大將着大庭幄座、有召參入、承不出御之仰者、失也、

十八日、刑部卿不蒙仰旨直到南庭、令射、□遺、奇異亦也、賭射、右近・右兵衞勝、

廿日、呼朝忠朝臣、昨日臙二奉入大內、賜錄祿歸來、

廿二日、甲子、外記政始、有□奏、右中辨、

十六日、節会例の如し。但し大臣（藤原仲平）・大納言 各 病 に依り不参。右大将（藤原実頼）内弁の事を行う。外弁に納言無し。

十七日、右大将大庭の幄の座に着す。召有りて参入し、出御せざるの仰せを 承 る者。失なり。

十八日、刑部卿（藤原顕忠）仰せの旨を蒙らず直に南庭に到る。射せしむ。射遣。奇異の事なり。賭射。右近・右兵衛勝つ。

廿日、（藤原）朝忠朝臣を呼す。昨日鷹二つ大内に入れ奉る。禄を賜わり帰り来たる。

廿二日、甲子。外記政始。官奏有り。右中弁（源 相 職）。

御修法

廿四日、丙寅、內御修法、義海律師始行、廿一人、

虹現ハル

卅日、虹立官正廳囚、

除目

廿八日、除目議始、裙芳坊、

六十算賀卷數ヲ持來ル

藤原忠文忠平

廿六日、修理大夫忠文朝臣將來於興福寺為予所修卷數等、祈筭之意也、

二月

御修法僧二度者ヲ賜フ

一日、除目議、丑四剋了、御修法僧等賜度者、緣義海律師申請也、加之今年可慎也、

二日、家法、阿闍梨延昌施度者一人之由、面告、

廿四日、丙寅。内の御修法。義海律師始行す。廿一人。

廿六日、修理大夫（藤原）忠文朝臣来たる。興福寺に於いて、予の為に修する所の巻数等を将来す。折算の意なり。

廿八日、除目議始む。桂芳坊。

三十日、虹官の正庁の内に立つ。

天慶二年二月

一日、除目議、丑の四剋了ぬ。御修法の僧等に度者を賜う。義海律師の申請に縁るなり。加之、今年慎むべきなり。

二日、家の法。阿闍梨延昌に度者一人を施すの由、面に告ぐ。

　三日、天見長星、常住寺別當師將來所算卷數、施興□大衣一領、

　四日、仁王會事、來十日可定行事、可進諸國米事、大納言來、便仰、

　五日、夜地震二度、

　五日、宣旨給相弁、敏通奏試事在此、

　八日、夜度〻鳴動、

　□日、大納言定仁王會事、

　十二日、大納言來、便示明日可直物事、仁王會檢校・呪願文事、可催宮垣事、可問召將門使事、

長尾現ハル
常住寺別當忠
平算賀卷數ヲ
持來ル

地震

仁王會定

平將門ヲ召問
スルノ使

三日、天に長星見ゆ。常住寺別当師祈算の巻数を将来。□大衣一領を施し与う。

四日、仁王会の事。来たる十日定め行うべき事。諸国の米を進むべき事。大納言（平伊望）来たる。

便ち仰す。

五日、夜地震二度。

五日、宣旨を相弁（源相職）に給う。（橘）敏通奉試の事此の中に在り。

八日、夜度々鳴動す。

十日、大納言仁王会の事を定む。

十二日、大納言来たる。便ち示す。明日直物すべき事。仁王会の検校・呪願文の事。宮垣を催

すべき事。（平）将門を問い召すべき使の事。

直物
秩父御牧別當
敍位
忠平高麗國牒
ヲ大江朝綱ニ
付ス
園韓神祭
(3張)

十三日、有直物事、又藤原惟修叙位、勤仕秩父御牧別當之上助國用也、

十五日、高麗牒付朝綱、(大江)

十七日、己丑、入夜外記貞(治部)用申云、今日祭、參議以上皆悉有憚不參云々、依大原野祭無上行例、〔障木〕
可行之狀仰了、〔由木〕

十八日、外記貞用申云、昨夜罷治部卿家告事由、卿參入行祭事、丑剋罷退出云々、是貞用以意(藤原雅軽)
招取老公也、何隨仰旨乎、已申老卿有病不堪之由、非有消息、何任意呼出乎、

廿一日、民部卿奉仰、欲行給囹官事、而依內記等不候、囮朝綱朝臣、明朝可作進勅書之狀云□、(平伊望)〔任木〕〔（） 〕

〔條刀〕

十三日、直物の事有り。又、藤原惟条の叙位あり。秩父の御牧の別当を勤仕せるの上、国用を助くるなり。

十五日、高麗の牒を（大江）朝綱に付く。

十七日、己丑。夜に入り外記（物部）貞用申して云く、今日の祭（園韓神祭）、参議以上、皆悉く障有りて不参と云々。大原野祭を上無く行うの例に依り、行うべきの状仰せ了ぬ。

十八日、外記貞用申して云く、昨夜治部卿（藤原当幹）の家に罷り事の由を告ぐ。卿参入し祭の事を行う。丑剋に畢りて退出すと云々。是貞用意に任せて老公を招き取るなり。何ぞ仰せの旨に随わんや。已に老卿病有りて堪えざるの由を申す。消息有るにあらず。何ぞ意に任せて呼し出ださんや。

廿一日、民部卿（平伊望）仰せを奉り、年官を給う事を行わんと欲す。而に内記等候ぜざるに依り、朝綱朝臣に明朝勅書を作り進むべきの状を催すと云々。

臨時仁王會

忠平ヲ三宮ニ
准ジテ年官ヲ
賜フ

廿二日、甲午、臨時仁王會、地震爲攘三合災也、

廿八日、年官勅書出、

三月

（底本、前行ニ續ク、今改行ス）

武藏介源經基
興世王不將門
等ノ謀坂ヲ奏
ス

三日、源經基告言武藏事、使左衛門督返賜昨表、被物如例、
（藤原師輔）

忠平ノ准三宮
ノ辭表ヲ返シ
給フ

四日、令齋主祈申坂車東兵事、神社數在祈文、大衞府官人・舍人等、不別當直・他直可候之狀、令
（祈）
（大中臣興生）

右大將仰、
（藤原貞頼）

祭主ヲシテ坂
東兵革ヲ賭社
ニ祈ラシム

六日、有震動、以前日～又如此、

地震

廿二日、甲午。臨時仁王会。地震、三合の災を攘わんが為なり。

廿八日、年官の勅書出ず。

天慶二年三月

三日、源経基武蔵の事を告言す。左衛門督（藤原師輔）を使して昨の表を返し給う。被物例の如し。

四日、祭主（大中臣奥生）をして、坂東の兵事を祈り申さしむ。神社の数祈文に在り。六衛府の官人・舎人等、当直・他直を別たず候ずべきの状、右大将（藤原実頼）をして仰せしむ。

六日、震動有り。以前の日々又此の如し。

十一社祈禱及
ビ延暦寺修法
ヲ行フ
忠平飛香舍ニ
宿ス

九日、祈禱十一日社、又台山二壇法始、座主・義海等爲阿闍梨、是緣經基告言也、夜參入、宿飛

香舍、伺侍同宿、

藤原貴子女饗
ヲ行フ

十日、伺侍女官饗、掌侍以下藏人以上在飛香、自舍在縫殿高殿、

十一日、地震、

十三日、地震、

藤原仲平上表

十四日、從内賜左大臣辭二官表、見即返奉、

季御讀經

十五日、季御讀經、一分宜旨給元方朝臣、

九日、十一社（じゅういっしゃ）に祈祷（きとう）す。又台山（たいざん）に二壇法（にだんぼう）を始（はじ）む。座主（ざす）（尊意（そんい））・義海等阿闍梨為（た）り。是経基の告言

に縁るなり。夜参入し、飛香舎（ひぎょうしゃ）に宿（しゅく）す。尚侍（ないしのかみ）（藤原貴子（たかこ））同宿（どうしゅく）す。

十日、尚侍の女官（にょかん）の饗（きょう）あり。掌侍（ないしのじょう）以下蔵人（くろうどいじょう）以上飛香に在り。自余縫殿（じょないどの）の高殿（たかどの）に在り。

十一日、地震。

十三日、地震。

十四日、内（朱雀天皇）従（よ）り左大臣（さだいじん）（藤原仲平）二官（にかん）（左大臣・左大将（さだいしょう））を辞（じ）するの表を賜う。見

て即（すなわ）ち返し奉る。

十五日、季御読経（きのみどきょう）。一分（いちぶ）の宣旨を（藤原）元方朝臣（もとかた）に給う。

一分召

諸國臨時春米

忠平仁號ニ茶
ヲ勸ム

忠平陰陽師ヲ
シテ太一式祭
ヲ行ハシム

仁和寺圓堂會

公卿不參ト雖
モ日本紀ヲ講
ゼシム

四月

十六日、一分召、今年無卿家内議、（式部卿敦實親王）

十七日、左大辨來、諸國臨時春米事云〻、召濟江問築垣國〻事、（源肇茂）（御給）

廿日、仁數律師寫經・誦經等令修願文將來、仍勸茶、施祿、白褂一重、

廿二日、召惟香・武兼、同可□□兵乱事、武兼申文一式祭尤可宜者、仰可奉仕狀了、（出雲）（父）（問力）（太）（大）云〻

廿七日、仁和寺圓堂會、

廿九日、講日奉記事、雖公卿不參、令仰可讀事、（矢田部公望）（本紀）

十六日、一分召。今年は卿（式部卿敦実親王）の家内の議無し。

十七日、左大弁（源是茂）来たる。諸国臨時春米の事と云々。（御船）済江を召し築垣の国々の事を問う。

廿日、仁・律師写経・誦経等の願文を修せしめ将来す。仍ち茶を勧め、禄を施す。白褂一重。

廿二日、（出雲）惟香・（文）武兼を召し、兵乱を□すべき事を問う。武兼申して云く、太一式祭尤も宜かるべし者、奉仕すべきの状仰せ了ぬ。

廿七日、仁和寺円堂会。

廿九日、日本紀を講ずる事、公卿不参といえども、読むべき事を（矢田部公望）仰せしむ。

貞信公記抄

句卒座

齋院御禊前驅

定

擬階奏

端午節會ノ有
無ヲ定ム

出羽介保利ヲ
城司トナス

賀茂祭河水ニ
ヨリテ齋院節
渡河シ得ず

（4張）

一日、(朱雀天皇)上不御南殿、

二日、定禊前驅、右大將、(藤原實頼)仁和寺円堂會舞童令儛御覽、式部」(教實親王)卿。王依召參候、親王・公卿・樂人

等賜祿有差、

七日、奏成選目錄、(藤原實頼大將)

十一日、定五月節有無事、以出羽介保利朝臣爲城司宣旨、仰相職朝臣、(源相職)

十四日、賀茂祭、終日雨下、齋日參向、(王)河水之反出、渡人有煩云〻、即(源)■右中弁入夜馳來云、齋王(媄子内親王)(近衛府)(内侍司)並諸司使更不能渡河、皆留逗、明朝待得使〻將來可遂給、但諸司使乘舟、今夜内可參向奉幣、(樂)

一八六

天慶二年四月

一日、上（朱雀天皇）南殿に御せず。

二日、禊の前駈を定む。右大将（藤原実頼）。仁和寺円堂会の舞童を俛わしめ御覧ず。式部卿親王（敦実親王）召に依り参候す。親王・公卿・楽人等に禄を賜うに差有り。

七日、成選の目録を奏す。大将（藤原実頼）。

十一日、五月の節の有無の事を定む。出羽介保利朝臣を以て城司と為すの宣旨、（源）相職朝臣に仰す。

十四日、賀茂祭。終日雨下る。斎王（婉子内親王）参向す。河水の反えり出で、渡る人煩有りと云々。即ち右中弁（源相職）夜に入りて馳せ来たりて云く、斎王並に諸司（内侍司）の使更に渡河能わず。皆辺に留る。明朝使々の将来を待ち得て、遂げ給うべし。但し諸司（近衛府等）の使舟に乗り、今夜の内に参向し奉幣すべし。

夜和忠平六十
算賀卷數ヲ持
來ル

當番殿上人ヲ
勘本ニ處ス

出羽國俘囚ノ
叛亂ヲ奏ス

邦司讀奏

出羽解文ヲ定
ム

十五日、早旦使內舍人在舒奉聞齋王、夜來行事公忠朝臣（源）傳示齋王御報旨、又云、咋夜將來、爲

告仰旨令求使等、不知其所在、今朝各出來、參社頓了、

十六日、一和師將來祈籌卷數、請前施祿、去　五六日番人可勘之事仰義方（良峯）、庶明（源）・敦忠（藤原）・在衡（藤原）・公

忠・兼忠（源）等也、

十七日、出羽國馳驛言上凶賊乱逆与秋田城軍合戰事等、左衞門督（藤原師輔）入夜參入、彼關解文令外記

送家、

十八日、參職（職曹司）、令候陣公卿定出解文事、

廿日、讀奏、

十五日、早旦内舎人在舒を使し斎王に聞え奉る。夜来の行事（源）公忠朝臣斎王の御報の旨を伝え示す。又云く、昨夜将来す。仰せの旨を告げんが為使等を求めしむ。其の所在を知らず。今朝各出で来たり、社頭に参り了ぬ。

十六日、一和師祈算の巻数を将来す。前に請い禄を施す。去る五六日の番人を勘ずべきの事（良峯）義方に仰す。（源）庶明・（藤原）敦忠・（藤原）在衡・（源）公忠・（源）兼忠等なり。

十七日、出羽国の馳駅凶賊乱逆し秋田城軍と合戦せる事等を言上す。左衛門督（藤原師輔）夜に入り参入す。彼の国の解文外記をして家に送らしむ。

十八日、職（職曹司）に参る。陣に候ずる公卿をして出羽の解文の事を定めしむ。

廿日、読奏。

御修法

貞救忠平算賀
卷數持來ル

東大寺別當忠
持來ル

平算賀卷數ヲ

忠攝政准三
宮ヲ辭ス
平ノ殿上人
勘事ス
ヲ宥
出羽城介ヲ
シテ早ク赴任セ
シム
ハ忠平勅答ヲ賜
ル

廿三日、甲午、内御修法、於山上座主奉仕、廿一僧、

廿五日、貞救師於長谷寺所修卷數持來ル、依有祈箏之志、施祿、

廿六日、東大寺別當明弥祈箏卷數將來、施祿、

辭攝政・年官等之表、使師氏朝臣奉之、勘事殿上人等令官、出羽城今保利朝臣申云、隨仰可
罷向者、召前仰可早赴之狀、衆賜酒・祿・馬等、

廿八日、中使師氏朝臣來賜勅書、依例被物、

廿三日、甲午。内の御修法。山上に於いて座主（尊意）奉仕す。廿一僧。

廿五日、貞救師長谷寺に於いて修する所の巻数を将来す。祈算の志有るに依り、禄を施す。

廿六日、東大寺別当明珍祈算の巻数を将来す。禄を施す。

摂政・年官等を辞するの表、（藤原）師氏朝臣を使して之を奉る。勘事の殿上人等を宥さしむ。

出羽城介保利朝臣申して云く、仰せに随いて罷り向うべし者、前に召し早く赴くべきの状を仰す。兼ねて酒・禄・馬等を賜う。

廿八日、中使師氏朝臣来たりて勅書を賜う。例に依り被物。

大索

廿九日、令六衛府・左右馬寮等搜索京中盜、

地震

卅日、夜半地震、

五月

坂東諸國ヲシ
テ部內ヲ肅清
セシムベキコ
ト等ヲ定ム

五日、民部卿（平伊望）來、便示下官符、可責坂。諸國（東）部內不肅清事、祈禱諸祉、讀經諸寺等事、可定行狀、

出羽國重ネテ
俘囚ノ反亂ヲ
奏ス

六日、出羽國馳驛使來、其解文云、賊徒到來秋田郡、開官舍、掠取官稻（倉カ）、燒亡百姓財物、又牽奕（異カ）
類可來云〻、

院成上皇北邊
院ニ競馬ヲ行
ヒ給フ

七日、北邊院有競馬事、

地震

十日、地震、

廿九日、六衛府・左右馬寮等をして　京中の盗を捜索せしむ。

三十日、夜半地震。

天慶二年五月

五日、民部卿（平伊望）来たる。便ち示す。官符を下し、坂東の諸国の部内を粛清せざるを責む

べき事。諸社に祈祷し、諸寺に読経する等の事を定め行うべきの状なり。

六日、出羽の国の馳駅使来たる。其の解文に云く、賊徒秋田郡に到来す。官倉を開き、官稲を掠取し、百姓の財物を焼亡す。又異類を率いて来たるべしと云々。

七日、北辺院に競馬の事有り。

十日、地震。

太一式祭　（日付順序本ノ二）十六日、太一式於八省院修、武徙、（交）

諸社奉幣
武藏守等ヲ任ズ　（5弨）十五日、奉幣諸社使立、祈軍賊事也、參職、令任武藏守等、十五日、（職事司）（百済王貞連、連一作連）

位記召給　廿日、位記召給、

賑給使定　廿三日、定賑給使、左金、（藤原師輔）

廿七日、早旦地震、夜又地震、

維摩會講師ヲ定ム　廿八日、當年維摩講師可請濟源事、使公忠宿祢、不及左閤、（三桃）（示）（藤原仲平）

十六日、太一式八省院（はっしょういん）に於いて修す。（文）武兼。

十五日、諸社に奉幣する使立つ。軍賊（ぐんぞく）の事を祈るなり。職（職曹司）に参る。武蔵守（むさしのかみ）（百済王貞運（くだらのこきしていうん））等を任ぜしむ。十五日。

廿日、位記（いき）召し給う。

廿三日、賑給使（しんごう）を定む。左金（さきん）（藤原師輔）。

廿七日、早旦地震。夜又地震。

廿八日、当年の維摩（ゆいま）の講師（こうし）済源（さいげん）を請うべきの事。（三統）（みむねの）公忠宿祢（きんただすくね）を使して、左閤（さこう）（藤原仲平）に示し及（およ）ぶ。

諸社寺讀經
法琳寺太元帥
法太政官應不着
座セザルニヨ
リ勘責ス

推問武藏密告
使ヲ補ス

御讀書竟宴

源經基ヲ左衞
門府ニ禁錮セ
シム

六月

一日、諸社・諸寺讀經、又法琳寺大元法等始行、

五日、官朝應不着事、勘責朝・相兩界弁、各申云、候日前後日可着亦相定了云〻、仰云、何定此日

可着乎、猶可念日〻着、但人非木石、何無不着之日、

七日、呼衆忠朝臣、告示左閣、今日可定問密告使事、亦可隨例不狀、参職曹司、令候陣公卿定問

密告使、晩頭民部卿將來諸卿略定使等夾名、仍公卿盍出内裏、

八日、御書竟宴、有所労不参、

九日、大納言來令見可禁告人忠明勘文、即示可令禁經基左衞門府事、諸輿・寂茂等可爲押領使、

天慶二年六月

一日、諸社・諸寺の読経、又法琳寺の大元法等を始行す。

五日、官の朝庁に着せざる事、朝（大江朝綱）・相（源相職）両少弁を勘責す。各申して云く、候日・前後の日着すべきの事相定め了ぬと云々。仰せて云く、何ぞ其の日を定めて着すべけんや。猶日々着することを念ずべし。但し人は木石にあらず。何ぞ着せざるの日なからんや。

七日、（源）兼忠朝臣を呼し、左閤（藤原仲平）に告げ示す。今日間密告使を定むべきの事、亦例に随うべきやいなやの状なり。職曹司に参る。陣に候ずる公卿をして間密告使を定めしむ。晩頭民部卿（平伊望）諸卿の略定せる使等の夾名（長官源俊）を将来す。仍ち公卿尽く内裏を出ず。

八日、御書竟宴（御注孝経、藤原元方）。所労有りて不参。

九日、大納言（平伊望）来たりて、告人を禁ずべき（檜前）忠明の勘文を見せしむ。即ち示す。（源）経基を左衛門府に禁ぜしむべきの事。（小野）諸興・（橘）是茂等押領使と為すべし。但し五

112

但以五位充例可勘、又推問使官符可令早仰事、

押領使ヲ補ス

月次祭神今食
祈雨ノタメ臨
時幣ヲ加フ

十一日、付月次祭使有臨時幣、王使相加也、是為祈甘雨、又申天変之事等也、神今食付所司令
行、緣欲幸中院、西方塞也、

諸社祈雨奉幣

十二日、壬午、祈雨諸社使立、宣命辞別有天変事、

延曆寺延命院
二御修法大般
若御讀經アリ

地震

十三日、癸未、大内御修法於山御願堂始行、（延命院）座主為阿闍梨、（弁意）伴僧廿口、又大般若三部、三ヶ日間［ヶ］

毎日一部、但御修法七日也、由天変可愼給也、近日地震數～、

虹現ハル

十五日、未時虹處～立、内膳・左衛門陣前・作物所云～、

臨時御讀經請
僧定

十六日、大納言定臨時御讀經請僧、

位を以て充つる例を勘ずべし。又推間使の官符早く仰せしむべき事。

十一日、月次祭の使に付けて、臨時の幣有り。王使相加うるなり。是甘雨を祈らんが為、又天変の事を申す等なり。神今食所司に付け行なわしむ。中院に幸せんと欲するに、西方塞るに縁るなり。

十二日、壬午。祈雨の諸社の使立つ。宣命の辞別に天変の事有り。

十三日、癸未。大内の御修法山の御願堂（延命院）に於いて始行す。座主（尊意）阿闍梨為り。伴僧廿口。又大般若三部。三个日の間、毎日一部。但し御修法七日なり。天変に由り慎み給うべきなり。

近日地震数々あり。

十五日、未時虹処々に立つ。内膳・左衛門陣前・作物所と云々。

十六日、大納言臨時の御読経の請僧を定む。

臨時御讀經

〔御殿カ〕
忠平源經基ノ
密告狀等ヲ辨
ニ下ス
忠平辨史ノ上
日ヲ注進セシ
ム

廿日、庚寅、臨時讀經於大極殿修之、爲祈甘雨・年穀並天下平安也、

廿三日、曉地震、御讀經今日可結願、而依不雨、延二日、

〔源相職〕
廿八日、宣旨給相弁、又下經基告狀、外記勘申祈雨例、尠付相弁、

〔史〕
廿九日、召言鑒、仰去月弁・吏官朝廳並結政所上日可注進亟、
〔冠カ〕

七月

五龍祭
龍穴社奉幣讀

〔亟カ〕
二日、辛丑、爲祈雨、令陰陽寮修五龍祭、又奉幣上龍穴、又令讀經、未時雷雨、伊勢守繁時依肥後
〔繁實〕

廿日、庚寅。臨時の御読経大極殿に於いて之を修す。甘雨・年穀並に天下平安を祈らんが為なり。

廿三日、暁地震。御読経今日結願すべし。而に雨ふらざるに依り二日を延す。

廿八日、宣旨を相弁（源相職）に給う。又経基の告状を下す。外記の勘申せる祈雨の例を、暫く相弁に付く。

廿九日、（尾張）言蜜を召し、去月の弁・史の官の朝庁並に結政所の上日を注進すべき事を仰す。

天慶二年七月

二日、辛丑。祈雨の為、陰陽寮をして五龍祭を修せしむ。又上の龍穴に奉幣し、又読経せしむ。未時雷雨。伊勢守（藤原）繁時肥後の功課に依り正五位下に叙す。去る正月此のこと有るべし。

而に一年の調庸の惣返抄を請わざるに依り叙せず。然而ども前例に准拠し、今日之を叙す。又愁い申すこと有るなり。

功課叙正五位下、去正月可有此、而依一年調庸惣返抄不請不叙、然而准據前例、今日叙之、

伊勢守藤原朝臣
時敍位

又有愁申也、

五日、祈雨御讀經始、海律修法始、藏人祭山法間候、此等爲東亂也、

祈雨御讀經
御修法

八日、令相職朝臣告民部卿云、祈雨事重定行者、晩頭使外記公忠宿祢送神祇・陰陽等占卜文云、

左右隨命者、報曰、先度祈不入諸祉可祈申、

九日、左右獄所未斷四人輕犯者合放免之、奉幣諸祉、爲祈雨也、是依昨夕報旨所行也、

獄所未斷輕犯
囚宥ス
祈雨賂祉奉幣

十日、己酉、十五大寺・延暦寺並有供寺ゝ從明從日轉讀仁王經三箇日間、可祈廿雨之狀、令仰

綱所、

十五大寺延暦
王寺等ヲ轉讀仁
王經ヲシテ轉讀セ
シム

五日、祈雨の御読経始む。海律（義海律師）御修法を始む。蔵人登山し法の間候ず。此東乱の為なり。

八日、（源）相職朝臣をして民部卿（平伊望）に告げしめて云く、祈雨の事重ねて定め行え者。晩頭外記（三統）公忠宿祢を使して神祇・陰陽等の占卜の文を送りて云く、祈雨の為なり。是昨夕報じて曰く、先度（六月十二日）の祈に入らざる諸社に祈り申すべし。

九日、左右の獄所の未断の囚人の軽犯の者之を放免し、諸社に奉幣せしむ。祈雨の為なり。是昨夕の報の旨に依り行う所なり。

十日、己酉。十五大寺・延暦寺並に有供の寺々明後日従り仁王経を三箇日間転読し、甘雨を祈るべきの状、綱所に仰せしむ。

忠平祈雨ノコトヲ辨ニ命ズ

十二日、辛亥、從今日三箇日讀經祈雨、

出羽國重ネテ俘囚ノ反亂ヲ奏ス

十三日、呼相職朝臣、祈雨事又〻可定行狀、合告上達部、

季御讀經
譽游法御修法

十五日、出羽馳驛言上賊戰行事、季御讀經、從大極殿始行、是爲祈雨所旱修也、令山座主修尊

勝法、同請雨也、廿一僧也、

地震

十六日、丑尅地震、依召大納言等參入、定可給出羽報符事、雖然不遂議定、戌尅退出、

出羽國へノ報符ヲ定ム

十七日、賜出羽國符案言鑒、宿祢將來、御讀經結願、賜座主

御修法僧ニ座者ヲ給フ

廿一日、山座主所行御修法之師等施度者、相撲召合以廿七日可有事、仰所司、

十二日、辛亥。今日より三箇日読経し雨を祈る。

十三日、相職朝臣を呼す。祈雨の事又々定め行うべきの状、上達部に告げしむ。

十五日、出羽の馳駅賊と戦を行う事を言上す。季御読経。大極殿に於いて始行す。是祈雨の為早く修する所なり。山座主（尊意）をして尊勝法を修せしむ。同じく請雨なり。廿一僧なり。

十六日、丑剋地震。召に依り大納言（平伊望）等参入す。出羽に報符を給うべき事を定む。然と雖も議定を遂げず。戌剋退出。

十七日、出羽国に賜う符案を（尾張）言鑒宿祢将来す。御読経結願。座主に〔　〕を賜う。

廿一日、山座主行う所の御修法の法師等に度者を施す。相撲召合は廿七日を以て有るべき事、所司に仰す。

廿七日、相撲召合、不奏音樂、

閏七月

五日、（藤原仲平）左大臣參入、任備前介・（藤原子高）參河守等云々、相職（源）朝臣令告事由、

八日、修善畢、阿闍梨[宥]別祿、結願之後加持之間、感淚自降、若尊乱向欲、[影迎ヵ]今日小念誦如例、從

近會所不能行也、

廿三日、文章生改判今日定行、合三度、而不成停止者、

廿七日、相撲召合。音楽を奏せず。

天慶二年閏七月

五日、左大臣（藤原仲平）参入す。備前介（藤原子高）・参河守等を任ずと云々。（源）相職朝臣事の由を告げしむ。

八日、修善畢ぬ。阿闍梨に別禄有り。結願の後加持の間、感涙自ら降る。若は尊影の迎うるか。今日小念誦例の如し。近曾従り行うこと能わざる所なり。

廿三日、文章生の改判今日定め行う。合せて三度。而に成さず停止す者。

122

御修法

　　　　　八月

　　　　　三日、辛丑、內御修法始、龍慧・延昌爲阿闍梨、

　忠平橘直幹ニ
　巡方帶ヲ與フ　　七日、烏犀純方帶一腰給內記直幹、閒無帶、
ク
　烏時杭ヲ喫拔　　八日、辰時烏咋拔時杭、
釋奠內論義　　　十日、ᵒ論議、不御南殿、
　　　　　　　　　　　內〔卷〕

尾張守共理射　　十一日、尾張守共理被ᵈ射敏之狀告來、出羽飛驛來、又尾張〕飛驛入夜來、
殺セラル　　　（藤原カ）
出羽尾張ノ飛　（7張）
驛至ル　　　　十二日、參入職曹司、見尾張・出羽解文、

天慶二年八月

三日、辛丑。内の御修法始む。覚慧・延昌阿闍梨為り。

七日、烏犀純方の帯一腰を内記（橘）直幹に給う。帯無きを聞く。

八日、辰時 烏時 杭を咋い抜く。

十日、内論義。南殿に御せず。

十一日、尾張守（藤原）共理射殺せらるるの状告げ来たる。出羽の飛駅来たる。又尾張の飛駅夜に入り来たる。

十二日、職曹司に参入す。尾張・出羽の解文を見る。

行十二皇祈羽惟忠章
ヒ算后ヲ年兵扶平明
給於遺法穀乱ニ陸親
フ忠法性及ノ饌奧王
　平性寺出コス守御
　寺六　　トヨ平元
　　　　　リ幣帛使　服

十三日、賜國〻官符案左大弁將來、頗受取捨歸去、
（源惟淺）

十四日、十三親王元服、
（章明親王）

十七日、往白河家、饌陸奧守惟扶朝臣、聊有管絃之興、又賜祿有差、
（甲午）

十八日、祈（年）穀並出羽兵乱事幣帛使從八省院立、大納言行事、

廿日、戊午、中宮爲予於法性寺有法事、銀佛・金泥經・七僧法服・余雜具等如例、又四尺屏風四
（藤原穠子）　　　　　　　　　　　　　　　　（伊望）　　　　　　　　　自
帖・沉香折敷六敷・銀器・同瓶子・地敷・於莚等被惠、左丞相勸盃、三四巡後將惠、
　　　　　　　　　　　　　　　　　　（指）　　　　　　（藤原仲平）　　　〔ろ〕

廿四日、曉賜中宮御書云、主上煩給云〻、
　　　　　　　　　　　（朱雀天皇）

十三日、国々に賜う官符の案を左大弁（源是茂）将来す。頻る取捨を受け帰去す。

十四日、十三親王（章明親王）元服す。

十七日、白河の家に往き、陸奥守（平）惟扶朝臣に餞す。聊か管絃の興有り。又賜禄に差有り。

十八日、祈年穀並に出羽の兵乱事等の幣帛使八省院従り立つ。大納言（平伊望）行事。銀仏・金泥経・七僧の法服・

廿日、戊午。中宮（藤原穏子）予の為に法性寺に於いて法事有り。自余の雑具等例の如し。又四尺屏風四帖・沈香の折敷六枚・銀器・同瓶子・地敷・指筵等を惠まる。

左丞相（藤原仲平）勧盃。三四巡の後将恵まる。

廿四日、暁中宮の御書を賜わるに云く、主上（朱雀天皇）煩い給うと云々。

天台座主ヲシテ調伏法ヲ修セシム

廿五日、率廿口伴僧参入、山座主御修法始、明日後夜時可始可之状仰了、而依調伏法、半夜始

者、

廿六日、参入大内、

公卿召除目

廿七日、参入大内、於御前有任公卿議、只与左丞相二人侯、議了召右大将、令清書、

九月

宜陽殿忠平ノ座紛失

一日、宜陽殿吾座縁失之由、左衛門督見問陣官・掃部等、不知其由者、

紀淑光薨ズ

十一日、伊勢例幣依有犬死穢延之、宮内卿薨、

廿五日、廿口の伴僧を率いて参入し、山座主（尊意）御修法を始む。明日の後夜の時始行すべきの状仰せ了ぬ。而に調伏法に依り、半夜始む者。

廿六日、大内に参入す。

廿七日、大内に参入す。御前に於いて公卿（大納言藤原実頼等）を任ずるの議有り。只左丞相と二人候ず。議了りて、右大将（藤原実頼）を召し、清書せしむ。

天慶二年九月

一日、宜陽殿の吾座紛失の由、左衛門督（藤原師輔）陣官・掃部等を見問す。其の由を知らず者。

十一日、伊勢例幣犬の死穢有るに依り之を延す。宮内卿（紀淑光）薨ず。

忠平師經
忠平病ム

伊勢例幣

貞救ヲシテ
園社ニ南海遊
行ノコトヲ祈
ラシム

忠平橘實利ヲ
シテ平扶ニ
庭立奏ヲ受習
セシム

十三日、伊勢例幣、[今日]令奉進、

十四日、七寺令誦經、爲息也、[次說カ]施物頗增例數、從午時許、如熱發煩、依左[ミ]又三寺令誦經、以水沃[此カ]

首廿楾、平損、

廿六日、甲午、令貞救祈禱祇園、[祇欽]自今日七箇日、南海監行事、

廿八日、左中弁將來賜五畿七道制兵、[藤原在衝]官符案、[之カ]云、[橘][平]

廿九日、八月廿二日令公忠宿祢仰實利公惟扶朝臣在宇治、須向彼宅、受習庭立奏、必奉仕十月朔日云、、

129

十三日、伊勢例幣。今日奉遣す。

十四日、七寺に誦経せしむ。息災の為なり。此に依り又三寺に誦経せしむ。施物顔る例数に増さる。午時 許 従り熱発の如く煩う。

廿六日、甲午。貞救をして祇園に祈禱せしむ。今日自り七箇日。南海 濫行 の事なり。水を以て首に沃ぐこと 廿 檪。平損す。

廿八日、左中弁（藤原在衡）五畿七道に賜う制兵の官符案を将来す。

廿九日、八月廿二日（三統）公忠宿祢をして（橘）実利に仰せしめて云く、（平）惟扶朝臣宇治に在り。須らく彼の宅に向い、庭立奏を受け習い、必ず十月朔日に奉仕すべしと云々。

忠平旬ノ式ヲ
奏ス
旬

十月

一日、（藤原仲平）左丞相入坐、今日事相定、奉付出居侍從等略定夾名、又旬儀。出書、爲令奏聞、上御南殿、（朱雀天皇）
〔茅殿カ〕
次

秉燭之後、有諸衛・少納言等奏、每事多失礼云〻、（橘實利）

五節ヲ出スべ
キ人々ヲ定ム

二日、可貢五節儸妓之事、仰新任宰相四人、（藤原元方・源高明・伴保平・藤原敦忠）皆承之狀、使朝忠朝臣有被仰之事、〻、（藤原）
〔間〕

推問武藏密告
使申請雜事ヲ
定ム

（8張）

三日、（藤原在衡）左中弁來云、昨日諸卿定申云、推間使申發兵事、不可」然、又加主典事、止前法家、可任後（阿蘇）
〔神〕
〔左カ〕

申人、請醫師隨將師事、不可給者、令告故問、（廣邊）

臨時御讀經請
僧定

忠平病ム

十日、（平伊望）戶部定臨時御讀經請僧、今日熱發、以冷水沃頂卌楝、依熱猶不盡、覆冷布、

天慶二年十月

一日、左丞相（藤原仲平）入坐す。今日の事相定む。出居の侍従等の略定の夾名を付け奉る。又旬儀の次第書き出す。奏聞せしめんが為なり。上（朱雀天皇）南殿に御す。秉燭の後、諸卿・

少納言（橘実利）等の奏有り。毎事失礼多しと云々。

二日、五節の傀儡貢ずべきの事、新任の宰相四人（藤原元方・源高明・伴保平・藤原敦忠）に仰す。皆承るの状。（藤原）朝忠朝臣を使して仰せらるるの事有り。

三日、左中弁（藤原在衡）来たりて云く、昨日諸卿定め申して云く、推問使發兵を申す事、然るべからず。又主典を加わうる事、前の法家を止め、後に申す人（阿蘇広遠）を任ずべし。醫師を将帥に随えんと請う事、給うべからず者。左閤に告げしむ。

十日、戸部（平伊望）臨時御読経の請僧を定む。今日熱発す。冷水を以て頂に沃ぐこと四十槵。熱猶尽きざるに依り、冷布を覆う。

極樂寺菊會

十二日、己酉、極樂寺菊會、有樂、依病不參、

臨時御讀經

十四日、辛亥、臨時御讀經在綾綺殿、僧數卅口、緣有天変也、

法性寺法華十
講

〔八〕
十四日、乙卯、法性寺十講始、

諸問密告使長
推問
官軍士發長
ザルヲ欲ク
臭太后御惱ニ
ヨリ十寺御讀
經ヲ行ヲ度ス

廿二日、俊朝臣等來申云、依諸卿定申、不發軍士事甚有恐云〻、

（藤原糧子）
廿三日、依中宮危急煩給、忍物忌馳參、御内藏寮十寺令行御讀經、又六十人度者爲六道可度之
（卯カ）
事、令義海律師祈申、卯時退出、

臭太后御修法

廿四日、中宮御修法、日中結願、從初夜又始行、

十二日、己酉。極楽寺菊会。楽有り。病に依り不参。

十四日、辛亥。臨時御読経綾綺殿に在り。僧数四十口。天変有るに縁るなり。

十八日、乙卯。法性寺十講始。

廿二日、（源）俊朝臣等来たり申して云く、諸卿定め申すに依り、軍士を発せざる事甚だ恐れ有りと云々。

廿三日、中宮（藤原穏子）危急に煩い給うに依り、物忌を忍びて馳せ参る。内蔵寮に仰せて十寺に御読経を行わしむ。又六十人の度者六道の為度すべきの事。義海律師をして祈り申さしむ。卯時退出。

廿四日、中宮御修法。日中結願。初夜従り又始行す。

廿六日、癸亥、依中宮重煩給參入、宿申、台山給自今日三箇日、奉爲宮令轉讀大般若三部、於法

延暦寺大般若
經轉讀御修法

法性寺御修法

性寺又有御修法、

天皇ノ爲ノ息
災法

廿七日、甲子、令山座主奉爲大內修息灾法、即山上行之、僧廿一口、
〔筆意〕
〔朱筆天皇〕

興福寺維摩會

廿九日、與福寺申維摩會不足斫先給之外卅石大和國宜旨、給左中弁、
〔給脱カ〕 〔正税脱カ〕

不税料ヲ給フ
正太后ニ大和

卅日、參入中宮、令義海、律師祈申六觀音・普賢像、可修法花三昧等事、奉造幷、長一時、
〔ア〕 〔ミ〕

觀音普賢ノ
義海ニ祈ラシ
六
メ

十一月

一日、智淵師將來慈覺大師門徒所修卷數、請前施祿、又有寶幢院卷數、於而所施定絹、此事並
〔四七〕 〔こ〕 〔以下藤原は〕

四仁門徒及ビ
寶幢院卷數

廿六日、癸亥。中宮重く煩い給うに依り参入す。禁中に宿す。台山今日自り始めて三箇日、宮の奉為

大般若三部を転読せしむ。法性寺に於いて又御修法有り。

廿七日、甲子。山座主（尊意）をして大内（朱雀天皇）の奉為息災法を修せしむ。即ち山上に之を

行う。僧廿一口。

三十日、中宮に参入す。義海律師をして六観音・普賢像に祈り申さしむ。法花三昧等を修する事。

廿九日、興福寺申す維摩会の不足料、先給の外三十石大和国正税を給うの宣旨、左中弁に給う。

天慶二年十一月

一日、智淵師慈覚大師（円仁）門徒修する所の巻数を将来す。前に請い禄を施す。又宝幢院の巻数

有り。所に於いて疋絹を施す。

不堪佃田奏

頼私記カ
多、而先〻不記、

二日、癸不堪佃田文、

忠平鼻太后ノ
御病ヲ訪ヒ來
ル

七日、參大內、牽問中宮御病、其次奏聞式部卿・左大臣乗車免等巫、即仰左衛門督、

教賞親王ノ
仲平鼻車ヲ
許不ス病ム

九日、今日今夜重煩、

忠鼻上鼻ノ御
天鼻上鼻ノ御
見舞アリ

十日、中使義方朝臣罔、有恩問、陽成院有御使、檢非違使勘申不供材木可沒官事、仰左衛門督、

沒官ノ材木工衆ヲ
修理職ノ木村ヲ

但相分修理職・木工寮可給、

勘二頒ツ職ノ
木村工衆

十一日、勸覺院後別當不依擧狀補例可勘事、仰左中弁、

勘學院後別當
ノ補任ニツキ
勘ヘシム

十二日、宣旨十一事仰相弁、推新使遲發巫、尾張不言敏芟巫、搜勘之由可責巫等在此中、

二日、不堪佃田文を奏す。

七日、大内に参る。中宮（藤原穏子）の御病を問い奉る。其の次いで式部卿（敦実親王）・左大臣（藤原仲平）輦車・免列等の事を奏聞す。即ち左衛門督（藤原師輔）に仰す。

九日、今日今夜重く煩う。

十日、中使（良峯）義方朝臣来たる。恩問あり。陽成院（陽成上皇）御使有り。検非違使勘申せる、供せざる材木沒官すべき事、左衛門督に仰す。但し修理職・木工寮に相分ちて給うべし。

十一日、勧学院後別当挙状に依らず補する例勘ずべきの事、左中弁（藤原在衡）に仰す。

十二日、宣旨十一枚相弁（源相職）に仰す。推問使遅発の事。尾張殺害（藤原共理）を言わざる事。捜勘の由責むべき事等此の中に在り。

推問武藏密告
使遲發ノコト
等ヲ實ム

御讀香始

鳥太后ノタメ
神寶ヲ諸社ニ
水ル

平伊衆慈ズ

源宗于卒ス

五節舞姫參入
遲ル

新嘗祭

賢明節會
天皇不豫

御讀經

（9張）「十四日、辛巳、御書始、以衡[剄]臣爲博士、（三枕）元夏爲尚復、史記、

十五日、壬午、公家所祈申、奉爲中宮別寶等差使殿上大夫等分奉、

十六日、民部卿薨、

廿二日、宗于卒、藏人信明蒙仰來云、五節妓異常遲參事、又仰參入前後令行例御前何云〻、

廿四日、辛卯、上不御中院、縁大臣・納言等各有障不參候也、只源中納言一人在小齋、仍付所司、

廿五日、節會如例、但不卷御簾、縁御體頗不預也、

廿七日、甲午、大內御讀經於台山修之、大般若三部、

十四日、辛巳。御書始。（藤原）在衡朝臣を以て博士と為す。（三統）元夏尚複為り。史記。

十五日、壬午。公家祈り申す所、中宮の奉為の別宝等殿上の大夫等を差し使して分け奉る。

十六日、民部卿（平伊望）薨ず。

廿二日、（源）宗于卒す。蔵人（源）信明仰せを蒙りて来たりて云く、五節の妓常に異りて遅参せる事。又仰す。参入の前後御前に行列せしむるは何んと云々。

廿四日、辛卯。上（朱雀天皇）中院に御せず。大臣・納言等各障り有りて参候せざるに縁るなり。只源中納言（是茂）一人小斎に在り。仍りて所司に付く。

廿五日、節会例の如し。但し御簾を巻かず。御体頗る不予に縁るなり。

廿七日、甲午。大内の御読経台山に於いて之を修す。大般若三部。

郡司讀奏

廿八日、讀卷、[奏]

賀茂臨時祭

十二月

一日、丁酉、賀茂臨時祭、依納言以上皆有障不參、參議顯忠朝臣（藤原）奏宣命、緣有覽平・延喜他日之（ヒ）例也、

二日、依欽（狀）可主上愼給、使相弁示（源相職）送可行神明祈事之狀於左大臣（藤原仲平）、而稱心神惱不逢、仍空歸也、（朱雀天皇）

人臣之節豈如此欽、

四日、俊（沒）朝臣來、進可發人兵文、仰付奉行此事之弁可進之狀、返給、

天皇御愼ニヨリ神明祈ヲ行ハントス不忠ヲ仲平ニ難ズ不臣平ニ

推問密告使長官忠平ニ人兵ヲ發スベキコトヲ請フ

廿八日、読奏。

天慶二年十二月

一日、丁酉。賀茂臨時祭。納言以上皆障り有りて不参に依り、参議（藤原）顕忠朝臣宣命を奏す。

寛平・延喜他の例有るに縁るなり。

二日、坎に依り主上（朱雀天皇）慎み給うべし。相弁（源相職）を使して神明の祈を行うべき事の状を左大臣に示し送る。而に心神悩むと称し逢わず。仍りて空しく帰るなり。人臣の節豈此の如きか。

四日、（源）俊朝臣来たる。人兵を発すべきの文を進む。此の事を奉行せるの弁に付け進むべきの状を仰せ、返し給う。

陰陽助等新曆
ヲ忠平ノ許ニ
持來ル

忠平兩京窮因
者ニ賑給ス

神今食

郡司召

天變ニヨリ祭
主ヲ祈テ十二
社ニ祈讓セシ
ム

五日、辛丑、陰陽助惟香率允・屬等、置新曆高机將來云、有可准三宮宣旨云々、聞其由、不慊答、

九日、差遣家人於東西京、令見窮因者、収有賑給、

十一日、付所司令行神今食、左中弁來云、左丞相令告云、伊勢齋國可遙拜之狀、大神宮有申、是

緣損來也者、依先々例、可定行狀答了、

十五日、左丞相參入陣外〆召齋主賴基、依天變可愼給之狀令祈二十二社、緣穢停止奉幣事也、但明日辰時可祈申、

十六日、任郡司、

五日、辛丑。陰陽助（出雲）惟香允・屬等を率い、新暦を置ける高机を将来して云く、三宮に准ずべきの宣旨有りと云々。其の由を聞き、慌に答えず。

九日、家人を東西京に差し遣し、窮困の者を見せしむ。聊か賑給有り。

十一日、所司に付け、神今食を行わしむ。左中弁（藤原在衡）来たりて云く、左丞相告げしめて云く、伊勢祭主（大中臣頼基）遥拝すべきの状、大神宮申すこと有り。是損年に縁るなり。者。先々の例に依り定め行うべきの状答え了ぬ。

十五日、左丞相参入す。陣外に祭主頼基を召し、天変に依り慎み給うべきの状十二社に祈らしむ。穢に縁り奉幣を停止せる事なり。但し明日辰時祈り申すべし。

十六日、郡司を任ず。

伊豫國蒋原純
女ノ反亂ヲ奏

御修法
荷前ノ

推問密使進
疑スベキヲ奏

王經ヲ讀
諸寺ニテ仁
兵亂ニヨリテ

純友ノコトニ
御仏名

符ヲ給フ官
ヨリ諸國ニ

明年維摩會ノ
講師ヲ定ム

師輔ニ忠平ヲ
算輔ニ修ス
乙兄寺ニ賀平六十
天性與忠平ヲ
ヒノ御誦經ヲ
給フ

（10張）

十七日、伊豫國申純友乗船欲出海上、被早召上云〻、（藤原）

十八日、大内有御修法始事、荷前、雨儀行也、皇帝不御、左大臣修之、（朱雀天皇）（臨）

十九日、推問使進今月廿八日可發申文、宣旨五枚給相弁、又仰從廿五日可令有供寺〻讀仁王經（源相職）（陽）
祈兵事、三个日、

廿一日、御仏名始、相職朝臣將來依純友事給國〻之官符草、便仰明方・彦真・安生等、可早進（源）（藤原）（伴）（平）
逆事、

廿二日、以與福寺定岑爲明年維摩講師宣旨、仰公忠宿祢、但可仰明宣旨、（三枝）（日藏ヵ）

廿五日、辛酉、乙兄於法性寺爲我修仏事、造佛寫經、晝讀經、夜佛名、問所爲愚、六寺令（藤原師輔）（藤原實頼）（忠平）（問所爲愚也、私記是臈）（朱雀天皇）
行誦經、與福・延暦各五百端、束・西・極樂・法性寺等各三百端、以殿上大夫爲使者、

十七日、伊豫国申す、（藤原）純友船に乗り海上に出でんと欲す。早く召し上げられよと云々。

十八日、大内御修法始の事有り。荷前。雨儀に行うなり。皇帝（朱雀天皇）御せず。左大臣之に臨む。

十九日、推問使今月廿八日発すべきの申文を進む。宣旨五枚を相弁（源相職）に給う。又廿五日より有供の寺々をして仁王経を読み兵を祈らしむべきの事を仰す。三个日。

廿一日、御仏名始。（源）相職朝臣純友の事に依り国々に給うの官符の草を将来す。便ち（藤原）明方・（伴）彦真・（平）安生等を早く進め遣すべき事を仰す。

廿二日、興福寺の定岑を以て明年維摩の講師と為すの宣旨、（三統）公忠宿祢に仰す。但し明日宣旨を仰すべし。

廿五日、辛酉。乙兄（藤原師輔）法性寺に於いて我の為に仏事を修す。造仏写経。昼は読経。夜は仏名。公家（朱雀天皇）愚の為、六寺に誦経を行わしむ。興福・延暦各五百端。東・西・極楽・法性寺等各三百端。殿上の大夫を以て使者と為す。

除目
藤原子高純友
ノ士卒ニ虜ト
セラル

忠平御師經卷
數ヲ給ハル
度者六十人ヲ
給ハル

信濃飛驛
ヨリ諸國ニ勅
符官符ヲ下ス

仰行賞ノコトヲ
長谷寺ニ御立
願アリ

廿六日、咋今左閤〔藤原仲平〕始除目儀、而今日稱有所勞不被參入、仍議停、子高朝臣〔藤原〕從者馳來云、子高於
攝津國〔攝津國〕、爲純友兵士被虜云々、囘之招公卿令定所行之事、

廿七日、曉參入桂芳坊、有除目議〔藤原文元等〕、丞相以下依例會集、議未畢、左閤稱病退出、丑剋俇了〔讃〕、

廿八日、中使敦忠朝臣〔藤原〕來、賜六寺御讀經卷數、兼有賜度者六十人仰下、仍被物白袿一重・女裝
束一襲、

廿九日、依信濃飛驛到來馳來、令行賜國々勅符・官符等事、大將〔藤原實頼〕奉行、丑剋退出、宿職曹司、

卅日、召賀茂忠行仰、若有功者、殊可賞之事、請救〔救力〕師長谷御立願事、

廿六日、昨今左閣（藤原仲平）除目議を始む。而に今日所労有りと称し参入せられず。仍りて議停む。（藤原）子高朝臣の従者馳せ来たりて云く、子高摂津国（葦屋駅）に於いて、純友の兵士（藤原文元等）の為に虜せらると云々。之に因り公卿を招き行う所の事を定めしむ。

廿七日、暁桂芳坊に参入す。除目議有り。丞相以下例に依り会集す。議未だ畢らざるに、左閣病を称し退出す。丑剋議了ぬ。

廿八日、中使（藤原）敦忠朝臣来たり、六寺の御読経の巻数を賜う。兼て度者六十人を賜うことの仰せ下し有り。仍りて被物白掛一重・女装束一襲。

廿九日、信濃の飛駅到来に依り馳せ来たる。国々に賜う勅符・官符等の事を行わしむ。大将（藤原実頼）奉行す。丑剋退出す。職曹司に宿す。

三十日、賀茂忠行を召し仰す。若し功有らば、殊に賞すべきの事。貞救師に長谷御立願を請う事。

The Second Year of the Tengyō Era: Year 939,
A Translation from the Teishinkōki

The First Month

The first
His Majesty [Suzaku Tennō] was present in the Southern Hall {alt. Naden, for the First Day Royal Banquet}, but those in charge were remiss in their duties. The Inner Left Guards claimed that they did not have the right apparel and so the gates were opened late. The Yinyang officials arrived late as well.[1] The second-in-command of the Ministry of Residential Palace Affairs was present but did not appear {in timely fashion}. Because of all this, the officials were late in attending.

The second
The Kasuga Shrine emitted a noise like the beating of drums. There were also sounds like whistling arrows.[2]

The fourth
My senior minister's grand banquet took place {at my residence}.[3] Since I have been feeling indisposed since the end of last year, I did not go out from behind the blinds. Senior Counselor [Taira no Koremochi] designated the banquet coordinators on my behalf.

The sixth
Decisions concerning promotions in rank in the Keihōbō.[4]

The seventh
Due to a taboo, His Majesty was not present in the Southern Hall [for the White Horse Royal Banquet] and his blinds were left down.[5] After leading the white horses past the Southern Hall, officials are supposed to lead them before His Majesty {in the Ryōkiden}. Instead the horses were distributed before they were paraded before

His Majesty, and only seven remaining horses were led past when the summons came.[6] Since the third-level managers from the Left and Right {Stables} were absent, I instructed Senior Counselor {Taira no Koremochi} to reprimand them.[7]

The eighth

The Ceremony for Women's Promotion in Rank took place.[8] In addition, two men received promotions in rank. Senior Counselor officiated.

The eleventh

Earthquake.

The sixteenth

The {Dance and Song} Royal Banquet took place as usual.[9] But Minister {of the Left} [Fujiwara no Nakahira] and Senior Counselor were unable to attend due to illness. Therefore Senior Right Captain [Fujiwara no Saneyori] served as master of ceremonies inside the Shōmei Gate.[10] There were no counselors posted outside the gate {to keep order}. {The names of} nine extra chamberlains were written down, and I had Senior Captain memorialize the list {to His Majesty}.[11]

The seventeenth

I heard that Senior Right Captain {Fujiwara no Saneyori} arrived at his seat in the tent in the Great Courtyard {for the Grand Archery Ceremony} but that then there was a summons.[12] When he entered {the residential palace}, he was told His Majesty would not be present {for the proceedings}. It was a blunder.[13]

The eighteenth

It was odd that Minister of Justice [Fujiwara no Akitada] did not receive the royal order but rather went directly to the Southern Courtyard to commence Continuation Rounds {of the Grand Archery Ceremony}.[14] Then there were the Archery Matches, where the Right Inner Palace Guards and the Right Palace Guards won.

The twentieth
I summoned Sir [Fujiwara no] Asatada. Yesterday he presented two hawks to the throne {on my behalf}, received the reward, and returned.

The twenty-second
Kōshi day. The ceremony marking the annual beginning of duties in the Council Secretariat took place.[15] There was {also} a Council memorial to the throne (*kansō*).[16] Middle Right Controller [Minamoto no Sukemoto] took charge.

The twenty-fourth
Heiin day. An esoteric rite for His Majesty {began in the residential palace}. Master of Discipline Gikai initiated proceedings.[17] Twenty-one monks {participated}.

The twenty-sixth
The director of the Repairs Agency, Sir [Fujiwara no] Tadafumi, brought the lists of sutras and prayers read on my behalf at Kōfukuji. The prayers were to celebrate my long life.[18]

The twenty-eighth
Beginning of the Ceremony for Assigning Posts in the Keihōbō.[19]

The thirtieth
A rainbow appeared at the main hall of the Council of State Office.[20]

The Second Month

The first
Discussions concerning assignment of posts ended in the small hours of the morning.[21] At Master of Discipline Gikai's request, the right to have one novice ordained was given to monks who participated in the esoteric rite {for His Majesty}.[22] In addition, His Majesty must take special precautions this year.[23]

The second
A Buddhist rite {was held} at my residence. I myself informed Enshō, the officiant, about the ordinand he has been granted.[24]

The third

A comet was seen in the firmament. The abbot of Jōjūji brought a list of sutras and prayers recited for my long life.[25] I {thanked him by} giving him a surplice.

The fourth

Senior Counselor [Taira no Koremochi] arrived and I gave him orders concerning the Benevolent King Assembly that must have its planning ceremony on the tenth, and concerning contributions of polished rice from various provinces {for its support}.[26]

The fifth

There were two earthquakes during the night.

The fifth

I gave Controller Sō [Minamoto no Sukemoto] royal orders.[27] [Tachibana no] Toshimichi's license to take the exam was one of these.[28]

The eighth

There were sounds and movements several times during the night.

The tenth

Senior Counselor [Taira no Koremochi] conducted the planning ceremony for the Benevolent King Assembly.

The twelfth

When Senior Counselor {Taira no Koremochi} arrived, I directed him to take care of the following: tomorrow's Ceremony for Modification of Appointments; decisions regarding the master-in-charge and votive petition for the Benevolent King Assembly; expediting work on the walls of the greater palace precincts; and seeing to the agents to summon and interrogate [Taira no] Masakado.[29]

The thirteenth

The Ceremony for Modification of Appointments was held. Also, Fujiwara no Koreeda was promoted.[30] He has been head of the royal pasture at Chichibu and has greatly benefitted the realm.[31]

The fifteenth
I passed the missive from [the realm of] Kōryō to [Ōe no] Asatsuna.[32]

The seventeenth
In the evening Council Secretary [Mononobe no] Sadamochi reported to me that all those of advisor rank and higher were unable to attend today's festival {for the Sono and Kara deities} for various reasons.[33] I ordered him to have it performed in accord with precedents from occasions when the Ōharano Festival has been conducted without a noble-in-charge.

The eighteenth
The Council secretary Sadamochi came and reported, "Last night I went to the residence of the Minister of Civil Affairs [Fujiwara no Masamoto] and informed him of the situation. The minister {then} went to the palace and took charge {of the Sono and Kara deities' festival}. It ended in the small hours and {then} he returned home." This means Sadamochi, acting on his own initiative, summoned the old gentleman! Why didn't he do as I ordered? The elderly minister had explained to me that he was ill and unable to bear the strain. Why did Sadamochi act on his own without my instructions?

The twenty-first
I heard that Minister of Popular Affairs [Taira no Koremochi] received a royal order to the effect that I was granted the right to recommend a person for posting every year.[34] Since there was not a palace secretary present, Sir {Ōe no} Asatsuna was told to have the royal edict prepared and submitted by tomorrow morning.[35]

The twenty-second
Kōgo day. There was an extraordinary Benevolent King Assembly because of an earthquake and to ward off the ill omen of triple alignment.[36]

The twenty-eighth
The royal edict granting me the right to recommend someone for office annually was issued.[37]

The Third Month

The third

Minamoto no Tsunemoto made accusations concerning events in Musashi.[38] {Also} His Majesty had the director of the Left Palace Guards [Fujiwara no Morosuke] return my previous missive declining {the honor of status equal to the three queens}.[39] My token of regard to him {Morosuke} was as usual.

The fourth

I had the Ise head ritualist [Ōnakatomi no Ōsei] say prayers concerning the fighting in the Bandō.[40] The number of shrines {where prayers are to be said} is written in the votive petition. I instructed Senior Right Captain [Fujiwara no Saneyori] to order officials and members of the six guard units to be on duty whether or not it is their shift.[41]

The sixth

The earth shook, just like over the past several days.

The ninth

Prayers were offered at eleven shrines. Also, two-altar rites began on Mount Hiei. The abbot [Son'i] and Gikai served as officiants. The rites were occasioned by {Minamoto no} Tsunemoto's accusations. In the evening I went to the palace and stayed in the Higyōsha. Director of Female Chamberlains [Fujiwara no Takako] stayed there as well.[42]

The tenth

There was a banquet for female officials {given by} the Director of Female Chamberlains {Fujiwara no Takako}. Those with third-level posts (*Naishi no jō*) down to those serving as female royal secretaries ({*nyo*} *kurōdo*) sat in the Higyōsha. Others sat in the Takadono vicinity of the Bureau of the Wardrobe.[43]

The eleventh

Earthquake.

The thirteenth

Earthquake.

Figure 10. The *Tennō's* Residential Palace

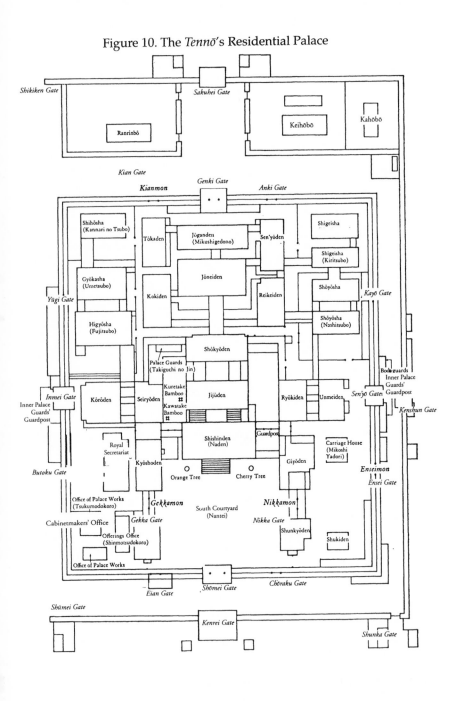

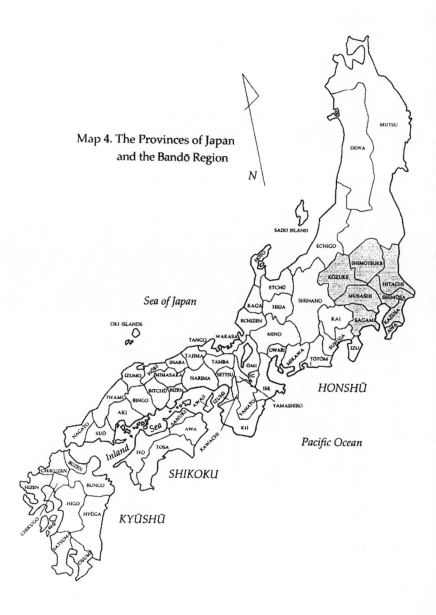

Map 4. The Provinces of Japan and the Bandō Region

The fourteenth
His Majesty sent me Minister of the Left's [Fujiwara no Nakahira] missive resigning his two posts [Minister of the Left, Senior Left Captain]. Having seen it, I immediately returned it.[44]

The fifteenth
The Seasonal Sutra Reading took place.[45] I passed royal orders concerning the Ceremony for Appointing Lowest Ranking Posts to [Fujiwara no] Motokata.[46]

The sixteenth
The Ceremony for Appointing Lowest Ranking Posts took place. But this year it did not take place in the residence of the Minister [of Personnel Prince Atsumi].

The seventeenth
Senior Left Controller [Minamoto no Koreshige] arrived and reported concerning the extraordinary {shipment of} polished rice from various provinces.[47] I summoned [Mifune no] Saikō and asked about {progress made by} the provinces {repairing} the walls {of the greater palace precincts}.

The twentieth
Master of Discipline Ninkō brought the dedicatory text that he had had prepared, [listing] scriptures copied and recited {for me}. Accordingly, I offered him tea and gave him a set of women's white robes as reward.

The twenty-second
I summoned [Izumo no] Koreka and [Fumi no] Takekane and asked {what to do} about the fighting [in the Bandō]. Takekane said that the most appropriate thing would be to perform the Taiitsu Rite.[48] I ordered him to do so.

The twenty-seventh
A ritual assembly in the Ninnaji Octagonal Hall took place.[49]

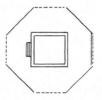

The twenty-ninth
Although no senior nobles attended the reading and lecture on the *Chronicles of Japan* {at court}, I gave orders [for Yatabe no Kinmochi] to read and lecture.

The Fourth Month

The first
His Majesty [Suzaku Tennō] was not present in the Southern Hall.[50]

The second
Naming of outriders for the {Kamo Priestess'} Lustration—Senior Right Captain [Fujiwara no Saneyori] officiated.[51] His Majesty had boy dancers from the Ninnaji Octagonal Hall Assembly perform in his presence.[52] Minister of Personnel [Prince Atsumi] attended, in accord with His Majesty's summons. The princes, senior nobles, and musicians received rewards according to their status.

The seventh
The list of those qualified for promotions in rank was memorialized {to His Majesty}.[53] Senior Captain [Fujiwara no Saneyori] was in charge.

The eleventh
The senior nobles discussed whether or not to hold a Fifth-month Banquet.[54] I gave Sir [Minamoto no] Sukemoto the royal order to commission the second-in-command in Dewa, Sir Yasutoshi, as commander of the {Akita} Stockade.[55]

The fourteenth
Kamo Festival.[56] Rain fell all day. The Kamo Priestess [Princess Tsuyako] set out, but the river was flooded and I heard that people had trouble crossing.[57] In the evening, Middle Right Controller [Minamoto no Sukemoto] hurried over saying that neither the Kamo

Priestess nor the other messengers [of the Office of Female Chamberlains] could cross the river and that they were stranded. I ordered that they should await the arrival of messengers tomorrow, and then continue on. But the messengers [from the Inner Palace Guards and other offices] should cross by boat this evening and deliver the votive strip offerings.[58]

The fifteenth
In the early morning I sent the attendant Zaijō to deliver a message to the Kamo Priestess. Sir [Minamoto no] Kintada, who was in charge of [the evening's] events, delivered a message from her that arrived last night. He also said that he had had someone look for the messengers in order to transmit my orders but that no one was found. Then this morning they appeared and everyone set out for the shrine.

The sixteenth
Master Ichiwa brought the list of sutras and prayers read for my long life. I called him before me to give him a reward. I [also] ordered [Yoshimine no] Yoshikata to reprimand those who had been on duty on the fifth and sixth days, namely [Minamoto no] Moroakira, [Fujiwara no] Atsutada, [Fujiwara no] Arihira, [Minamoto no] Kintada, and [Minamoto no] Kanetada.

The seventeenth
An express courier from Dewa Province reported a rebellion and battle against forces from Akita Stockade.[59] The Director of the Left Palace Guards [Fujiwara no Morosuke] went to the palace in the evening {to hear the report}.[60] He had a Council secretary send the report to my residence.

The eighteenth
I went to my office in the Queen-consort's Agency.[61] I had the senior nobles assemble at the guardroom to deliberate on the report from Dewa.[62]

The twentieth
Memorializing {of nominations for appointments to the post of district chieftain}.[63]

The twenty-third
Esoteric rite for His Majesty, performed by the abbot [Son'i] on Mount Hiei. Twenty-one monks {participated}.

The twenty-fifth
Master Jōgu brought the list of sutras and prayers performed at Hasedera.[64] I gave him a reward because they were for my long life.

The twenty-sixth
The abbot of Tōdaiji, Myōchin, brought the list of sutras and prayers read for my long life. I gave him a reward. I sent Sir [Fujiwara no] Morouji to present my letter renouncing the office of regent and the right to recommend one appointee for an official post annually. I ordered that the reprimanded royal intimates be pardoned.[65] Yasutoshi, second-in-command of the Dewa Stockade, told me that he would proceed to Dewa in accordance with my orders.[66] I summoned him and told him to leave promptly. I had given him *sake*, other gifts, and horses earlier.

The twenty-eighth
The royal emissary Sir [Fujiwara no] Morouji came and transmitted a royal command. In accord with precedent I gave him a token of regard.

The twenty-ninth
I had officials from the six guards units and from the Left and Right Stables conduct a search for thieves throughout the capital.[67]

The thirtieth
Earthquake during the night.

The Fifth Month

The fifth
The Minister of Popular Affairs [Taira no Koremochi] came and I ordered {first} that Council directives be prepared to the effect that {provincial headquarters in} Kantō provinces be reprimanded for not strictly controlling the territories they govern.[68] {Next,} I ordered that the matter of shrines offering prayers and temples reading sutras be decided.

The sixth
An express courier came from Dewa.[69] The report stated that rebels arrived at the Akita District office. They broke open storehouses, stole the rice, and burned local cultivators' property. It is even said that they brought demons with them.

The seventh
Horse races took place in the Hokuhen'in.[70]

The tenth
Earthquake.

The sixteenth
A Taiitsu Rite was held in the State Halls Compound.[71] [Fumi no] Takekane {officiated}.

The fifteenth[72]
Messengers set off to various shrines with votive strip offerings. This was for prayers concerning the rebels. I went to my office in the queen-consort's quarters. I had them {the senior nobles} appoint the Musashi provincial governor [Kudaranokokishi Teiun] and others.[73]

The twentieth
Certificates of rank were granted {to the summoned recipients}.[74]

The twenty-third
Agents for charitable distributions were appointed.[75] {The noble-in-charge was the} head of the Left Palace Gate Guards [Fujiwara no Morosuke].

The twenty-seventh
Early morning earthquake. Another at night.

The twenty-eighth
Concerning this year's Vimalakirti Assembly, Seigen is to be invited as lecturer.[76] I sent Sir [Mimune no] Kintada to communicate this to Minister of the Left [Fujiwara no Nakahira].[77]

Sixth Month

The first
Sutra readings at various temples and shrines as well as the Taigen Rite at Hōrinji commenced.[78]

The fifth
I reprimanded two junior controllers, [Ōe no] Asa{tsuna} and [Minamoto no] Suke{moto}, for absenteeism in the offices of the Council of State. The two said that they had decided among themselves which {officials} would come on the days of required service and on the days before and after. I censured them, "How could you decide about attendance for those days? Mind you attend every day." But since a man is not made of wood and stone, how can there not be days when there are absences?[79]

The seventh
I summoned Sir [Minamoto no] Kanetada and had him transmit the following to the Minister of the Left [Fujiwara no Nakahira]: first, that agents to investigate allegations of trouble {in the Kantō} be appointed; second, concerning the above, there is need to decide whether to follow precedent in this matter. I went to my office in the queen-consort's quarters and instructed the senior nobles to appoint the investigative agents. In the evening Minister of Popular Affairs [Taira no Koremochi] brought the list of appointees decided by the senior nobles.[80] Then the senior nobles all left the residential palace.

The eighth
There was a banquet celebrating the completion of the classics reading in His Majesty's presence [the *Annotated Classic of Filial Piety*, Fujiwara no Motokata].[81] Feeling unwell, I did not attend.

The ninth

Senior Counselor [Taira no Koremochi] came and showed me [Hinokuma no] Tadaaki's report that the initiator of the allegations should be placed under arrest.[82] In response, I gave him the following instructions: {Minamoto no} Tsunemoto should be detained in the headquarters of the Left Palace Gate Guards; and [Ono no] Morooki and [Tachibana no] Koreshige should be appointed Envoys to Subdue the Territory.[83] However, precedents for appointing persons of the fifth rank for this purpose should be verified. I ordered that a Council directive be drafted immediately appointing investigative agents.

The eleventh

Extraordinary offerings were sent with the agent for the Tsukinami Festival.[84] A prince was added to the party sent {to Ise Shrine} to pray for rain and to make supplications concerning disturbing celestial events. I had the appropriate officials perform the Jinkonjiki Rite {in the *tennō*'s stead}. Although His Majesty wanted to go to the Chūin, there was a westerly directional taboo {and he could not go}.

The twelfth

Jingo day. Messengers left {with offerings} for rain prayers at various shrines. To the royal proclamation was appended a special appeal concerning the disturbing celestial events.

The thirteenth

Kibi day. The esoteric rite for His Majesty began at Enryakuji's royal vow hall [Enmeiin].[85] The abbot [Son'i] served as officiant with twenty assistant monks. They will also read the Great Wisdom Sutra three times over three days, once each day. However, the esoteric rite for His Majesty will last seven days. Due to the disturbing celestial event, His Majesty must be cautious. There have been many earthquakes lately.

The fifteenth

In the early afternoon a rainbow appeared in different places: at the Office of the Royal Meal, in front of the headquarters of the Left Inner Palace Guards, and at the Cabinetmakers' Office.[86]

The sixteenth

Senior Counselor {Taira no Koremochi} appointed the monks who will serve in the extraordinary sutra-reading ceremony.[87]

The twentieth

Kōin day. An extraordinary sutra-reading ceremony was held at the Throne Hall. The purpose was to pray for rain, a good harvest, and peace in the realm.[88]

The twenty-third

Earthquake at daybreak. The sutra-reading ceremony was to conclude today, but because it has not rained it was extended two days.

The twenty-eighth

I gave the royal order to Junior Controller [Minamoto no] Sukemoto. I also gave him [Minamoto no] Tsunemoto's accusation;[89] and I passed on the precedents for rain prayers researched by Council secretaries.

The twenty-ninth

I summoned [Owari no] Genkan.[90] I ordered him to tally up the days that controllers and junior secretaries of the Council of State had reported for work last month in the Council Office and Preparatory Office.[91]

The Seventh Month

The second

Shinchū day. I ordered the Yinyang Bureau to conduct a Five-Dragon Festival to pray for rain.[92] I also ordered votive strip offerings at Kami no Ryūketsu {Shrine} as well as sutra readings.[93] In the early afternoon there was thunder and rain. The governor of Ise, [Fujiwara no] Shigetoki, was promoted to the senior fifth rank for {his previous} meritorious service in Higo.[94] He should have been promoted in the first month, but he did not obtain the comprehensive receipt for one year's taxes in kind and labor and so he was not promoted.[95] However today he was promoted because there were precedents for doing so and also because he submitted a complaint.

The fifth
Sutra readings for rain began. And the esoteric rite for His Majesty conducted by Master of Discipline {Gi}kai began. A royal secretary went to Mount Hiei to be present for the duration of the rite. This was because of the rebellion in the east.

The eighth
I ordered Sir [Minamoto no] Sukemoto to tell Minister of Popular Affairs [Taira no Koremochi], "Conduct prayers for rain again." In the evening, the Minister sent a reply through Sir [Mimune no] Kintada containing divinations forwarded by the Council on Shrine Affairs and the Yinyang Bureau with the assurance that, "I {Taira no Koremochi} am following your orders completely."[96] I sent word, "You should conduct prayers again at shrines not previously included [on the twelfth day of the sixth month]."

The ninth
I ordered amnesty for those prisoners in the Left and Right Prisons who had committed minor offenses and had not yet been judged. And I ordered votive strip offerings for various shrines to pray for rain. I did this on the basis of the report received the previous evening.

The tenth
Kiyū day. I ordered the Prelates' Office to have the fifteen great temples and Enryakuji, along with state-supported temples, perform an abbreviated reading of the Benevolent King Sutra for three days, beginning the day after tomorrow.[97] This is to pray for rain.

The twelfth
Shingai day. Today, and for three days, there were sutra readings to pray for rain.

The thirteenth
I summoned Sir [Minamoto no] Sukemoto. I ordered him to inform the senior nobles to decide on more rain prayers.

The fifteenth
An express courier from Dewa reported on the fighting with rebels. Seasonal sutra readings were begun at the Throne Hall. These were

performed early to pray for rain. I had the abbot of Mount Hiei [Son'i] perform the Sonshō Rite to pray for rain.[98] Twenty-one monks participated.

The sixteenth

There was an earthquake in the small hours of the morning. In response to my summons, the Senior Counselor [Taira no Koremochi] and others proceeded to the residential palace. There was a discussion concerning a Council directive responding to the report from Dewa, but no decision was reached.[99] They {senior nobles} went home between seven and nine in the evening.

The seventeenth

Sir [Owari no] Genkan brought me the draft of the Council directive to be sent to Dewa Province. Seasonal Sutra Readings concluded.[100] I gave the abbot {a reward}.

The twenty-first

Ordinands were granted to the monks performing the esoteric rite led by the Abbot {Son'i}. I gave orders to the relevant officials concerning the Sumo Matches in His Majesty's presence to be held on the twenty-seventh.[101]

The twenty-seventh

The Sumo Matches in His Majesty's Presence took place. There was no music.[102]

The Intercalary Seventh Month

The fifth

The Minister of the Left [Fujiwara no Nakahira] went to the palace and they {senior nobles} appointed the vice-governor of Bizen [Fujiwara no Sanetaka] and the governor of Mikawa. Sir [Minamoto no] Sukemoto had someone report to me.

The eighth

Private rites concluded. I gave a special reward to the officiant. After the concluding prayers, during the empowerment rite, I was moved to tears.[103] Perhaps it was because a numinous image seemed to appear to me?[104] Today my brief prayer session was as usual—I have not been able to do it recently.[105]

The twenty-third
Results of the university students' examinations were reviewed.[106] There have now been three such re-evaluations. However, discussion broke up without agreement.

Eighth month

The third
Shinchū day. An esoteric rite for His Majesty {in the residential palace} began. Kakue and Enshō served as officiants.[107]

The seventh
I gave the palace secretary [Tachibana no] Naomoto a lacquered leather belt decorated with square pieces of rhinoceros horn.[108] This was because I heard he didn't have one.

The eighth
In the morning a crow seized a clock peg in its beak.[109]

The tenth
The annual Residential Palace Debate {for the Memorial for Confucius}.[110] {His Majesty} was not present in the Southern Hall.

The eleventh
News arrived that the governor of Owari, [Fujiwara no] Tomomasa, had been shot and killed by an arrow.[111] An express courier from Dewa {also} arrived. And another express courier from Owari came in the middle of the night.

The twelfth
I went to my office in the Queen-consort's {Fujiwara no Yasuko} quarters and looked at reports from Owari and Dewa.[112]

The thirteenth
Senior Left Controller [Minamoto no Koreshige] brought drafts of Council directives for various provinces.[113] I approved some and rejected others, and he withdrew.

The fourteenth
The thirteenth prince [Noriakira Shinnō] had his coming-of-age ceremony.[114]

The seventeenth
I went to the Shirakawa residence and hosted a departure banquet for the governor of Mutsu, Sir [Taira no] Koresuke.[115] We had a bit of playing of flutes and strings. Appropriate rewards were distributed.

The eighteenth
Messengers bearing votive strip offerings for prayers for a plentiful harvest and for suppression of the Dewa uprising departed from the State Halls Compound.[116] Senior Counselor [Taira no Koremochi] was in charge.

The twentieth
Bogo day. The Queen-consort [Fujiwara no Yasuko] held a Buddhist service on my behalf at Hosshōji.[117] The silver Buddha, a sutra written in gold ink, robes for seven monks, and other miscellaneous implements were as usual. In addition, the four-foot-high folding screens, the six trays for offering scented aloeswood, silver implements, silver flagons, floor coverings, and under-cushions were lavishly presented. Minister of the Left [Fujiwara no Nakahira] offered the cup. After three or four rounds…(the next clause in the text is indecipherable)

The twenty-fourth
A missive from the Queen-consort arrived at dawn, saying that His Majesty [Suzaku Tennō] was in discomfort.

The twenty-fifth
Bringing twenty assistant monks with him into the residential palace, the abbot of Mount Hiei [Son'i] began an esoteric rite for His

Majesty. I had ordered that the rite commence before dawn tomorrow. But because it was a subjugation rite, it started before midnight, I heard.[118]

The twenty-sixth
I went to the residential palace.

The twenty-seventh
I went to the residential palace. The ceremony to name senior nobles was held in the presence of His Majesty.[119] Minister of the Left [Fujiwara no Nakahira] and I were present. At its conclusion we summoned Senior Right Captain [Fujiwara no Saneyori] and had the formal record prepared.

The Ninth Month

The first
Since my cushion seat has disappeared from the Giyōden, Director of the Left Guards [Fujiwara no Morosuke] questioned the guardroom staff and those in the Custodial Office. But they said they knew nothing about it.[120]

The eleventh
The annual votive strip offerings for Ise {Grand Shrine} were postponed because of defilement caused by the death of a dog. Minister of the Royal Household [Ki no Yoshimitsu] died.

The thirteenth
The delayed annual votive strip offerings for Ise {Shrine} were dispatched today.

The fourteenth
I ordered sutra readings at seven temples for my health and safety. The number of goods I donated greatly exceeded the norm. Around noon I came down with a fever. Thus I ordered additional sutra readings at three temples. I doused my head with twenty flagons of water and the fever abated.

The twenty-sixth
Kōgo day. I had Monk Jōgu say prayers at Gion {Shrine}.[121] Today is the first of seven days of prayers occasioned by the violence in the Nankai circuit.[122]

The twenty-eighth
Middle Left Controller [Fujiwara no Arihira] came and delivered the drafts of Council directives for deployment of troops in the five Home Provinces and the Seven Circuits.[123]

The twenty-ninth
[Previously,] on the twenty-second of the eighth month I had Sir [Mimune no] Kintada inform [Tachibana no] Sanetoshi that he should go to the residence of [Taira no] Koresuke in Uji and receive instruction in the protocols for Presenting a Memorial from the Southern Courtyard. He must perform {that ceremony} on the first day of the tenth month.

The Tenth Month

The first
Minister of the Left [Fujiwara no Nakahira] went to the residential palace and determined today's agenda. In short order he selected and recorded the extra ceremonial chamberlains {to be present for the Seasonal Ceremony} and then submitted the list to His Majesty.[124] I also wrote down the sequence of events for the Seasonal Ceremony to memorialize His Majesty. His Majesty [Suzaku Tennō] was present in the Southern Hall. After the lighting of the lamps, the guards and Lesser Counselor [Tachibana no Sanetoshi] presented memorials. In all this I heard that there were many violations of protocol.

The second
I ordered the four new advisors [Fujiwara no Motokata, Minamoto no Takaakira, Ban no Yasuhira, Fujiwara no Atsutada] to provide female dancers for the Gosechi Dance Performance.[125] All complied. It was Sir [Fujiwara no] Asatada who received the royal command to serve as emissary.

The third
Middle Left Controller {Fujiwara no Arihira} came to report that yesterday the senior nobles decided on the following: "The special investigative agent's request to raise troops is not approved. As for the addition of a fourth-level manager, the former legal scholar is terminated, and the person who spoke for the posting subsequently [Aso no Hirotō] should be appointed. As for the request that a physician should accompany the military commander, it is not approved." I ordered that all this be reported to Minister of the Left {Fujiwara no Nakahira}.[126]

The tenth
Minister of Popular Affairs [Taira no Koremochi] selected monks to be invited to perform an extraordinary sutra reading for His Majesty.[127] Today I came down with a fever. I doused my head with forty flagons of cold water, but since the fever still did not abate, I put on a chilled cloth.

The twelfth
Kiyū day. Chrysanthemum Assembly at Gokurakuji.[128] There was music. But due to my illness, I did not attend.

The fourteenth
Shingai day. There was an extraordinary sutra reading for His Majesty in the Ryōkiden.[129] Forty monks participated. It was occasioned by a disturbing celestial event.

The eighteenth
Itsubō day. The Ten Lectures began at Hosshōji.[130]

The twenty-second
Sir [Minamoto no] Suguru {director of the royal investigative agents to Musashi Province} and others came and said that the decision by senior nobles against raising troops is most regrettable.[131]

The twenty-third
Since the Queen-consort [Fujiwara no Yasuko] suddenly fell dangerously ill, I dashed to the palace despite the taboo prohibiting me from social interaction. I ordered the Royal Provisions Bureau to commission sutra readings at ten temples. Also sixty new ordinands

should be permitted for the salvation of all on the six paths.[132] Master of Discipline Gikai was ordered to conduct prayers. I left the palace early in the morning.

The twenty-fourth
An esoteric rite for the Queen-consort concluded at mid-day. Another began in the early evening.

The twenty-sixth
Kigai day. Since the Queen-consort continues to be seriously ill, I went to the residential palace and stayed overnight. On Mount Hiei there will be three abbreviated readings of the *Great Wisdom Sutra* for her over three days. There will also be an esoteric rite at Hosshōji.

The twenty-seventh
Kōshi day. The abbot of Mount Hiei [Son'i] was ordered to conduct a rite for His Majesty's health and safety. It was conducted on Mount Hiei. Twenty-one monks participated.

The twenty-ninth
Concerning Kōfukuji's petition as to its inadequate resources for the Vimalakirti Assembly, I transmitted a royal order to Middle Left Controller {Fujiwara no Arihira} to the effect that Yamato Province should provide thirty additional bales of tax rice {from the provincial stores}.

The thirtieth
I went to the Queen-consort's Agency and commissioned Master of Discipline Gikai to address prayers to the Six Kannon and Fugen. And I ordered the Lotus Meditation to be performed.[133] I also commissioned an image of the bodhisattva to be made and presented.[134]

The Eleventh Month

The first
Master Chien delivered the list of sutras and prayers that had been read by the disciples of Great Master Jikaku [Ennin] {for my long life}.[135] I called him before me and rewarded him. There was also a list from the Hōdōin.[136] The rewards given were folded lengths of silk. {Saneyori's note:}[137] There were very many such occasions so I

won't include them all.

The second
The Derelict Field Surveys Memorial was memorialized.[138]

The seventh
I went to the residential palace. I inquired about the Queen-consort's [Fujiwara no Yasuko] indisposition. Then I presented a memorial concerning granting the right of entering the greater palace precincts by carriage and being excused from the line up of senior nobles {at royal banquets} to Minister of Personnel [Prince Atsumi] and Minister of the Left [Fujiwara no Nakahira].[139] I immediately transmitted these orders to the head of the Left Residential Palace Guards [Fujiwara no Morosuke].

The ninth
Day and night I was in terrible agony.

The tenth
The royal emissary, Sir [Yoshimine no] Yoshikata, came. He made inquiries about my health on behalf of His Majesty. There was also an emissary from Retired Tennō Yōzei. I gave orders to the head of the Left Gate Guards that undelivered lumber—concerning which the Royal Police office has issued a report—should be seized. It should be divided between the Repairs Agency and the Carpentry Bureau.

The eleventh
I instructed Middle Left Controller [Fujiwara no Arihira] to report concerning precedents for appointing sub-directors of the Kangakuin without a letter of recommendation.[140]

The twelfth
I gave Controller Sō [Minamoto no Sukemoto] eleven royal orders. Included among them was one concerning the delayed departure of investigative agents {to the Kantō}. Another concerned the lack of

reporting from Owari Province about the murder {of Provincial Governor} [Fujiwara no Tomomasa]. Investigation of the latter should be pressed.[141]

The fourteenth
Shinshi day. The ceremony commencing a Reading of the Classics was held in His Majesty's presence. Sir [Fujiwara no] Arihira served as lecturer, and [Mimune no] Motonatsu served as assistant reader. The text was *Records of the Historian.*[142]

The fifteenth
Jingo day. His Majesty ordered that, for the benefit of the Queen-consort, royal intimates of the fifth rank should be sent {to various shrines} with special treasures.

The sixteenth
Minister of Popular Affairs [Taira no Koremochi] passed away.

The twenty-second
[Minamoto no] Muneyuki passed away. The royal private secretary [Minamoto no] Nobuakira came from His Majesty to ask why the presentation of the Gosechi dancers was later than usual, and to inquire about the procession of female dancers in His Majesty's presence before and after the Gosechi presentation.[143]

The twenty-fourth
Shimbō day. His Majesty [Suzaku Tennō] did not go to the Chūin {for the First Fruits Service}.[144] This was because ministers and counselors all were indisposed and not in attendance. Of those divined to be minimally affected by ritual taboo, only Middle Counselor Minamoto [no Koreshige] was present. Appropriate officials took charge.[145]

The twenty-fifth
The royal banquet took place as usual.[146] However, the blinds of the royal quarters were left down. This was because His Majesty was extremely unwell.

The twenty-seventh
Kōgo day. Sutra readings for His Majesty were performed on Mount Hiei. There were three readings of the Great Wisdom Sutra.

The twenty-eighth
Memorialization {of nominations for appointments to the post of district chieftain}.[147]

The Twelfth Month

The first
Teiyū day. Extraordinary Kamo Festival.[148] Senior counselors and higher ranking senior nobles were all indisposed and did not attend. So Advisor [Fujiwara no] Akitada presented the royal proclamation following precedents from the Kampyō and Engi eras.[149]

The second
Because it was an inauspicious day, His Majesty [Suzaku Tennō] needed to take special care.[150] I sent Controller Sō [Minamoto no Sukemoto] to Minister of the Left [Fujiwara no Nakahira] to order him to arrange prayers to the deities. But saying that he was ill, {the Minister} did not receive him and Sukemoto returned without having carried out his charge. Is this any way for a minister of the throne to act?

The fourth
Sir [Minamoto no] Suguru came.[151] He presented a request that troops be raised. I returned it, directing that such matters be put forward by the controller-in-charge.[152]

The fifth
Shinchū day. Attended by the third- and fourth-in-command, [Izumo no] Koreka, second-in-command of the Yinyang Bureau, brought the high tables on which to place the new calendar {at my mansion}.[153] He said there was a royal order granting me status equal to the three queens.[154] Hearing this, I said nothing definite.

The ninth
I sent servants to the east and west sectors of the capital to look for the poor and suffering. I sent them alms.[155]

The eleventh

I directed that the Sacred Meal be carried out by the appropriate officials.[156] Middle Left Controller [Fujiwara no Arihira] came. He said the Minister of the Left {Fujiwara no Nakahira} had directed him to report that Ise Shrine requested that its ritual director [Ōnakatomi no Yorimoto] direct his prayers from the palace to the Grand Shrine because of the poor harvest this year.[157] I replied that it should be decided on the basis of many precedents.

The fifteenth

Minister of the Left {Fujiwara no Nakahira} went to the residential palace and summoned the Ise director, {Ōnakatomi no} Yorimoto, to present himself outside of the guardroom.[158] Because of disturbing celestial events, there is need for special precautions {by His Majesty} and prayers should be offered at the twelve shrines. But because of a defilement, the presentation of votive strip offerings [to shrines] is cancelled. Still, prayers should be offered tomorrow morning.

The sixteenth

Appointment of District Chieftains.[159]

The seventeenth

Iyo Province reports that [Fujiwara no] Sumitomo is preparing to board ships and take to the sea. Let him be quickly summoned to the capital.[160]

The eighteenth

At the residential palace an esoteric rite for His Majesty commenced. {Then there was} presentation of tribute items for the royal mausolea using rainy day protocols. His Majesty [Suzaku Tennō] was not present. Minister of the Left {Fujiwara no Nakahira} presided.

The nineteenth

The investigative agents submitted a report saying that they would set out on the 28th. I gave five royal orders to Controller Sō [Minamoto no Sukemoto]. I also directed that state-supported temples read the Benevolent King Sutra and pray for three days commencing on the 25th day to end the fighting.

The twenty-first

Commencement ceremony for the Litany of the Buddhas' Names.[161] Sir [Minamoto no] Sukemoto brought drafts of Council directives concerning Sumitomo for various provinces. I directed that [Fujiwara no] Akikata, [Tomo no] Hikozane, and [Taira no] Ansei be sent out as soon as possible.[162]

The twenty-second

I gave the royal order to [Mimune no] Kintada to the effect that Master Jōshin of Kōfukuji serve as lecturer at next year's Vimalakirti Assembly. The order is to be issued tomorrow.

The twenty-fifth

Shinyū day. My second son [Fujiwara no Morosuke] conducted Buddhist services on my behalf at Hosshōji. He had images made and sutras copied. During the day there were sutra readings and at night there was the Litany of the Buddhas' Names.[163] {Saneyori's note:} This was done by my honored father.] His Majesty [Suzaku Tennō] ordered sutras read at six temples on my behalf. Kōfukuji and Enryakuji each received five hundred *tan* {of cloth}; Tōji, Saiji, Gokurakuji, and Hosshōji each received three hundred *tan*.[164] Royal intimates of the fifth rank served as emissaries.

The twenty-sixth

Yesterday and today Minister of the Left [Fujiwara no Nakahira] commenced the Ceremony for Assigning Posts. But today, saying that he was ill, he did not come to the residential palace. So the event was cancelled. Followers of Sir [Fujiwara no] Sanetaka hastened to report that Sanetaka had been taken captive by Sumitomo's men [Fujiwara no Fumimoto] in Settsu Province [at Ashiya Post Station].[165] So I assembled the senior nobles to discuss what to do.

The twenty-seventh

At dawn I entered the Keihōbō for the Ceremony for Assigning Posts.[166] The senior nobles from the great ministers on down assembled according to precedent. When the ceremony was not yet over, Minister of the Left {Fujiwara no Nakahira} withdrew due to illness. The ceremony was completed in the small hours of the morning.

The twenty-eighth

The royal emissary, Sir [Fujiwara no] Atsutada, came and presented the list of sutras read at the six temples. He also had a royal order granting me sixty ordinands.[167] As gifts I presented him with a set of white robes and formal courtwear for a woman.

The twenty-ninth

The express courier from Shinano Province arrived at a gallop.[168] I commanded the promulgation of royal orders and directives of the Council of State to the various provinces. Senior Right Captain {of the Inner Palace Guards} [Fujiwara no Saneyori] officiated. I retired in the small hours and spent the night in the Queen-consort's Agency.

The thirtieth

I summoned Kamo no Tadayuki and ordered him that if there were deserving ones, they should be rewarded. I made a request of Master Jōgu regarding His Majesty's vow for Hasedera.[169]

Map 5. The Kinai Region

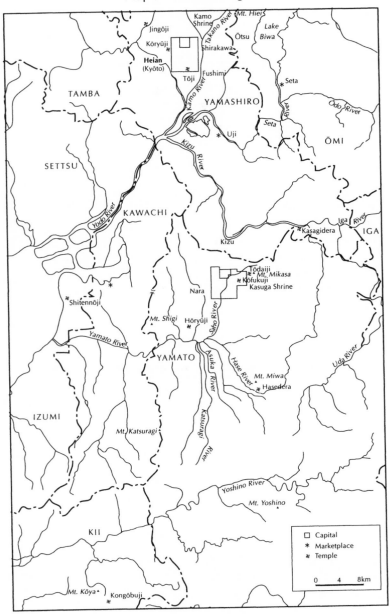

Kamo Shrine · Jingōji · Kōryūji · **Heian** (Kyōto) · Tōji · Shirakawa · Ōtsu · Lake Biwa · Takano River · Mt. Hiei · Fushimi · Seta · Kamo River · YAMASHIRO · Seta River · Odo River · TAMBA · SETTSU · Kizu River · Uji · ŌMI · Yodo River · KAWACHI · Kizu · Iga River · Kasagidera · IGA · Tōdaiji · Mt. Mikasa · Kōfukuji · Kasuga Shrine · Nara · Shitennōji · Mt. Shigi · Hōryūji · Saho River · YAMATO · Yamato River · Asuka River · Hase River · Mt. Miwa · Hasedera · Uda River · IZUMI · Mt. Katsuragi · Katsuragi River · Yoshino River · Mt. Yoshino · KII · Mt. Kōya · Kongōbuji

☐ Capital
* Marketplace
ㆍ Temple

0   4   8km

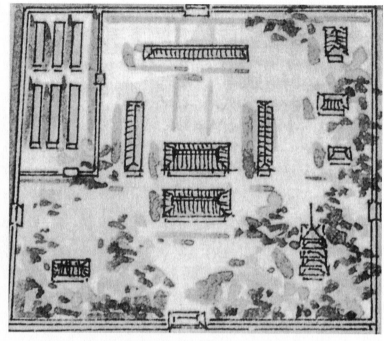

Figure 11. The Buddhist Sphere of Realm Protection

As regent, Tadahira frequently ordered rites at official temples such as Enryakuji on Mount Hiei and others of the 15 great temples that appear frequently in entries of the journal. He and his colleagues and kinsmen also patronized plentiful rites for themselves and members of their families. What might the precincts and halls of such temples have looked like? Above is a sketch of early Tōji, and below is a recontructed hall based upon archaeological finds from Heian-period Ninnaji.

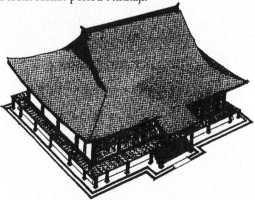

NOTES

Our English translation is faithfully based on the Dai Nihon kokiroku edition. For further details about it, see Yoshida Sanae's essay in this volume. In the translation, we have preserved its annotations in square brackets. And we have marked with curly brackets personal and geographical names added by our translation group. Glossaries of names and terms as well as an index of names and Japanese terms from journal entries of 939 can be found at the back of the volume, along with a chronology of Tadahira's life.

¹ . Ceremonies celebrating the new year were extremely important at court. The First Day Royal Banquet (*Ganjitsu no sechie*) began when the ranking senior minister (*ichi no kami*) presented the *tennō* with a list of provincial officials in attendance (*Genin no sō*). Later an official from the Yinyang Bureau (Onmyōryō) presented the *tennō* with the calendar for the new year. The Southern Hall (Naden) was the main reception hall of the royal residential palace (see Figure 10). After 818 it was also known as the Shishinden. It measured nine bays long and three bays wide with a porch (*hisashi*) all around. At the First Day Banquet attendees assembled in the south courtyard (*nantei*) before taking their seats for feasting. Ritual music and dancing was followed by reading of a royal proclamation (*semmyō*).

For useful descriptions of the various events that comprised the yearly ritual cycle, see Abe Takeshi et al. 2003.

² . Kasuga Shrine was the family shrine of the Fujiwara. It is located in the old eighth-century capital of Nara, south of Heiankyō (Kyoto today). For the history of both Kasuga Shrine and the Fujiwara family temple, Kōfukuji, see Grapard 1992.

³ . Such ministerial grand banquets were hosted by grand (senior) ministers (*daijin*) of the left and right—or by an inner palace minister (*naidaijin*)—during the first month of every year and at the time of their appointment. Princes and senior nobles attended such events, which were held at the minister's own mansion. Tadahira was then residing at his West Fifth-ward Mansion (Nishi Gojō tei), located at the southwest corner where Higashi no Tōin Avenue and Shijō Avenue crossed. For details based on archaeological excavation, see Tsunoda Bun'ei and Kodaigaku kyōkai/Kodaigaku kenkyūjo 1994, 265; and Murai Yasuhiko 1995, 88-89. The "Five Toast Ceremony" (*Gokon no gi*) and music and dance provided by the Bureau of Music (Gagakuryō) were important elements at such banquets. One toast consisted of the passing of the wine cup (*sakazuki*) to participants according to their status. For a report concerning ceramic wares used at such

banquets, see Kamiya Masaaki 1998.

Note: In our translation we have differentiated post names used as personal appellations, as in this case, by omitting the article.

[4]. In preparation for promotions in rank for those of the fifth rank or higher, senior nobles met to discuss who should be promoted. Such discussions were called *Joi no gi*. Final decisions were to be made by the *tennō* or the regent, acting for the *tennō*. The certificates of rank (*iki*) confirming such promotions were then distributed at the Aouma Banquet on the seventh day of the first month. During Tadahira's regency, such meetings were often held in the Keihōbō, a small hall northeast of the residential palace (See Figure 10).

[5]. "Taboo" is a frequent English translation for *monoimi*, which means conducting oneself so as not to attract misfortune. This might entail avoiding a certain activity or limiting one's outside contact. Normally one would place a wooden tag with the characters for *monoimi* either on one's cap or on one's blinds. One would then withdraw to one's own house or to another site designated through divination, close the gates, and receive no visitors. On this day, the *tennō* closeted himself in the Ryōkiden despite the fact that it was the day of the White Horse Royal Banquet. He could thus not be present in the Southern Hall where the banquet was conducted.

Monoimi meant refraining from specific activities in order to avoid calamity, for which a forewarning had been identified in bad dreams, mysterious phenomena, or celestial events. A yinyang master would use divination to identify the nature and severity of the calamity. In this way the type and duration of the *monoimi* would be decided. *Monoimi* was also regularly required on certain days of the year. In either case, the aim was less to prevent calamity than to avoid it. Thus the term *monoimi* was also applied to the custom of cloistering oneself in one's own home at times of defilement or during periods of mourning. The root expression, *imi*, is also rendered as "taboo." The practice of *kataimi* (directional taboo) involved avoiding certain directions and took many forms. One, which was particularly common in the Heian Period, entailed avoiding directions inhabited by certain deities, most notably Daijin, Daiitsu Taihaku, and Taiitsu. Avoidance of this type of *imi* was known as *katatagae* and involved proceeding to one's destination along a detour not including the direction of ill omen. *Kataimi* might also refer to construction activities taking place in areas inhabited by these deities.

[6]. The White Horse Royal Banquet (*Aouma no sechie*) was held annually on the seventh day of the new year. For it, the *tennō* was to appear in the Southern Hall to watch white horses paraded in front of him by officials from the Bureau of the Left and Right Stables. The horses were to be led from the Kenshun Gate (Kenshunmon) past the Southern Hall, through the Mumei Gate (Mumeimon), and then to the royal residence in the Ryōkiden.

[7] . A recent article concerning the practice of reprimands at court is Tsugei Yukio 2001.

[8] . In Heian times the Ceremony for Women's Promotion in Rank, the *Onna joi*, was a distinct event from that in which men were promoted, called the *Joi*. The former was overseen by the Ministry of Residential Palace Affairs (Nakatsukasashō). See Okamura Sachiko 1993; and Yoshikawa Shinji 1990.

[9]. The Song and Dance Royal Banquet (*Tōka no sechie*) was one of the major annual banquets hosted by the *tennō*. An early reference dates from 903, although such festivities held in the Office of Music Female Dancers and Musicians (Naikyōbō) date back to Nara times. In early Heian times the banquet featured dancing, singing, and feasting to celebrate the new year, and it was typically held on the fourteenth and sixteenth days of the first month. The dances for men took place on the fourteenth. On the sixteenth, dances for women were held. In 939, however, it seems that the banquet was held only on the sixteenth.

[10] . The Shōmei Gate (Shōmeimon) was the main entryway into the residential palace, the Dairi. See Figure 10.

[11] . For special events, extra ritual chamberlains (*jijijū*) were appointed in addition to regular chamberlains (*jijū*).

[12] . The Great Courtyard (Ōba, alt. Ōniwa) was the open area in front of the residential palace and outside the Kenrei Gate. According to the usual calendar of court events, the Grand Archery Ceremony (*Jarai*) was to be held annually on the seventeenth day of the first month to assure good fortune in the coming year. See Obinata Katsumi 1993b.

[13] . The *Dai Nihon kokiroku* editor of our text provides additional context for this phrase by quoting a later Heian ritual handbook, the *Hokuzanshō*, authored by Fujiwara no Kintō between 1012 and 1020. It cites the *Teishinkōki* entry and explains that Saneyori should not have gone directly to the Great Courtyard before receiving word that the *tennō* would not attend the event.

[14] . These Continuation Rounds (*Inokoshi*) of the Grand Archery Ceremony (*Jarai*) accommodated archers from the Six Guards unable to participate on the preceeding day. The rounds were demonstrations, in contrast with subsequent Archery Matches meant for sport and called *Noriyumi*. Fujiwara no Akitada was the second son of Tadahira's elder brother, Tokihira, and therefore a potential rival of Tadahira. Tokihira's first son and heir, Yasutada, had died in 936, however, leaving Tadahira reasonably unimpeded in his leadership at court.

[15] . The annual opening of such activities was termed *Gekisei hajime*. *Gekisei* refers to discussion and decision-making by the senior nobles (as members of the Council of State were called in the Heian Period). Such discussions took place in the Council's Secretariat Office, the Gekichō, and

concerned matters reported by the provinces or official agencies. The first extant reference to *Gekisei* is found in a royal order (*senji*) of 822 to be found in the late Heian compendium of such orders, the *Ruijū fusenshō*. The latter is included in the original *Shintei zōho Kokushi taikei* series of historical sources. See page 134 there. For details concerning the nature of such classical sources, including printed texts, see Piggott et al. 2006.

[16] . A *kansō* was a formal memorial made by the Council of State to the throne. Procedures for such memorials were outlined in the eighth-century *ritsuryō* codes, but in Heian times the protocols were abbreviated and otherwise modified. See Okamura Sachiko 1999.

[17] . Master of Discipline Gikai, a monk from Enryakuji on Mount Hiei, was already a member of the Prelates' Office (Sōgōsho) in 939. On Gikai and Son'i, another prelate and Enryakuji's abbot in 939, see Groner 2002, 42-43. Regarding the Prelates' Office, see Piggott 1997, 94-5 and passim; Abe 1999, 30-33 and passim, esp. 465 n. 36; and Groner 1984, 281-85.

[18] . The actual occasion for such prayers was Tadahira's sixtieth birthday, which occurred in 939.

[19] . Senior nobles met for a series of discussions to consider who should receive new postings, an event known as the *Jimoku no gi*. There were various stages in these discussions—here we refer to the entire process as "Ceremony for Assigning Posts" in 939. Final decisions concerning these nominations were made by the *tennō* or regent (on the *tennō*'s behalf). The most important postings were decided in the first month, at the Spring *Jimoku*. Given its focus on provincial offices, it was also termed the *Agatameshi jimoku*. In 939 it began on the twenty-eighth day of the first month and finished on the first day of the second month. The next important discussions concerned postings in the capital (*Kyōkan jimoku*). Also known as *Tsukasameshi no jimoku*, they were originally held early in the second month, but over time they came to be held later, during the fall and winter. In 939 they began on the twenty-fifth and ended on the twenty-seventh of the twelfth month. In addition to these annual events, there were occasional extraordinary discussions for new postings.

In 939 Tadahira records that discussions took place in the Keihōbo (see Figure 10), a venue that was important to the regent and his family. The crown prince, who would eventually take the throne as Murakami Tennō, was born to his sister Queen Yasuko there in 926. It was used on occasion as the regent's quarters (*chokuro*). See Okamura Sachiko 1996, esp. 5-6.

[20] . The Council of State originally had its main office in the State Halls Compound (Chōdōin, alt. Hasshōin), southwest of the residential palace. In the Heian Period the Council of State office was relocated east of the State Halls Compound (see Figure 7).

[21] . The text reads, "in the fourth segment of the Hour of the Ox," which is about 2:30 A.M.

[22] . This esoteric rite (*mishiho*) had been held in the residential palace on 1/24. Here each of the celebrants was rewarded with the privilege of passing one follower into monkhood, a tax-free status that only the state could authorize.

[23] . The astronomical occurrence that occasioned this call for caution was the triple alignment of Jupiter, the Sun, and the Guest Star.

[24] . Enshō had served as an officiant (*ajari*) at Tadahira's own Hosshōji since 935 and he was appointed abbot of that temple in 939. Per the *Tendai zasu ki* list of Enryakuji abbots, Enshō later became the fifteenth abbot of Enryakuji in 946 (see *Zokugunshoruijū*, Bu'ninbu). A year earlier he was appointed a master of discipline (*risshi*) in the Prelates' Office, according to the *Sōgō bunin* (Nanjō Bun'yū 1915, 63).

As for Hosshōji, it was built by Tadahira some time prior to 924, the date of its earliest mention in *Teishinkōki*. It was situated in Yamashiro's Kii District. During his reign, Daigo Tennō sponsored construction of additional halls; and in 945 Queen-consort Yasuko presented the temple with a miniature pagoda containing a complete copy of the scriptures. It became a royal vow temple (*goganji*) during the reign of Suzaku Tennō (930-46). Hosshōji was the site of Tadahira's funeral, and it continued to receive the patronage of his descendants and other members of the Fujiwara family, especially Michinaga (966-1027).

[25] . The temple known as Jōjūji (alt. Nodera) was located in Kadono District of Yamashiro Province, which is today's Kitano district in Kyōto. It seems to have been an extremely old establishment with ties to Kanmu Tennō (737-806, r. 781-806) and the early Tendai school. See Hayashiya Tatsusaburō 1970-, vol. 1, 142, 234, 296; and Groner 1984, 65, 136.

[26] . The Benevolent King Assembly (*Ninnōe*) was a realm-protecting ritual focused on the *Benevolent King Sutra* (*Ninnōkyō*). It was held regularly under court auspices in the spring and autumn. The planning ceremony including decisions on personnel and timing for the spring event.

[27] . A royal order (*senji*) could be either oral or written. At this time Regent Tadahira decided and issued orders on the *tennō*'s behalf. Here Tadahira was sending various orders to either the noble-in-charge or other officials through Controller Sō (Minamoto no Sukemoto).

[28] . Presumably this means that Toshimichi could now sit for the civil service exam administered by the Ministry of Personnel (Shikibushō). On these exams see Ceugniet 2000, 51-82.

[29] . Taira no Masakado (?-940) was a provincial warrior descended from the monarch Kanmu Tennō (r. 781-806). His home was in the province of

Shimōsa in the Bandō, within today's metropolitan Tokyo region (see Map 4). During the previous year (938), after a long-running dispute with his relatives, Masakado had been summonded to the capital to explain himself. Although found guilty, he had been pardoned. In 939 another dispute flared between Minamoto no Tsunemoto, Prince Okiyo, and Musashi no Takeshiba. Masakado unsuccessfully attempted to mediate. Tsunemoto went to the capital, where he accused Masakado of launching a rebellion. The court decided to send in investigative agents (*suimonshi*). In late 939 Masakado joined provincial warriors who persuaded him to attack the Hitachi provincial headquarters in the eleventh month. Masakado then reportedly declared himself "the new *tennō*" (*shinnō*) of the east. The court then had no option but to label him a rebel, and his revolt was quashed by other provincial warriors acting in the name of the court. See the entry and note above for 03/03. A new analysis of Masakado 's rebellion and its significance is Friday 2008.

[30] . The ceremony for modification of appointments was known as the *Naoshimono*. Concerning Fujiwara no Koreeda, see *Dai Nihon shiryō*, Series 1, vol. 6, entry for Shōhei 3 (933) 04/02; and *Sonpi bunmyaku* 2, 292 (in the *Shintei zōho Kokushi taikei* series of historical sources).

[31] . Our earliest extant record concerning the Chichibu royal pasture in Musashi Province dates from 933. Koreeda was already its director (*bettō*). On the pasture see Kokuritsu rekishi minzoku hakubutsukan 1997, 355.

[32] . Per some manuscripts of the *Nihon kiryaku*, the delegation from Kōryō (Jap. Kōrai), a kingdom that had unified much of the Korean peninsula, was sent home from the Dazaifu in Kyūshū on the eleventh day of the third month. The *Nihon kiryaku* is published in the *Shintei zōho Kokushi taikei* series of historical sources. Ōe no Asatsuna was the left junior controller (*sashōben*) at this time, per the *Benkan bu'nin*. See Iiakura 1982-, vol. 1, 70.

[33] . The deities propitiated at the time of the Sono-Kara Festival were two: the Sono deity and the Kara deity. The festival is listed in the *Engi shiki* (completed in 927, promulgated in 967) as a lesser one. It was celebrated twice annually, in the second and eleventh months, by the Council of Shrine Affairs (Jingikan). It included offerings of horses as well as song and dance to entertain the *kami*.

[34] . Among the perquisites and privileges given to the three queen-consorts (*sangō*)—to which Tadahira had been recently dubbed equivalent in status (*jusangō*, alt. *jusangū*)—was the privilege of *nenkyū*. It made it possible for him to recommend a person for promotion in rank (*nenshaku*) or official posting (*nenkan*) every year.

[35] . In other words, normally the royal command would have been put down on paper by a residential palace secretary (*naiki*), but in the absence of that official, controller Ōe no Asatsuna was charged with the task.

36 . See the entry and note for 02/01 above.

37 . See the entry and note for 02/21 above.

38 . See the entry and note for 02/12 above, concerning Taira no Masakado. As noted there, Minamoto no Tsunemoto and a prince called Okiyo became involved in a dispute with a local magnate named Musashi no Takeshiba. Masakado tried to mediate and even petitioned the court for recognition of his efforts. When Takeshiba surrounded Tsunemoto's base, however, Tsunemoto thought that Okiyo had allied himself with Masakado and Takeshiba. Tsunemoto then fled to Kyoto to accuse them of rebellion. Tsunemoto was eventually judged guilty of slander. When Masakado moved towards a more rebellious stance, Tsunemoto joined in the campaign to defeat Masakado. He later achieved further fame for helping to put down Fujiwara no Sumitomo's insurrection in the Inland Sea. On these events see Friday 2008, esp. 79-83.

39 . Concerning *nenkan*, see the entry and note for 02/21 above. Fujiwara no Morosuke was Tadahira's second son.

40 . The provinces of the Bandō region were Musashi, Sagami, Kai, Izu, Awa, Kazusa, Shimōsa, Hitachi, Kōzuke, Shimotsuke (see Map 4).

41 . Fujiwara no Saneyori was Tadahira's eldest son.

42 . The Higyōsha was a hall to the west of the Back Palace (see Figure 10). Fujiwara no Takako was Tadahira's daughter.

43 . The Bureau of the Wardrobe (Nuidonoryō) was located just north and outside of the residential palace. See Figure 7.

44 . Fujiwara no Nakahira was Tadahira's elder brother. It was customary for high ranking officials like Nakahira to offer to resign their posts, but such resignations were rarely accepted by the *tennō* (or his regent).

45 . Seasonal Sutra Readings (*Kinomidokyō*) were held on appropriate days during the second and eighth months to pray for the health of the *tennō* and safety in the realm. One hundred monks were invited to the palace to page through the Great Wisdom Sutra (*Daihannyakyō*). The event lasted four days and took place either in the Throne Hall or in the Southern Hall of the residential palace. After the mid-ninth century, the event was sometimes held in the *tennō*'s own living quarters.

46 . This event, called *Ichibumeshi*, was held annually by the Ministry of Personnel to appoint provincial secretaries (*shishō*).

47 . The use of this rice is not clear. Perhaps it was to be used to feed construction workers rebuilding the palace wall. See *Dai Nihon shiryō*, Series 1, vol. 7, 427.

48 . Both officials were members of the Yinyang Bureau, which was staffed by specialists in yinyang learning and divination. See Bock 1985. The Taiitsu Rite was performed by members of the Yinyang Bureau to bring peace to the realm. Protocols required the officiant to isolate himself from

the world for three days. A royal mirror was employed as a votive object to absorb pollution or defilement. Extant documents indicate that the Taiitsu Rite was actually performed in the State Halls Compound on the sixteenth of the fifth month by Takekane (also see the entry for 5/16 below). See further details in *Dai Nihon shiryō*, Series 1, vol. 7, 452. On the Yinyang Bureau as described in the *Engi shiki* of 927, see Bock 1985, 9-22 and 29-48.

[49] . The assembly is called the Endōe in the entry. According to other records, the Endō at Ninnaji, a royal temple located northwest of the capital, had just been renovated. See *Dai Nihon shiryō*, Series 1, vol. 7, 429. On Ninnaji as a royal vow temple (*goganji*), see Hiraoka Jōkai 1981-1988, vol. 1, 529-41; and on the *goganji*, see Adolphson et al. 2007, 217-18 and passim.

[50]. Formerly held on the first, eleventh, and twenty-first of each month, the *Shun* ceremony brought officials before the *tennō* to report on matters of governance. (*Shun* literally denotes a period of ten days; the month was divided into three such periods.) On those occasions, the *tennō* also held banquets for courtiers. In the tenth century, the *Shun* occurred only on the first day of the fourth and tenth months. Moreover, the *tennō* frequently did not attend these occasions, which were then called *Shun no hiraza*, "*Shun* without the *tennō* in attendance." When the *tennō* was unable to attend an important court function at the Shishinden due to illness or taboo, senior nobles would attend a separate banquet in the Giyōden (see Figure 10).

[51] . Ritual ablutions (*misogi, harae*) were an important part of many of the most important religious rites, but no lustration was as conspicuous as the *misogi* performed on the banks of the Kamo River by the Kamo Priestess on either the Day of the Horse or the Day of the Ram preceding the annual Kamo Festival. Selection as one of the outriders was a sign of honor since the horsemen and their mounts (as well as the ox chosen to pull the Priestess's carriage) were inspected by the *tennō* himself beforehand at the Shishinden, and the lustration ceremony was a major spectacle attended by many courtiers. See also note 56 below.

[52] . See above entry and note for 3/27 concerning Ninnaji.

[53] . Promotions in rank for those below the sixth rank were listed in a *jōsen*, a document presented to the *tennō* in the course of the Memorial Concerning Promotions (*Gikai no sō*), a ceremony held annually on this day. On the eleventh day of the second month, a list would be drawn up of all persons of the sixth rank and below who were due for promotion. For civilian officials, the list was drawn up by the Ministry of Personnel; and for military officials, it was drawn up by the Ministry of Defense. These lists were then sent to the senior nobles on the first day of the fourth month. They drafted their own proposal based on this information, and this latter document together with reports from the two ministries were submitted to the *tennō* on this day.

[54] . The Fifth-month Banquet (*Tango no sechie*) was celebrated on the

fifth day of the fifth month. As in China, where it originated, it was associated with military activities and also with good health—one element of the festivities included arranging bunches of medicinal irises around the eaves of houses to protect against disease. See also Masuo Shin'ichirō 1997; and Obinata 1993a.

55 . Akita Stockade was a military base in northeastern Japan built to guard against uprisings by Emishi tribesmen. It was located in northern Dewa Province, Akita District. There have recently been extensive archaeological excavations at the site, and at the Akita provincial headquarters (*kokufu*) as well.

56 . The Kamo Festival, alternatively called the Aoi Festival, was held annually on the middle Day of the Cock in the fourth month. (There was also an Extraordinary Kamo Festival that sometimes occurred on the last Day of the Cock in the eleventh month.) The festival sought protection and blessings from the Kamo deities, which were venerated at the Lower and Upper Kamo Shrines near the Kamo River (see Maps 2, 5). The Kamo Priestess set off from her residence in Murasakino, northeast of the capital, and proceeded along First Ward Avenue. From the palace, attendants and officials bearing offerings from the *tennō*, crown prince, queen-consort, and others, joined her procession. The procession became a spectacle that engaged the entire capital in its public display of courtly splendor.

57 . On Princess Tsuyako (904-69), see Kamens 1990.

58 . *Hōbei* refers to the act of offering gifts to shrine deities (*kami*). These gifts usually took the form of paper or cloth strips attached to a staff (*hei* or *heihaku*). Occasionally implements, weapons, and jewels might also be offered.

59 . On Akita Stockade, see the entry and note for 4/11.

60 . Morosuke, Tadahira's second son, was also serving as director (*bettō*) of the the Office of Royal Police and as a middle counselor on the Council. We can assume that the courier would have brought his report to a Council secretary, who would have contacted Morosuke, who contacted Regent Tadahira.

61 . Tadahira had his office within the Queen-consort's Agency (Chūgū shiki) in the Back Palace. At this time Tadahira's sister, Yasuko, who had been Daigo's senior consort and who was also Suzaku Tennō's mother, resided there.

62 In Heian times the *jin*, which were originally guardrooms used by the Left and Right Inner Palace Guards (Sakonoefu, Ukonoefu), came to be used as meeting places by the senior nobles and their staff. Such spaces and the meetings held there were thus called *Jin no za*. By mid-Heian times, however, the left guardroom, which was located in the corridor east of the Southern Hall of the residential palace, had come to be used most frequently

by the senior nobles.

[63] *Gunji dokusō*: Appointment of district chieftains (*gunji*) had become an annual court ceremony by the mid-ninth century. When a district chieftaincy became available, the provincial governor supplied a list of potential successors. There would be two sets of deliberations before one of the candidates was chosen. The senior nobles were required to meet before the twentieth day of the fourth month, and then they submitted their choices to the *tennō*. Successful candidates were summoned by the Council of State before the thirtieth of the sixth month to receive the appointment. The ceremony whereby senior nobles offered their nominations was called *Gunji dokusō*. The event in which successful candidates were summoned was called *Gunji meshi*.

[64] . Hasedera, in present-day Sakurai City of Nara Prefecture, is a temple housing a celebrated image of an eleven-headed Kannon. The temple was reportedly founded in the 720s and became a branch first of Tōdaiji and later of Kōfukuji. It was a popular site for aristocratic pilgrimage in the Heian Period. See Map 5.

[65] . The meaning of this reference is not clear.

[66] . The stockade referred to here is the same Akita Stockade in Dewa mentioned in the entry for 4/11.

[67] . On the Six Guards Headquarters (Rokuefu, alt. Efu), see Friday 1992, 56-61.

[68] . On the Bandō, see note 40 above, and Map 4. And for this directive, see *Dai Nihon shiryō*, Series 1, vol. 6, 4-5.

[69] . The term *chieki* (alt. *hieki*) referred to express courier service. According to the *ritsuryō* codes, such a courier could pass through ten post stations in a day and was to be used in the event of important governmental crises, omens, illness, or diplomatic news.

[70] . Such races (*kurabeuma*) originally had an important spiritual significance. They were held on the fifth and sixth days of the fifth month annually in the palace precincts, in tandem with mounted archery contests and offerings of medicinal sweet flag. For more on the history and significance of these fifth month activities, see Obinata Katsumi 1993a. A number of important shrines also conducted horse races, including the Kamo Shrine. As we see here, in 939 such races were held on the seventh day of the fifth month at the Hokuhen'in, once a retirement palace occupied by Yōzei Tennō (r. 876-84).

[71] . On the Taiitsu Rite and Takekane's role, see the earlier entry and note for 3/22. Concerning the Yinyang Bureau, see note 48 above. The State Halls Compound was the original venue for everyday ceremonial activities of the Council of State (see Figure 7). But by mid-Heian times it was used only for certain ceremonial occasions. See Kamiya Masaaki 1991. Furuse

Natsuko has discussed changes in the working venues of officials from Nara to Heian times. See Furuse Natsuko 1998, esp. 128-210.

72 . An appended note in the manuscript indicates that this entry was made out of phase.

73 . Unusually this provincial governor was being transferred from Kazusa to Musashi. For further details see *Dai Nihon shiryō*, Series 1, vol. 7, 452.

74 . See the entry and note for 4/7. A certificate of rank (*iki*) was prepared by a senior residential palace secretary (*dainaiki*) and then handed out to the person promoted as confirmation. The certificates of rank given out on 5/20 reflected promotions memorialized on 4/7.

75 . According to *ritsuryō* law, there were to be alms of rice and salt occasionally distributed to the poor, the ill, and the elderly in the capital. Such charitable distributions were called *shingō*. The capital was divided into blocks that were assigned to agents who distributed the provisions. Eventually *shingō* became just another custom carried out annually in the fifth month, as described here.

76 . The annual Vimalakirti Assembly at Nara's Kōfukuji consisted of a series of debates on the *Vimalakirti Sutra* (*Yuimakyō*). Its history was long—establishment is attributed to Fujiwara no Kamatari, founder of the Fujiwara family. Together with the annual lecture on the *Suvarnaprabhasa Sutra* (*Konkōmyō saishōōkyō*)—known as the *Gosaie*, which took place at the palace—and Yakushiji's annual lecture on the same text (called the *Saishōe*), the three comprised the most prestigious of annual official Buddhist events, the *San'e*. For a late tenth-century description of the Vimalakirti Rite, see Minamoto no Tamenori's *Sanbōe kotoba*, translated in Kamens 1990, 353-54. On the *Saishōe*, see 286; and on the *Gosaie*, see 251-52.

77 . Mimune no Kintada was a senior secretary (*daigeki*) serving the Council of State—here he was acting as Tadahira's liaison with the leader of the senior nobles, Tadahira's elder brother, Nakahira. In his journal Tadahira frequently used Tang appellations (*tōmyō*), such as *sakō*—meaning "minister of the left;" and later, on the twenty-third of the sixth month, he referred to his son Morosuke as *sakin*, the Tang name for the head of the Left Palace Gate Guards.

78 . The Taigen Rite (*Taigenhō*) is one of the most important Shingon rituals for the protection of the state performed from Heian to modern times. Dedicated to the Buddhist guardian-deity Taigen-myōō (alt. Daigen), this esoteric rite was introduced by the Shingon monk Jōgyō (d. 866) after his return from China in 839. In the sixth month of 840, Jōgyō was granted permission to enshrine Taigen as the main deity at the Hōrinji in Ogurusu, in the Uji District of Yamashiro Province. Tradition has it that the rite was first performed in Japan in the twelfth month of that year, at the Jōneiden in

the royal residential palace. The Taigen Rite was performed regularly at Hōrinji until around 1135, after which the main locus for the rite was moved to Daigoji's Rishōin due to the deterioration of Hōrinji. See Tsunoda Bun'ei 1994, 1441-2, 2303; Grapard 1999, esp. 535-36. And for a detailed analysis of Taigen and the Taigen Rite, see Duquenne 1983.

[79]. This derives from a well-known Chinese saying to the effect that "to be human is to sometimes be absent."

[80]. A note by the *Dai Nihon kokiroku* editor states that the leader of the investigative agents was to be Minamoto no Suguru.

[81]. Regular readings of Chinese classics for the *tennō* were performed at court. In the case of a child *tennō*, such readings would have played an important part in the monarch's education. Another later occasion saw reading of a Chinese history classic, the History of Han (J. *Kanjo*, Ch. *Hanshu*) — see the entry for 11/14. Banquets held after the completion of a full cycle of readings were called *kyōen*, during which poems were composed on themes from the preceding readings and lectures.

[82]. See the earlier entry for 03/03, when Tsunemoto first made the allegations.

[83]. On these "envoys to subdue the territory" (*ōryōshi*), see Friday 1992, 123-24, 141-48.

[84]. The Tsukinami Festival was celebrated semi-annually in the sixth and twelfth months, at court and at Ise Shrine in Ise Province. The palace ceremony involved summoning heads of major shrines to the palace. The *tennō* would then eat sacred rice in the presence of the deity during the Jinkonjiki ("meal in the divine presence"). The ceremonies at Ise Shrine were ranked among the three main rites performed there every year, and they required the presence of a princess-priestess, the *saiō*, sent by the court. See Bock 1972 80, 123-85.

[85]. The Enmeiin was the royal vow temple built by Suzaku Tennō in the east sector of Mount Hiei. Construction was overseen by the prelate Son'i in 936. It had a staff of seven healer monks (*zenji*), and its main Buddha images (*honzon*) were those of Fugen Bosatsu and Enmei Bosatsu, deities known to bring about long life.

[86]. A rainbow was considered an omen, and reports of them appear frequently in the *Teishinkōki*. The time recorded here was *hitsuji no toki*, between one and three in the afternoon. Appearance of such an omen required divining to determine cause and response. See for instance Friday 2008, 84.

[87]. We can suspect here that Koremochi acted as "noble-in-charge" (*shōkei*) for this event.

[88]. According to the *Honchō seiki*, a historical compendium from the later Heian period, this was part of a three-day reading of the Great Wisdom Sutra (*Daihannyakyō*). See *Dai Nihon shiryō*, Series 1, vol. 7, 461. Sutra-read-

ings continued after the twentieth as well.

⁸⁹ See former references to Minamoto no Tsunemoto and his complaints of criminal activity in Musashi in earlier entries dated 2/12, 3/3, and 3/9.

⁹⁰. In those cases where pronunciation of the Japanese name is uncertain, the custom is to read the name using the "Chinese" pronunciation (on'yomi) of the characters. We have done so here.

⁹¹. Concerning the Council of State Office in the residential palace, see the note for 1/30 above. The Preparatory Office (Katanashidokoro) was the place where controllers (ben) and Council junior secretaries (shi) organized materials for discussion by the senior nobles. It was located in the Council Office compound outside the Kenshun Gate (see Figure 10).

⁹². There are various explanations. According to one, the five dragons differed in color—blue, red, yellow, white, and black. Chinese legend has them controlling rainfall. In times of drought it was customary to propitiate the deity by sending votive strip offerings while Buddhist monks read sutras. The Five Dragon Festival generally was performed in the royal park, the Shinsen'en.

⁹³. This shrine was more commonly known as the Murōryūketsu Jinja, located in Nara Prefecture, Uda District, Murō. During years of drought the tennō (or his regent) would order prayers there. On Murōji, see Fowler 2005.

⁹⁴. According to the process called zuryō kōka sadame, provincial governors were evaluated in terms of their service. They submitted reports of their previous tenure, which were then collated by the director (bettō) of the Royal Secretariat (Kurōdodokoro). A report was then made to the tennō, who ordered senior nobles to debate the merits and demerits of the candidate. See Kiley 1999.

⁹⁵. The taxes indicated here were the chō and yō taxes—taxes in kind and labor. For details, see the corresponding entries in Tsunoda Bun'ei 1994. The "comprehensive receipt" was the sōhenshō, an important element in the end-of-term evaluation procedures for provincial governors seeking a new posting.

⁹⁶. Mimune no Kintada was a Council secretary (geki), in the Council secretariat (Gekikyoku).

⁹⁷ Here "abbreviated reading" (tendoku) refers to a ritualized paging through and recitation of a sutra, in which only designated parts are read out, such as the sutra title and the chapter titles, or a few lines from the beginning, middle and end of each chapter.

⁹⁸. The Sonshō Rite focused on the Sonshō Mandala and was intended to ward off calamity.

⁹⁹. Hofu were Council orders in response to reports from the provinces

or the Kyushu Headquarters (Dazaifu).

[100] . There may be confusion in the text here. Other sources, such as the *Honchō seiki*, indicate that the sutra readings concluded on the eighteenth. See *Dai Nihon shiryō*, Series 1, vol. 7, 472.

[101] . In the second and third months messengers were sent out from the capital seeking champions to compete; and during the seventh month, wrestlers were sent to the capital from across Japan. However, most wrestlers belonged to the Inner Palace Guards' Headquarters (Konoefu). According to the Miscellaneous Laws (*Zōryō*) in the eighth-century *ritsuryō* codes, such matches were to be held on the seventh day of the seventh month every year. But by mid-Heian times it had become customary for them to be held later in the month.

[102] . Music was omitted from such ceremonies at inauspicious times.

[103] . According to esoteric Buddhist teachings, *kaji* is the power of a buddha or bodhisattva transferred to (*ka*) and retained by (*ji*) the practitioner—an "empowerment" effected through the ritual use of mudras, mantras, and mandalas. See Nakamura Hajime 1981 146; and Tsunoda Bun'ei 1994, 479. Thus the term can be used, as it is here, to refer to a rite or prayer for such empowerment. The officiant is invoking the buddha's or bodhisattva's power on Tadahira's behalf.

[104] . Lack of clarity in the text makes our translation tentative here.

[105] . Here we have translated *nenzu* (alt. *nenju*) as "prayer session." *Nenzu* refers to "invoking the name of a deity, meditating on his *shingon* (true word), (and) reading scriptures dedicated to him."See Iwano Masao 1999, 236.

[106] . University students who had just completed a prescribed course in Chinese history and literature were termed *monjōshō*. Evaluation was carried out by professional scholars at the Bureau of the University (Daigakuryō). For more on the Heian university system in English, see Borgen 1986, esp. 93-112; Wetzler 1977, 16-44; and in French, Ceugniet 2000.

[107] . Kakue appears elsewhere in the *Teishinkōki* as an officiant at palace rites, but no further information on him could be found. For Enshō, see note 24 above.

[108] . Tachibana no Naomoto, here a palace secretary (*naiki*), is a scholar who is the subject of stories in collections of court lore such as the *Jikkunshō*, *Chomonjū*, and *Gōdanshō*. There is even an illustrated scroll, *Naomoto mōshibumi emaki*, made in the fourteenth century. Ceugniet makes several references to him in Ceugniet 2000: 55, 59, 63, 67, 99, 110, 138, 153, 311.

[109] . *Tatsu no toki* designates one of the twelve two-hour intervals making up a day, specifically the interval from 7 to 9 A.M. The clock peg (*toki no kui*) mentioned here was apparently part of a time-marking device used in the residential palace. It seems to have consisted of a plaque into which pegs were inserted to mark the passing hours. There are other entries in the

Teishinkōki where such omen-like occurrences are recorded.

¹¹⁰. *Uchirongi*, translated here as "Residential Palace Debate," could be of two kinds. There were annual debates conducted by Buddhist scholars in the *tennō*'s presence on the fourteenth of the first month at the conclusion of the *Gosaie* (alt. *Misaie*, "Annual Royal Vegetarian Assembly"). And there were annual lectures concerning the Chinese classics conducted by university-trained professors (*hakase*) in the eighth month, after the fall memorial for Confucius, the *Sekiten*.

¹¹¹. There is a frustrating lack of information concerning this murder of the Owari provincial governor in 939. What is clear is that the post of provincial governor could be dangerous. Readers familiar with Ki no Tsurayuki's *Tosa nikki* will remember his harrowing trip home from the province of Tosa in Shikoku in 934. Moreover, historian Abe Takeshi has charted incidences of violent attacks against governors and has identified 59 such events between 795 and 1104. See Abe Takeshi 1974, 329-32. Owari remained a hub of discontent over time. In 865 and 866 provincial governors in both Owari and Mino complained of violence against them and their staff by district chiefs; and of course, Owari is also famed for a strong protest against a provincial governor in 988.

¹¹². Regarding the *Shikino(mi)zōshi*, see the entry and note for 4/18. And see Okamura Sachiko 1996.

¹¹³. Minamoto no Koreshige (886-941) was a son of Kōkō Tennō (r. 884-887). His mother was the daughter of Fujiwara no Kadomune. Koreshige was granted the surname Minamoto at the age of four. In 939 he was senior left controller (*sadaiben*). Later in 939 he was made a provisional middle counselor and Minister of Popular Affairs.

¹¹⁴. Prince Noriakira (934-990) was a son of Daigo Tennō (r. 897-930) by Fujiwara no Kanesuke's daughter, Kuwako. He was thus the reigning Suzaku Tennō's younger half-brother. Most boys went through their coming-of-age ceremony (*genpuku*) between the ages of 11 and 15. For an excellent description of the *genpuku* rite, see Ury 1999, 372 n. 13.

¹¹⁵. Taira no Koresuke was the governor of Mutsu at the time of Masakado's rebellious activities in the Bandō (see Map 4). The account of Masakado known as the *Shōmonki* (alt. *Masakadoki*) describes Koresuke as a close friend of Taira no Sadamori, who was Masakado's cousin and foe. Later in the autumn of 939 the two friends led an unsuccessful effort to quell Masakado. For an English translation of the *Shōmonki*, and on Koreshige, see Rabinovitch 1986, esp. 98.

¹¹⁶. Messengers bearing votive strip offerings for a good harvest (*kinenkoku hōbei*) delivered their offerings to various shrines. A list of shrines that usually received them was included in the tenth-century *Engi shiki*. See the "Register of Deities" in Bock 1972, vol. 2, 141-71.

[117] . On Hosshōji, see note 24 above.

[118] . Subjugation rites (*chōbukuhō*, alt. *jōbukuhō*), a variant of the fire-offering ritual (*goma*) and one of the four or five kinds of esoteric rites (*shishuhō*, or *goshuhō*), were aimed at overcoming physical enemies as well as demons, angry spirits, and internal obstacles. For more detail see the entry for *chōbukuhō* in Nakamura Hajime 1989.

[119] . Among others, Fujiwara no Saneyori was appointed a senior counselor (*dainagon*) at this time.

[120] . The seat may have been stolen or simply misplaced, in either case a serious business. The Giyōden was a hall in the residential palace just southeast of the Southern Hall and bordering the Southern Courtyard on the east (see Figure 10). Seats occupied by the senior nobles during their discussions, called the *kugyō no za*, were situated at its north end. That was also the site of the announcement of new postings as well as readings of the eighth-century court annal, the *Nihon shoki*. Senior nobles also feasted there during banquets for which the *tennō* was not in attendance, termed *hiraza*. See note 50 above. The Custodial Office (Kamonryō, Kanimoriryō) was responsible for palace maintenance and supplying props needed for various events and activities. The "cushion seat" mentioned here would have consisted of multiple layers of seating material.

[121] . Gion Shrine in Heiankyō, also known as Yasaka Shrine, is dedicated to the deity-brother of Amaterasu, Susanoo no Mikoto. The most reliable accounts date its founding to 876. Tadahira's father, Mototsune, sponsored construction of several of its buildings during the Gangyō era (877-885) and called it the Gangyōkanshin'in. It was one of the twenty-two shrines where offerings were made and prayers performed by the court in Heian times, and was generally associated with thaumaturgy. Tadahira's journal notes offerings sent to it in 920 when he was ill. During Tadahira's lifetime it remained a branch of Nara's Kōfukuji, over which Tadahira presided as Fujiwara family head.

[122] . This would seem to refer to Fujiwara no Sumitomo's pirate activities in the Southern Sea Circuit, made up of the provinces of Kii, Awaji, Awa, Sanuki, Iyo, and Tosa. Sumitomo was the son of the Junior Vice-governor of Dazaifu (*shōni*) Fujiwara no Yoshinori. In 932 Sumitomo was appointed a third-level governor (*jō*) of Iyo, and in 936 he was ordered to pacify the Inland Sea, leading to a brief reduction in piracy there. But by 939 he was himself considered the leader of the pirates. Later that year, in the twelfth month, his forces abducted a deputy to the vice-governor (*suke*) of Bizen Province (see the entry for 12/26). And yet in 940 the court gave Sumitomo a promotion to the junior fifth rank, to attempt coopting him. Sumitomo's reply was to burn government offices in Iyo and Sanuki; he also burned warships of Bizen and Bingo. In 941 Sumitomo was finally defeated at the Dazaifu, and he and his son later died in Iyo. For a discussion

of Sumitomo's piracy in historical context, see Farris 1992, 149; and Friday 2008, 110-114, 143-146.

¹²³ . The "five home provinces" (*Gokinai*) and the "seven circuits"(*Shichidō*) denote the two spatial components of the *tennō*'s realm. The home provinces were Yamashiro, Yamato, Settsu, Kawachi, and Izumi—all surrounding the capital at Heiankyō. The seven circuits, which linked all the provinces with the capital, were the Eastern Sea Circuit (Tōkaidō), Eastern Mountain Circuit (Tōzandō), North Coast Circuit (Hokurikudō), Shadow-side Circuit (San'indō), Sunny-side Circuit (San'yōdō), South Sea Circuit (Nankaidō), and Western Sea Circuit (Saikaidō). See Map 4.

¹²⁴ . These "extra ceremonial chamberlains" were the *dei no jijū*, who served various ceremonial tasks during the twice yearly *Shun no gi*, about which see the note for the entry of 4/1 above.

¹²⁵ . The *Gosechi* Dance Performance, in which young women danced before the *tennō*, was one part of the year-end thanksgiving celebration known as the Niinamesai. See Bock 1972 vol. 2, 92.

¹²⁶ . For further background see Farris 1992 140. For related sources see *Dai Nihon shiryō*, Series 1, vol. 7, including the relevant entry in *Honchō seiki* (939 10/07) concerning another investigative agent, the *mikkokushi*. The *Honchō seiki* annal of court events, which covers the period from 935 to 1153 and was compiled in the later twelfth century, is included in the *Shitei zohō Kokushi taikei* series of historical sources.

¹²⁷ . Here Tadahira refers to the minister by the Tang appellation for the *Minbushō* (Ministry of Popular Affairs), which was *Kobu*.

¹²⁸ . Fujiwara no Mototsune, Tadahira's father, founded Gokurakuji during the late ninth century. Located in Fukakusa in the Fushimi district of Kyoto, the temple took some two to three hours to reach by horse from the palace. In this relatively removed place, tombs of *tennō* and their consorts can be found, including those of Mototsune's mother and daughter. The Amida Hall of this temple was probably built to pray for the salvation of the deceased nearby. In Tadahira's day, the temple became associated with Mototsune, just as Hosshōji came to be known as Tadahira's temple. The Chrysanthemum Assembly commemorated Mototsune, buried at Fukakusa, and included prayers for his repose. Its name implies the use of chrysanthemums in the service.

¹²⁹ . East of the Jijūden and north of the Giyōden, the Ryōkiden in the residential palace served as an occasional dwelling and ritual space for the *tennō* (see Figure 10).

¹³⁰ . The Ten Lectures (*Jukkō*) probably consisted of ten lectures over five days focusing on the *Lotus Sutra* as well as the *Sutra of Unfathomable Meanings* (*Muryōgikyō*) and the *Sutra of Contemplation on Samantabhadra* (*Fugenkangyō*), the latter two of which served as opening and concluding

texts for the *Lotus Sutra*. A similar series was the *Hokke hakkō*, Eight Lectures on the *Lotus Sutra*, which could be held over a four- or eight-day span. In English see Willa Tanabe 1994, 394; and Neil McMullin 1989, 129-30.

[131]. See *Dai Nihon shiryō*, Series 1, vol. 7, 456-57, for the relevant entry from *Honchō seiki* (939 06/07), when Minamoto no Suguru is mentioned as director of the investigating agents sent to Musashi Province.

[132]. In Buddhist teaching, the "six paths" (*rokudō*) refers to six realms of existence through which beings pass in the process of transmigration. Though the order can vary slightly, the six paths were generally arranged in a hierarchy of beings from hell-dwellers to hungry ghosts (beings with insatiable desires), animals, *asuras* (demons), humans, and gods. Good or bad deeds result in rebirth up or down the hierarchy, and salvation is attained when one reaches the state of a buddha or bodhisattva. See LaFleur 1983, 26-59.

[133]. The Six Kannon aid and save all sentient beings in the six paths of existence. The Lotus Meditation (*Hokke zanmai*) is a twenty-one or thirty-seven day contemplative practice based on the *Lotus Sutra* and the *Sutra of Contemplation on Samantabhadra*. Alternatively known as the Lotus Repentance Rite (*Hokke senbō*), it includes repentance, circumambulation of a buddha image or images, recitation of the *Lotus Sutra*, and seated meditation. The Lotus Meditation represents one form of the "part-walking, part-sitting medition" (*hangyō hanza zanmai*), the third of the "four kinds of meditations" (*shishu zanmai*) in Tendai-school Buddhism. For a detailed analysis based on Chinese sources see Stevenson 1986.

[134]. A few undecipherable characters follow.

[135]. Ennin (794-864), posthumously awarded the title Great Master Jikaku (Jikaku Daishi), was one of the most illustrious monks in Tendai history. He first entered Mount Hiei and became a disciple of the Tendai founder, Saichō (767-822), in 808. In 838, he went to China to study the T'ien-t'ai/Tiantai (in Japan, Tendai) tradition, esoteric Buddhism, and Sanskrit. After his return to Japan in 847, he was named one of the ten royal protector monks (*naigubu jūzenji*) in 848, and he became the head of the Tendai school as the third Enryakuji abbot (*zasu*) in 854. He was the founder of Tendai's Sanmon lineage and is particularly renowned for synthesizing esoteric and Tendai teachings and rituals, and strengthening the foundation of the Tendai school on Mount Hiei. His most famous work is the record of his journey to China (*Nittō guhō junreikōki*), which has been translated into English. See Reischauer 1955.

[136]. The Hōdōin was a cloister on Mount Hiei, planned as one part of Saichō's West Tower (Saitō). It was actually completed after a royal vow (*chokugan*) by Montoku Tennō (r. 850-858).

[137]. Internal evidence in the *Teishinkōkishō* (see the entry for 12/25) has

led scholars to conclude that this abstract of Tadahira's original journal was made by Tadahira's son and heir, Fujiwara no Saneyori. Therefore the translators have interpolated Saneyori's name as compiler and author of this and similar notes.

[138] . Every year provincial governors surveyed and reported the number of derelict fields in their province—those left barren due to bad weather. The Council of State would memorialize these reports to the throne as the *Fukandenden sō*; then the tax would be appropriately reduced for the distressed province. Later in the century, however, tax responsibilities were formalized and such survey reports became largely a matter of annual ceremony. See Kiley 1999, esp. 325. For an analysis of Tadahira's involvement in provincial policy, see Piggott 2007.

[139] . With the granting of this privilege the two ministers could enter the greater palace precincts in a special palanquin, the *teguruma*, designated for this purpose.

[140] . A part of the Heian university system, the Kangakuin was specifically affiliated with the Fujiwara, having been founded by Fujiwara no Fuyutsugu in 821. It partly served educational purposes, but it also housed Fujiwara students attending the royal university and took care of administrative work for the family temple, Kōfukuji, and also the family's Kasuga Shrine.

[141] . See the entry for 08/11.

[142] . See the entry for 06/08, when the *Annotated Classic of Filial Piety* had been read for a similar event.

[143] . See the entry for 10/02.

[144] . The Chūin was a locus for *kami* worship in the residential palace. The First Fruits Service (*Niinamesai*) thanked the gods for the fall harvest. The *tennō* would partake of the new grain and offer it to the gods. In the first autumn of a new monarch's reign, the grander Great Thanksgiving Service (*Daijōsai*) replaced the First Fruits Service.

[145] . The fact that Koreshige was divined to be minimally affected by taboo did not absolve him from undergoing rigorous purification rituals. Having been selected as one able to assume this role, he then had to guard doubly against impurity. *Omi*, written with ideographs meaning "small taboo," actually refers less to Koreshige's spiritual state than his designation as one who was chosen by divination to serve the *tennō* during the ritual. See McCullough and McCullough 1980, 291 note 142.

[146] . This was the "Flushed Faces Banquet" (*Toyo no akari no sechie*) that concluded the *Niinamesai* rites. Wine made from new rice was presented, and the Gosechi dances were performed. For more details see the English translation of *Eiga monogatari* : McCullough and McCullough 1980 375-78.

[147] . On the *Gunji dokusō* event, see the note for the 4/20 entry and note

63 above.

148 . Regarding this extraordinary Kamo Festival, see Abe Takeshi et al. 2003 179-80.

149 . In other words, precedents from the courts of Uda and Daigo were investigated and reported, whereupon Akitada was ordered to present the draft proclamation to the *tennō* for approval.

150 . It was a *kannichi*, an inauspicious day according to *Onmyōdō* thought.

151 . Minamoto no Suguru was the chief of the investigating agents appointed to look into violence in the Bandō involving Taira no Masakado. See the entry for 6/7.

152 . The Japanese text refers to the *bugyō seru no ben*, "the controller-in-charge."

153 . The calendar for the following year (*shinreki*) was prepared by the eleventh month. It was then memorialized to the throne and distributed to officialdom. As regent, Tadahira would have been one of the first officials to receive a copy of the document. See Yamashita Katsuaki 1984.

154 . Regarding Tadahira's status "equal to that of the three queens," see the entries for 03/03 and 12/05 , as well as notes 34 above.

155 . On alms for the poor (*shingō*), see the entry for 5/23 above.

156 . On the *Jinkonjiki*, or "Sacred Meal," see the entry for 6/11 and note 84 above. Felicia Bock terms the *Jinkonjiki* "a sacred communion, a together-tasting, of the year's rice and *sake* on the part of the new emperor and the ancestral deities and divine spirits." See Bock 1990, 307.

157 . The Japanese term for such prayers at a distance—in this case from the capital—is *yōhai*.

158 . On the guardroom (*jin*) as council chamber for the senior nobles, see note 62 above.

159 . According to a note by the *Dai Nihon kokiroku* editor, appointments included that for Tajima Province Mikumi District's lesser district chief (*shōryō*), Osakabe no Fukuhide. See the order in *Ruijū fusenshō* Tengyō 2, 5/22 (Shintei zōho Kokushi taikei).

160 . Concerning Fujiwara no Sumitomo, see notes 38 and 122 above.

161 . The Litany of the Buddhas' Names was an annual rite performed in the twelfth month. It generally lasted three days and nights and was performed in the royal palace as well as in the provinces. The service centered on reciting the names of the buddhas of the past, present, and future to repent and erase the year's transgressions. In earlier times 13,000 names were recited based on a *Sutra of the Buddhas' Names* (*Butsumyōkyō*) that was subsequently lost. By Tadahira's time, the service relied on the so-called *Sutra of Three Thousand Buddhas' Names* (*Sanzen butsumyōkyō*), a collection of three sutras listing 1,000 names each for the buddhas of the three ages. See Tsunoda 1994, Vol. 2, 2233. On the Litany of the Buddhas' Names (*Butsumyōe*)

as it was described by Minamoto no Tamenori in 984, see Kamens 1990 366-67.

162 . They were all sent down to the Inland Sea to negotiate with Sumitomo, and they seem to have included his relatives.

163 . See the entry for 12/21 above.

164 . The *tan* is a unit for measuring cloth—it was equal to the amount of cloth needed to make a robe for one person (2 *jō* 6 *shaku*, about 25 feet of a narrow width of cloth).

165 . A recently published discussion and analysis of this event is Friday 2008 109-14.

166 . See the entry for 1/28.

167 . See the entry for 7/21 concerning a grant of ordinands.

168 . For background see Friday 2008, 105-7.

169 . Concerning Hasedera, see note 64 above.

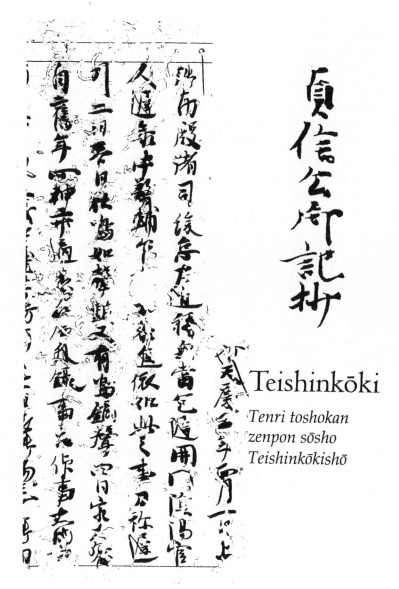

Teishinkōki

*Tenri toshokan
zenpon sōsho
Teishinkōkishō*

行き六日〇〇〇〇〇〇〇〇〇七日〇〇〇〇〇〇〇
〇〇〇老〇〇〇〇〇〇〇〇〇〇〇〇〇〇〇〇〇
〇〇〇〇〇〇〇〇〇〇〇〇〇〇〇〇〇〇〇〇
〇〇〇〇〇〇〇〇〇〇〇〇〇〇〇〇〇〇〇〇
上人〇〇〇〇執筆

十日〇〇〇
〇〇〇〇會〇〇〇〇〇〇〇〇〇〇〇〇〇
〇事〇辭無〇〇以〇〇〇〇〇〇〇〇〇
〇〇〇〇〇〇〇〇〇〇〇〇〇〇〇〇

三月一日、□月□日□□□□□□□□□□□□□□□度者、□□義海

候□□由□□□□□□□□

□辰清□□□□□□□□□度□□□□□□□

□天晴、長斗□任□□□□□□□□□□□□□□□□□□一巻、枝、絃□

大辰一傾、

昌仁□會事□、百□□□□□□□□田□□事□□

□候作

□夜□震二度、五□□□□□相□□□□□□事大□□

□夜度□□動

百□□□□□□仁□□□□□

南信同宿　十日南清女□□饗當停以下誡人以上

□□書自會在□殿南殿

十□地震　十□地震　□□川場在右新一□

裏見□□□奉□　□□□□陰陽□□□□言首□□□

朝□　十□□□今年□□□□□

□日左大將束滿回□□蔵束□□□□陽江川□項

□□　甘□□連□□□□□□夫大□□文將束□

勅差□□□白□□□□□□武高□□□□□□

廿□□□□武室同□□□□□主武高□□□□□□

□□作□□仕□□　□日仁和寺□堂□

師長座寺阿闍梨薨慎望々復有祈等之奏隨様

芸り東大寺別當明珍仍行年念歳將来々孫祿

諸國政年中出来々表白所司賴貴方之敢將来之勳々殿之人

大人々々所司城今保利朝々申々隨佛一々致回夫々正義

仰可宣封之狀並賜阿闍梨馬小

於三生使師戊戌々夫眠勳善假倒敕物

廿日人宗傳府左右醫寮本捜索京畢監

廿日夜主地震

来所

三月己巳朔丙申夫使王下官府一貴坂諸國龍仇和壽清々

新壽梢法貴仍清寺等事一二七々狀

新拝諸社読経諸寺導事二三々仍状

宵劣羽四肥蹄使を以珠齢父を職後到来秋田刺閼

定舎棟辰米稲焼上百姓財地又申矢藝軍を々

有此雌阮有䕃匿と

前地震

五々に一武先人有院収弐釜

五月季謝諸社役三新軍賊受起氣膾匕倍武蔵等

申卅五甘億乱起沂世苻一服沂使左全、支早旦地

震夜又地震廿六り當年經障係沂一清渚渾寄使

玄忠寵孫沂及左閉

二月

六月

一日諸松諸寺讀師又　　　　　五日天朝慶

着書勅責朝相有裏弁　　　　　　着

立　　　　　　　　着但人非

大石信立不着同

吉日呼車忠卿告于左同日同衆告使上隨倒

状僉議書司候陣衆告使賎以民物

卿橋未福略此使

月波寿見寄有　　　　左日　　　葉

明勅父　　業約甚左衛門届諸興宸

着押領使但　　足倒動又催問使官符

十月付月次祭使有御時贊使相尅是為祈有兩又東夫

愛之事也　此種今食付阿可之行低欲事小汶西方善也

十二日午剋雨諸社使者室弁将別有天変事

十二日夫水内殿此次老山陰就雲始行居之為�年候

像廿又大般若無三今日同毎日一部廿汶汰比七日也

内天変可候於七断日地震敬

十五日末府虹雲之三四暗左為門陰為作物而雲之

十五日大師之云膳陰陰汶請候

昔度廛此阿漬経敷大並汶候之石初廿兩年敷並天

二二四

九月

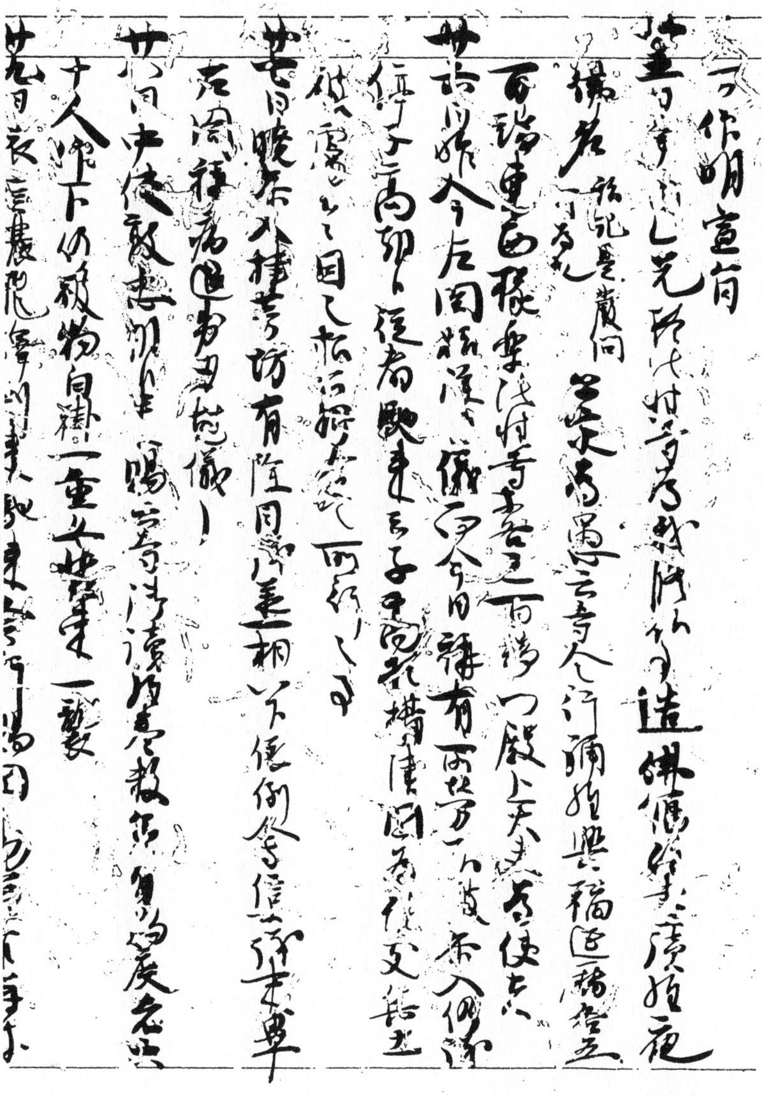

Year			
900	made Council advisor, resigns as advisor, right senior controller, takes Uda's daughter, Nobuko, as consort	Yasuko enters Daigo's palace	
901		birth of first son, Saneyori	exile of Michizane *Sandai jitsuroku* compiled
903	junior fourth rank, upper grade	Nakahira head of the Royal Secretariat Yasuko consort of Daigo Yasuko bears Prince Yasuakira	death of Michizane Prince Yasuakira made Crown Prince
904		birth of daughter, Takako	*Kokinwakashū* compiled
905		Yoshiko tonsured	*Engi shiki* compilation ordered
906		birth of daughter, Hiroko	
907		death of Yoshiko	
908	*Teishinkōki* entries remain from this year advisor, director of the Crown Prince's Agency, director of the Right Guard, director of the Royal Police; takes Minamoto no Akiko as consort (daughter of Minamoto no Yoshiari) junior third rank, provisional middle counselor, chieftain of the Fujiwara family, director of the Royal Secretariat, right senior captain, director of the Royal Police middle counselor	birth of second son, Morosuke	
909	senior counselor, resigned as director of the Royal Police	death of Tokihira	
910			
911			
912	ordered to continue compiling *Engi shiki*	birth of fourth son, Morouji	
913	senior third rank, left senior captain	Nakahira director of the Crown Prince's Agency	
914	minister of the right		Miyoshi's Twelve-clause Memorial
915		Saneyori's coming-of-age ceremony	
916			
917	junior second rank		
918	Prince Hiroakira born at Tadahira's mansion senior second rank, minister of the left not attending court late in year (Nobuko ill) charged with Crown Prince's upbringing (as maternal uncle)	Nakahira middle counselor, director of the Crown Prince's Agency Takako enters Crown Prince's palace Akiko bears fifth son, Moromasa Yasuko made Queen-consort	
920			
923			
924			
925		death of Nobuko	Hiroakira made crown prince
926	memorializes *Engi shiki* with others designated regent granted court attendants and escorts	Yasuko bears Nariakira Nakahira senior counselor Saneyori head of the Royal Secretariat Nakahira right senior captain	lightening strikes Seiryōden Tennō ill, Tadahira at palace Daigo Tennō abdicates
927			
930			

Tadahira's Life

Year	Event/Rank	Family	Political/Cultural Developments
880	born	father Minister of the Right Mototsune mother daughter of Prince Hitoyasu elder full brothers Tokihira, Nakahira elder half brother Kanehira full sister Yoriko (consort to Seiwa) full sister Kazuko (consort to Seiwa) half sister Yoshiko Mototsune presides over memorials	death of the tonsured monarch Seiwa
884			Yōzei Tennō abdicates Kōkō Tennō enthroned
885		birth of full sister Yasuko	
886		Tokihira's coming-of-age ceremony	
887		Tokihira made head of the Royal Secretariat Mototsune made chief-of-staff	death of Kōkō Tennō Uda Tennō enthroned Akō Debate
888			
890		Yoshiko enters palace as consort	
891		Nakahira's coming-of-age ceremony death of Mototsune	
892		Tokihira made Council advisor	Ruijū kokushi compiled Shinsenjikyō compiled Silla pirate attack
893		Tokihira middle counselor, right senior captain, director of the Crown Prince's Agency	
894			China embassy cancelled
895	coming-of-age ceremony (age 16), senior fifth rank, lower grade appointed chamberlain		
896			Uda Tennō abdicates Daigo Tennō enthroned
897		Tokihira senior counselor, left senior captain, chieftain of the Fujiwara family Tokihira assigned plenary royal powers with Sugawara no Michizane Yoshiko named Mother of the Crown Prince (kōtaifujin) Tokihira minister of the left Nakahira director of the Queen-consort's Agency	
899			Michizane minister of the right Retired Uda Tennō tonsured

Year			
931	Suzaku Tennō enthroned; death of retired Daigo Tennō	Saneyori made Council advisor; Morosuke head of the Royal Secretariat; Yasuko designated Queen-mother; Takako appointed head of the Wardrobe Bureau, moves to Higyōsha; Nakahira left senior captain; Nakahira minister of the right; Moromasa's coming-of-age ceremony; Saneyori made middle counselor; Morosuke made Council advisor	
932			junior first rank, permitted ox carriage
933	Inland Sea rife with pirates		
934	Ki no Tsurayuki's return from Tosa; Taira no Masakado kills his uncle, Kunika		
935		death of Kanehira	
936	Fujiwara no Sumitomo leads pirates in the Inland Sea; Masakado pardoned, defeats uncle	Nakahira minister of the left	prime minister, instructions to Morosuke
937	Masakado attacks Taira no Sadamori		Tadahira caps Suzaku Tennō during coming-of-age ceremony instructions to Saneyori
938		Saneyori made right senior captain; Morosuke provisional middle counselor; Takako head of female chamberlains (naishi)	
939	Masakado attacks Hitachi Province; Sumitomo leads pirates in the Inland Sea; Masakado's letter to Tadahira; Masakado killed by Sadamori and Fujiwara no Hidesato	Saneyori made senior counselor; Morosuke director of Queen-consort's Agency; Morouji head of the Royal Secretariat	60th year, granted privileges equivalent to the three queen-consorts
940	Ono no Yoshifuru defeats Sumitomo, Sumitomo killed	Queen-consort Yasuko ill, takes vows	Tadahira caps Nariakira during
941		Moromasa right middle controller; Morosuke senior counselor; Saneyori minister of the right; Morouji Council advisor; Moromasa head of the Royal Secretariat; Nakahira director of Crown Prince's upbringing; death of Hiroko, Nakahira tonsured; death of Nakahira	coming-of-age ceremony resigns as regent, made chief-of-staff
942			ill
944			ill
945			ill, receives various visitors, regular visits by palace emissary, robbers at Tadahira's mansion; ill
946	Suzaku Tennō abdicates; Murakami Tennō enthroned; death of Ki no Tsurayuki	Yasuko named Senior Queen-mother	
947		Saneyori minister of the left; Morosuke minister of the right	ill
948			ill
949			attempts to resign as chief-of-staff; death; posthumously awarded title, "Teishinkō"

Teishinkōki Name Glossary

Prince Atsumi (893-967)
Eighth son of Uda Tennō. After his coming-of-age ceremony in 907, he served as a provincial governor and minister of personnel (from 937).

Enshō (880-964)
Monk from Kaga Province who took vows at Enryakuji in 901. He became Hosshōji abbot and a royal protector monk (*naigubu jūzenji*) in 940. In 946 he was made Enryakuji abbot. He was on close terms with the Suzaku and Murakami monarchs.

Fujiwara no Akitada (898-965)
Fujiwara no Tokihira's second son and Tadahira's nephew. He was named an advisor on the Council in 937. In 939 he was serving as an advisor and as minister of justice.

Fujiwara no Asatada (912-966)
Began his career with service in the Inner Palace Guards and the Royal Secretariat; and then he served in various Guards and provincial posts. He was also a respected poet. Asatada appears to have been on close terms with Tadahira. He was in the Royal Secretariat and the Inner Guards in 939. He later became an advisor in 952 and was eventually called the "Tsuchimikado Middle Counselor."

Fujiwara no Arihira (892-970)
Grandson of Fujiwara no Yamakage. He rose through the university to receive his first appointment in 924. He was the left middle controller in 939. In 941, he was made an advisor on the Council, and he eventually rose to the post of senior minister.

Fujiwara no Atsutada (906-943)
Third son of Fujiwara no Tokihira, Tadahira's brother and court leader before Tadahira. Atsutada was known primarily as a poet (particularly as one of the Thirty-six Poetic Sages, the Sanjūrokkasen) and his works are found in various official anthologies. He was given the junior fifth rank in 921. Thereafter he served as a chamberlain and in various other posts until he was

named head of the Royal Secretariat in 935. In 939 he became an advisor on the Council but then died shortly after.

Fujiwara no Masamoto (864-941)
A scholarly member of the Fujiwara Southern House, he advanced from the palace university to posting as a guard and then to service in the Controller's Office. After serving in the Capital Agency and at the Dazaifu, he was named a Council advisor. When he was quite elderly he became minister of civil affairs, as he was in 939.

Fujiwara no Motokata (888-953)
Son of Council advisor Fujiwara no Sugane. He was a scholar who served in the Controller's Office and the Crown Prince's Agency before the prince took the throne as Suzaku Tennō in 930. In 939 Motokata was made an advisor on the Council of State and rose to serve as major counselor.

Fujiwara no Morosuke (908-960)
Tadahira's second son, born of Minamoto no Akiko, a daughter of Minister of the Right Minamoto no Yoshiari. He was Saneyori's half-brother. Morosuke was appointed to the fifth rank in 923, became head of the Royal Secretariat in 931, and was promoted to advisor in 935. As a senior noble he served as director of the Left Gate Guards, eventually rising to minister of the right in 939. Morosuke's descendents, the Kujō, came to hold the highest posts in the court. An active poet, thirty of Morosuke's extant poems are included in official anthologies.

Fujiwara no Morouji (913-970)
Tadahira's fourth son, and full brother of Morosuke and Moromasa. In 944 he was made a Council advisor, eventually rising to senior counselor in 970.

Fujiwara no Nakahira (875-945)
Tadahira's elder brother, he was minister of the left and senior captain of the Left Inner Palace Guards in 939. His home was the Biwa Mansion (Biwadono), and Nakahira is sometimes called by that name. With Tadahira as prime minister, Nakahira was the second highest ranker on the Council. Nakahira was more a poet than a politician, and many of his verses are preserved in official collections.

Fujiwara no Saneyori (900-970)

Tadahira's eldest son and heir, his mother was one of Uda Tennō's daughters. In 930 he was appointed head of the Royal Secretariat, and in 931 he became a Council advisor. In 939 he was serving as senior captain of the right. Much later (in 947) he became minister of the left, and still later prime minister (in 967). Saneyori is thought to have been the one who abstracted entries of the longer journal for the *Teishinkōkishō*.

Fujiwara no Takako (904-962)

Tadahira's eldest daughter and a consort of Crown Prince Yasuakira, Daigo Tennō's second son. She entered his palace in 918. She moved to the Higyōsha in 931, some years after the prince's death in 923. Some attributed that death to the menacing ghost of Sugawara no Michizane. She was subsequently appointed director in the Office of Female Chamberlains (*Naishi no kami*) in 938.

Fujiwara no Yasuko (885-954)

Tadahira's younger sister. She became a consort to Daigo Tennō in 901 and gave birth to Prince Yasuakira in 903. Though named heir to the throne, Yasuakira died in 923. Yasuko was named queen-consort in 923 and gave birth to the future Suzaku Tennō. After bearing the future Murakami Tennō in 924, Yasuko was made queen-mother (*kōtaigō*) in late 931, and then senior queen-mother (*taikōtaigō*) in 946. As the mother of two *tennō* and sister to the most powerful men at court, she exercised considerable influence.

Fumi no Takekane

An official of the Yinyang Bureau in 939, who proposed and later performed the Taiitsu Rite for peace in the realm.

Gikai (871-984)

A monk from Enryakuji on Mount Hiei, where he was a disciple of Son'i. He came from the Usa family of Buzen province in Kyushu. He was appointed to the Prelates' Office in 935; and by 939 he had been made master of discipline, the third-ranking post in that Office. In 940 he became Tendai abbot at Enryakuji.

Ichiwa (890-967)
A monk from Kōfukuji, he came from the Tajihi Family and served in the Prelates' Office from 958 onward.

Izumo no Koreka
A yinyang master and second-in-command of the Yinyang Bureau.

Kamo no Tadayuki
A celebrated specialist in Yinyang studies who recommended performance of certain rituals for realm protection during the Masakado and Sumitomo rebellions. He was also called to the palace for divining activities during the reign of Murakami Tennō.

Ki no Yoshimitsu (869-939)
Third son of the noted scholar and literary figure Ki no Haseo, he was named a controller in 919 and became a counselor on the Council in 934. He received junior third rank and was named head of the Royal Household Ministry in the eighth month of 939, only to die a month later.

Kudaranokokishi Teiun
A provincial governor who was serving in the Bandō in 939, he was moved from Kazusa to Musashi in the fifth month to help quell the violence there.

Mimune no Kintada (?-949)
A well-known scholar, in 936 he was promoted from fourth-in-charge at the Ministry of Popular Affairs to lesser Council secretary. In 938 he was made senior Council secretary, and in 939 he was given the junior fifth rank, lower grade.

Mimune no Motonatsu
A scholar and graduate of the university who participated in the Classics Reading. He was made third-in-command at the Ministry of Personnel in 937.

Minamoto no Kanetada (901-958)
Grandson of Seiwa Tennō. He received his first appointment to the junior fifth rank in 917 and served as a provincial governor before becoming a chamberlain, Guards member, and official in the Queen-consort's Agency. He also received additional appointments

as a provincial governor. Later, in the 950s, he was appointed an advisor on the Council of State.

Minamoto no Kintada (889-948)

Serving as royal secretary for the monarchs Daigo and Suzaku, he was left middle controller in 939. Talented as both an administrator and poet, he is one of the Thirty-Six Poetic Sages, with poems in the *Gosenwakashū* (951). He appears in anecdotes in the *Yamato monogatari*, *Kojidan*, and *Konjaku monogatarishū*.

Minamoto no Koreshige (886-941)

Son of Seiwa Tennō and designated a member of the Minamoto lineage. He served as left senior controller and advisor, and rose to middle counselor in 939.

Minamoto no Moroakira (903-955)

A descendent of Uda Tennō, he received his first appointment to the junior fourth rank, lower grade, in 924. He served as director of the Left Capital Agency and director of the Palace Guards before being promoted to junior fourth rank, upper grade, in 936. Thereafter he was made a senior noble with the post of Council advisor in 941.

Minamoto no Muneyuki (?-939)

Grandson of Kōkō Tennō and a well-known poet, he was first assigned junior fourth rank, lower grade, and later held various posts.

Minamoto no Sukemoto (901-943)

Son of a middle counselor (Minamoto no Masatoki) and grandson of a former minister of the right (Minamoto no Yoshiari), Sukemoto was an intimate of Tadahira's—his father's sister was one of Tadahira's consorts and she was the mother of Morosuke. In 939 Sukemoto held the post of right middle controller.

Minamoto no Suguru

Son of Right Senior Controller Minamoto no Tonau, he was appointed head of the agents investigating allegations in Musashi in 939.

Minamoto no Takaakira (914-982)
Tenth son of Daigo Tennō, his coming-of-age ceremony was held in 929. The following year he was given junior fourth rank, upper grade. In 939 he was made a Council advisor, rising to minister of the right in 966 and minister of the left in 967. Takaakira took the tonsure after the Anna Disturbance of 969; but he was later made Supernumerary Governor General of Dazaifu (*Dazai no gon no sochi*). This amounted to exile. Well versed in the practices of court and Council, he produced the *Saikyūki*, an important ritual handbook.

Minamoto no Tsunemoto (?-961)
Second-in-command in the provincial headquarters of Musashi in 939.

Mononobe no Sadamochi
Made a junior Council secretary 938, he rose to senior secretary in 942.

Myōchin (871-954)
Abbot of Tōdaiji in 939, he came from Izumi Province to enter Tōdaiji at the age of eighteen. In 936 he was made abbot there. In 940 he led prayer services in response to the threat of Masakado's rebellion.

Ninkō (875-949)
A monk and Hossō scholar from Nara's Kōfukuji, he also studied Tendai and esoteric Buddhism. He was appointed lecturer for the Vimalakirti Assembly (*Yuimae*) in 927, he entered the Prelates' Office in 931, and in 939 he was serving as Master of Discipline (*risshi*).

Prince Noriakira (924-90)
The fifteenth son of Daigo Tennō, his coming-of-age ceremony was held in 939.

Ōe no Asatsuna (886-957)
A scholar and poet known for his Chinese verses (*kanshi*). He served in provincial posts, at the university, and the Controllers Office before promotion to the Council as an advisor in 953. He was left junior controller with senior fifth rank, lower grade, in 939.

Ōnakatomi no Yorimoto (886-958)

Ritual director (*saishu*) at the Ise Shrine and a famous poet (one of the Thirty-Six Poetic Sages), he served as an official within the Council of Shrine Affairs. In 939 he was awarded the junior fifth rank for leading prayers contributing to the suppression of rebellions by Masakado and Sumitomo.

Saigen (882-964)

A scholar monk at Yakushiji in Nara. In 939 he was appointed lecturer for the Vimalakirti Assembly at Kōfukuji.

Son'i (866-940)

Tendai abbot at Enryakuji on Mount Hiei. He performed rituals on behalf of Daigo and Suzaku Tennō and was greatly trusted by Tadahira.

Tachibana no Naomoto

Served as a palace secretary in the Ministry of Residential Palace Affairs in 939. He was a noted scholar, and examples of his work appear in the eleventh-century compendium of Sino-Japanese materials, the *Honchō monzui*. After 939 he was made director of the university, professor of literature, and second-in-command at the Ministry of Personnel.

Taira no Koremochi (881-939)

A Kammu Heishi—that is, a descendent of one of Kanmu's princes who was given the family name of Taira—he was Tadahira's cousin and frequently served as a messenger between the residential palace and Tadahira. In 939, the year of his death, Koremochi held the junior third rank and was senior counselor on the Council of State, as well as head of both the Ministry of Popular Affairs and the Queen-consort's Agency.

Taira no Masakado (?-940)

A fifth-generation descendent of Kanmu Tennō and son of a professional warrior—his father had served as Pacification Commander (*chinjufu shōgun*) on the eastern frontier—Masakado clashed with his own relatives from 935 onward. He eventually rebelled against the Heian court and proclaimed himself a "new monarch" (*shinnō*) in 939. His rebellion was defeated in 940 by a coalition of forces that included other professional warriors from the Bandō area, including Taira no Sadamori and Fujiwara no Hidesato.

Princess Tsuyako (904-969)
Seventh daughter of Daigo Tennō. In 931 she was selected to become the Kamo Priestess and she kept that position until the death of Murakami Tennō in 967. Some contemporary records term her the Daisai'in, the Great Kamo Priestess.

Yatabe no Kinmochi
A scholar who graduated from the university, worked for the Ministry of Personnel, and moved to the Royal Archives in 929, he also served as a Council secretary. From 936 to 943 he lectured intermittently on the *Nihon shoki* at the residential palace.

Yoshimine no Yoshikata (?-957)
Son of Yoshimine no Moroki and a well-known poet, he attained the fourth rank and served as left middle captain of the Inner Palace Guards.

Teishinkōki Glossary

ajari	officiant
ben	controller (senior, junior, and middle; left and right)
bettō	director of an agency, office, or temple
Butsumyō	Litany of the Buddhas' Names
chieki	express courier
chō	missive
chōbukuhō	subjugation rite
chokusho	royal edict
chōyō	taxes in kind and labor
chūgū	queen-consort
Chūin	venue within the residential palace used for *kami* worship
chūshi	royal emissary
Daigokuden	Throne Hall; main hall in State Halls Compound
daijin	senior minister
daikyō	grand banquet
dainagon	senior counselor
Dairi	royal residential palace
dei	extra ceremonial role
dosha	ordinand; novice
e	defilement
Efu	Headquarters of the Six Guards units
Emonfu	Headquarters of the Palace Gate Guards (Left and Right)
Endōe	ritual assembly in the Endō Hall of Ninnaji
Fukandenden no fumi	Annual Survey Report of Barren Fields
ganmon	dedicatory text
geben	an area outside the Shōmei Gate and the courtiers who assembled there for ceremonies
gebumi	report
geki	Council secretary (senior and junior)
Gekisei	Preparatory Activities in the Council Secretariat Office
genpuku	coming-of-age ceremony
Giyōden	a residential-palace hall southeast of the Southern Hall, used primarily by senior nobles for discussions
Goryōsai	Five-Dragon Festival

Gosechi	Gosechi Dance Performance by young women before His Majesty, part of year-end thanksgiving celebrations
Gosho hajime	ceremony commencing the Reading of the Classics before His Majesty
Gosho kyōen	banquet in the residential palace celebrating completion of the court Classics Reading
Gōsho	Prelates' Office (alt. Sōgōsho)
Gunji dokusō	memorialization of nominations for district chieftain appointments
Gyōbushō	Ministry of Justice
hakase	lecturer
Hasshōin	State Halls Compound where Council of State activities originally took place in Nara times; later used ceremonially
hei	offerings
hieki	express courier
Higyōsha (alt. *Fujitsubo*)	one of five main halls in the Back Palace and northeast of the Seiryōden
hōbei	offering of gifts (usually paper strips) to shrine deities
hōka	legal scholar
hyakusei	commoner; cultivator
hyō	missive
Hyōefu	Headquarters of the Palace Guards (Left and Right)
Ichibumeshi	Ceremony for Assigning Lowest Ranking Posts
iki	certificate of rank
Inokoshi	Continuation Rounds of the Grand Archery Contest
Jibushō	Ministry of Civil Affairs
jijijū	extra chamberlains appointed for specific ritual activities
jijū	chamberlain
Jimoku	Ceremony for Assigning Posts
jin	guardroom; those of Inner Palace Guards were used as meeting rooms by senior nobles
Jin no mōshibumi	report (to the throne) of a Council discussion
Jingikan	Council on Shrine Affairs
Jinkonjiki	a meal taken by His Highness before the gods
jō	third-in-command official; a third-level manager
Joi	Promotions in Rank Ceremony
jōjitsu	days on which an official reported for work

Jōsen mokuroku   List of Individuals Qualified for Lower Rank Promotion

jōshi   commander of a stockade

juganmon   statement of prayers and vows

jusangū   status equivalent to that of the three queen-consorts

kaji   empowerment rite

Kamon(ryō)   Custodial Bureau

Kan no seichō   main hall of the Council of State Office (Daijōkanchō)

kanmon   a report; an opinion by a specialist submitted to the Council or throne

kanpu (alt. *dajō kanpu*)   Council directive

kansō   formal memorial by Council of State to the throne

kanzu   list of sutras and prayers performed for a patron and then presented to the patron

Katanashidokoro   Preparatory Office located near the Council Office where controllers (*ben*) and junior secretaries (*shi*) worked

kazukemono   gift or reward

Kebiishi(chō)   Royal Police (Office)

kechigan   conclusion of a Buddhist rite

Keihōbō   a small hall northeast of the royal residence

kengyō   master-in-charge of a Buddhist rite or court ceremony

Kinomidokyō   Seasonal Sutra Reading, particularly one taking place at the palace

Kinenkoku   Prayers for a Plentiful Harvest

kisan   prayers for a long life

kitō   prayer offerings

kiu   prayers for rain

kōji   reprimand

kokugen   accusations

Konoefu   Headquarters of the Inner Palace Guards (Left and Right)

kotowake   special appeal appended to a royal proclamation

kugyō   senior noble, members of the Council of State

Kunaishō   Ministry of the Royal Household

kurabeuma   horse races

Kuraryō   Royal Provisions Bureau (alt. Royal Storehouse Bureau)

kurōdo   royal secretary

kyojō	letter of recommendation
kyōmyō	list of appointees
maki	royal pasture
Meryō	Bureau of the Stables (Left and Right)
Minbushō	Ministry of Popular Affairs
mishiho	esoteric rite
misogi	lustration
Mokuryō	Carpentry Bureau
monmikkokushi	agent(s) in charge of investigating an allegation
monjōshō	student having completed university studies in Chinese classics
monoimi	taboo and associated period of abstinence, ritual cleansing, or isolation
mōshibumi	report, request to a superior
Naden (alt. *Shishinden*)	Southern Hall
naiben	senior nobles serving as masters of ceremony inside the Shōmei Gate
naiki	residential palace secretary
Naishishi	Office of Female Chamberlains
Naizenshi	Office of the Royal Meal
Nakatsukasashō	Ministry of Residential Palace Affairs
Naoshimono	Ceremony for Modification of Appointments
narikabura	whistling arrows
nenkan	annual right to recommend someone for official posting
Ninnōe	Benevolent King Assembly
Niwatachi no sō	Presentation of a Memorial from the Southern Courtyard
Noriyumi	Archery Matches
Nosaki	presentation of tribute items for a royal mausoleum
Nuidonoryō	Bureau of the Wardrobe, located north and outside the residential palace
Ōba	Great Courtyard, outside the Kenrei Gate and in front of the residential palace
omi	minimal impediment caused by a ritual taboo
Onmyōryō	Yinyang Bureau
Onna joi	Women's Promotions in Rank Ceremony
ōryōshi	envoy appointed to pacify a region
risshi	master of discipline in the Prelates' Office
rokudō	the six paths of existence (hell-dwellers, hungry ghosts, animals, *asuras*, humans, gods)

rokuji	banquet coordinator
Ryōkiden	hall in the residential palace located north of the Giyōden and used as occasional living and ritual space by His Majesty
saiō	Kamo Priestess (alt. *saiin*); Ise Priestess (alt. *saigū*)
saishu	Ise Shrine head ritualist
sakan	fourth-level manager
sangi	Council of State advisor
sangō	the triple alignment of Jupiter, the Sun, and the Guest Star, signifying an inauspicious omen
sechie	royal banquet hosted by His Majesty for leading court members and officials
Sekiten	biannual Memorial for Confucius
senji	written or oral statement of a royal command
senmyō	royal proclamation
sesshō	regent
shi	junior secretary working in Controller's Office
Shikino(mi)zōshi	office of the Queen-consort's Agency
Shikibushō	Ministry of Personnel
shindenzukuri	a style of noble residential building in Heian times
shingō	charitable distributions of rice and salt to the capital's poor, ill, or elderly
shōfuku	assistant reader
shōkei	noble-in-charge
shōnagon	junior counselor
shōzei	tax kept in provincial or district storehouses
Shun no gi	Seasonal Ceremony
Shurishiki	Repairs Agency
shuzen	private rites
sōhenshō	comprehensive receipt (issued to provincial governors at the end of term)
sokusaihō	rite to stop calamities
Sonshōhō	Sonshō Rite, a ritual to ward off calamities
suimonshi	investigative agent
suke	second-in-command official; second-level manager
Sumai no meshiawase	wrestling matches held before His Majesty
Taigen no hō	Taigen Rite, an important Shingon ritual for protecting the state
Taiitsushiki no matsuri	performance of the Taiitsu Rite by the Yin-yang Bureau to bring peace to the realm

taishō	senior captain of Inner Palace Guards (Left and Right)
tendoku	abbreviated sutra reading
tenjōbito	royal intimates
tenpen	disturbing celestial events
Tōka no sechie	Dance and Song Royal Banquet
toki no kui	clock peg
tone	officials of fourth-level managerial status (*sakan*) or higher
toneri	male attendants; servants; soldiers; lower members of Six Guards units
Tsukumodokoro	Cabinetmakers' Office
uchigi	woman's robe
Uchirongi	Residential Palace Debate
udoneri	male court attendant; official
zasu	abbot (particularly at Enryakuji)
zenku	outrider

Other Terms

Agatameshi jimoku	Appointment of Non-capital-based Officials
Aouma no sechie	White Horse Banquet
banki	plenipotentiary powers of rulership
chakushi	heir
Chōdōin	Halls of State
Chōga	New Year's Salutation to the *Tennō*
chōja	head of a noble family (*uji*)
Chūgūshiki	Queen's Household Agency
chūnagon	middle counselor
Chūyūki	Journal of the Nakamikado Minister of the Right
Daidairi	Greater Palace Precincts
daiji	official great temple
Daijōdaijin	prime minister, supreme minister
Daijōkan	Council of State
Daijōsai	Enbthronement Rite
Dairishiki	Protocols of the Residential Palace
Engishiki	Protocols of the Engi Era
fu	order
fugō no tomogara	local elites
Fukandendensō	Derelict Field Surveys Memorial

fuko	prebendal tax units
Ganjitsu no sechie	New Year's Banquet
ge	report, request to a superior
gekan	non-capital-based officials
gishiki	ceremony
gishikisho	a handbook on court ceremonial
Gisō	Emergency Stores
goi kurōdo	fifth-rank royal secretary
goryō	angry and destructive spirit of a political rival, enemy
gyōjisho	project planning team
gyōsei	administration
Hairei	New Year Salutation to the Regent
harae	cleansing ritual
hisangi	qualified-as-advisor (on the Council of State)
hōbeisha	an official shrine
Hokke Fujiwara	Fujiwara of the Northern House
Hokuzanshō	The Kitayama Minister's Notes on Court Proceedings
Hyōbushō	Ministry of Military Affairs
ie	lineage
in	retired monarch
Jarai	Grand Archery Meet
Jin no sadame	Council Discussion and Report to the Throne
jōi	royal abdication
joshaku	promotion to the fifth rank
Juzenshi	Minting Office
Kageyushi	Office to Oversee Provincial Governors' Performance
kami	a Japanese deity
kanbun	Sino-Japanese written language; writing in Chinese by a Japanese
Kanbutsue	Buddha's Birthday Assembly
kanji	Chinese characters
kanjin	officials
kanpaku	chief-of-staff
Katanashi	Preparatory Proceedings
kenmon seika	noble and powerful households
kirokutai	a special way of writing Chinese by courtiers in their daily journals that is close to actual Japanese
Kochōhai	Lesser New Year Salutation

Kōka sadame	Evaluation of Efficacy (for custodial provincial governors)
kokiroku	a category of historical record keeping: a daily courtier journal
Kōkyō	Classic of Filial Piety
Kujōdono no yuiikai	Kujō Lord's Testament
kyaku	supplemental legislation
mandokoro	household chancellery (of a noble household)
man'yōgana	Chinese characters used to express Japanese sounds, meaning
mappō	latter days of the Buddhist law
matsurigoto	government decision making
Matsurigoto hajime	Initiation of Governance
Midō kampakuki	Journal of the Midō Chief-of-staff
midōkyō	sutra reading
Misaie	New Year's Buddhist Assembly
naidaijin	inner palace minister
Naishi no kami	director of the Office of Female Chamberlains
nenjūgyōji	calendar of rites, annual ceremonial calendar
Nenjūgyōji no misōji	text of the Notes on the Annual Court Calendar inscribed on a screen at the entrance to the Hall of Royal Intimates in the royal residence
Nihon sandai jitsuroku	Veritable Record of Three Reigns in Japan
Nihon shoki	Chronicle of Japan
Niinamesai	First Fruits Festival
nikki no ie	houses possessing courtier journals
Ninnōkyō	Benevolent King Sutra
ōdo	realm
Ōharae	Major Purification Rite
Ōkurashō	Ministry of the Treasury
ōshinke	princely and noble houses
reki	calendar
Rekken	Inspection of Lower Rankers
ritsuryo	Chinese-style law, containing administrative and penal codes
rōchō	resume (of a custodial provincial governor)
rokui kurōdo	sixth-rank royal secretary
sabenkan	controller of the left
sadaijin	minister of the left
sadamebumi	Council report to the throne
Saikyūki	Notes from the (Minister of the) Western Palace

seimu	governmental administration
Sekkanke	Regents' Line
sen	downward transmission of an order
setsugyō	to steer, take charge
Shikiinryō	Law on Personnel (of the *ritsuryō* codes)
shōen	estate
Shōyūki	Jounal of the Ono Minister of the Right
shukke	taking Buddhist orders, withdrawing from the world
sō	memorial to the throne
Sokui	Royal Accession Rite
Tango no sechie	Fifth-month Royal Banquet
Teishinkō	Tadahira's posthumous title, the Sagacious and Trustworthy Lord
Teishinkōkishō	the abstracted Journal of the Sagacious and Trustworthy Lord
Tenjōnoma	Chamber of Royal Intimates in the *tennō*'s residential palace
tennō	Heavenly Sovereign, the Japanese monarch
ubenkan	controller of the right
udaiben	senior controller of the right
udaijin	minister of the right
uragaki	writing on the reverse side
Wamyōruijūshō	Categorized Notes on Japanese Terminology
zokubettō	lay director of a temple
zuryō	custodial provincial governors

INDEX

BIBLIOGRAPHY

PRIMARY SOURCES

Inoue Mitsusada. 1976. *Ritsuryō*. In *Nihon shisō taikei*, vol. 3. Tokyo: Iwanami shoten.

Iwai shishi hensan iinkai, Fukuda Toyohiko. 1996. *Taira Masakado shiryōshū tsuke Fujiwara Sumitomo shiryō*. Tokyo: Shinjinbutsu ōraisha.

Kojitsu sōsho henshūbu. n.d. *Hokuzanshō*. In *Shintei zōho kojitsu sōsho*. Tokyo: Meiji tosho shuppankai.

Kunaichō shoryōbu. 1981. *Kōshitsu seido shiryō: Sesshō*. 2 vols. Tokyo: Yoshikawa kōbunkan.

Kuroita Katsumi, ed. 1933. *Ruijū fusenshō*. In *Shintei zōho Kokushi taikei*. Tokyo: Yoshikawa kōbunkan.

Kuroita Katsumi and Kokushi taikei henshūkai. 1964. *Honchō seiki*. In *Shintei zōho Kokushi taikei*. Tokyo: Yōshikawa kōbunkan.

Kuroita Katsumi and Kokushi taikei henshūkai. 1974. *Honchō monzui, Zoku Honchō monzui*. In *Shintei zōho Kokushi taikei*. Tokyo: Yoshikawa kōbunkan.

Kuroita Katsumi and Kokushi taikei henshūkai. 1979-1981. *Nihon sandai jitsuroku*. 2 vols. In *Shintei zōho Kokushi taikei*. Tokyo: Yoshikawa kōbunkan.

Kuroita Katsumi and Kokushi taikei henshūkai. 1980. *Seiji yōryaku*. 3 vols. In *Shintei zōho Kokushi taikei*. Tokyo: Yoshikawa kōbunkan.

Kuroita Katsumi and Kokushi taikei henshūkai. 1984-85. *Nihon kiryaku*. 3 vols. In *Shintei zōho Kokushi taikei*. Tokyo: Yoshikawa kōbunkan.

Kuroita Katsumi and Kokushi taikei henshūkai. 1986. *Kugyō bu'nin*. 6 vols. In *Shintei zōho Kokushi taikei*. Tokyo: Yoshikawa kōbunkan.

Nanjō Bun'yū et al. 1915. *Sōgō bu'nin*. In *Kōfukuji sōsho 1, Dai Nihon bukkyō zensho*, vol. 123. Tokyo: Bussho kankōkai: 61-288.

Takeuchi Rizō, ed. 1973-1978. *Heian ibun*. 15 vols. Tokyo: Tōkyōdō.

Tenri toshokan zenpon sōsho hensan iinkai. 1980. *Teishinkōkishō, Kujōdono gyoki*. In *Tenri toshokan zenpon sōsho* Washo no bu vol. 42. Tenri: Tenri daigaku shuppanbu/Yagi shoten.

Tōkyō daigaku Shiryō hensanjo. 1901- . *Dai Nihon shiryō*. Tokyo: Tōkyō daigaku shuppankai.

Tōkyō daigaku Shiryō hensanjo. 1956a. *Kyūreki*. In *Dai Nihon kokiroku*. Tokyo: Iwanami shoten.

Tōkyō daigaku Shiryō hensanjo. 1956b. *Teishinkōki*. In *Dai Nihon kokiroku*. Tokyo: Iwanami shoten.

Yamada Munemutsu. 1992. *Nihon shoki*. 3 vols. Tokyo: Kyōikusha.

Yoneda Yūsuke and Yoshioka Masayuki, eds. 1974. *Rihōōki*. In *Shiryō sanshū*. Tokyo: Zokugunshoruijū kanseikai.

Secondary Sources

Abe Ryūichi. 1999. *The Weaving of Mantra*. New York: Columbia University Press.

Abe Takeshi. 1974. *Heian zenki seijishi no kenkyū*. Tokyo: Shinseisha.

Abe Takeshi et al. 2003. *Heian jidai gishiki nenjūgyōji jiten*. Tokyo: Tōkyōdō shuppan.

Adolphson, Mikael. 2007. "Institutional Diversity and Religious Integration: The Establishment of Temple Networks in the Heian Age," in *Heian Japan: Centers and Peripheries*, ed. M. Adolphson et al. Honolulu: University of Hawaii Press: 212-244.

Arakawa Reiko. 1996. *Shin sekkanke den*. Vol. 1- Tokyo: Zoku-gunshoruijū kanseikai.

Batten, Bruce. 1993. "Provincial Administration in Early Japan." *Harvard Journal of Asiatic Studies* 53 (1): 103-134.

Bock, Felicia. 1985. *Classical Learning and Taoist Practices in Early Japan: Books XVI and XX of the Engi Shiki*, Occasional Paper 17. Tucson: Center for Asian Studies, Arizona State University.

Bock, Felicia. 1972. *Engi Shiki*. 2 vols. Tokyo: Sophia University.

Bock, Felicia. 1990. "The Enthronement Rites." *Monumenta Nipponica* 45 (3): 307-337.

Borgen, Robert. 1986. *Sugawara no Michizane and the Early Heian Court*. Cambridge: Council on East Asian Studies, Harvard University.

Ceugniet, Atsuko. 2000. *L'Office des Etudes Supérieures au Japon du VIIIè au XIIè Siècle et les Dissertations de Fin d'Etudes*. Genève: Droz.

Duquenne, Robert. 1983. "Daigensui." *Hōbōgirin* 6: 610-40.

Endō Keita. 2000. "Shoku Nihon kōki to Jōwa no hen." *Kodai bunka* 52 (4): 238-246.

Farris, William Wayne. 1992. *Heavenly Warriors*. Cambridge: Harvard University Press.

Fowler, Sherry Diane. 2005. *Murōji: Rearranging Art and History at a Japanese Buddhist Temple*. Honolulu: University of Hawaii Press.

Frank, Bernard. 1998. *Kata-imi et Kata-tagae*. Paris: Collège de France, Institut des Hautes Études Japonaises.

Frédéric, Louis. 2002. *Japan Encyclopedia*. Cambridge: Harvard University Press.

Friday, Karl. 1992. *Hired Swords*. Palo Alto: Stanford University Press.

Friday, Karl. 2008. *The First Samurai*. Hoboken, NJ: John Wiley.

Furuse Natsuko. 1998. *Nihon kodai ōken to gishiki*. Tokyo: Yoshikawa kōbunkan.

Furuse Natsuko. 2001. "Sekkan seiji seiritsu no rekishiteki igi: sekkan seiji to bokō." *Nihonshi kenkyū* (463): 3-22.

Grapard, Allan G. 1992. *Protocol of the Gods: A Study of the Kasuga Cult in Japanese History*. Berkeley and Los Angeles: University of California Press.

Grapard, Allan G. 1999. "Religious Practices," in *Cambridge History of Japan, Vol. 2 Heian Japan*, ed. D. H. Shively and W. H. McCullough. Cambridge: Cambridge University Press:517-575.

Groner, Paul. 1984. *Saichō*. Berkeley: Center for South and Southeast Asian Studies, University of California.

Groner, Paul. 2002. *Ryōgen and Mount Hiei*. Honolulu: University of Hawaii Press.

Haruna Hiroaki. 1991. "Heianki daijōtennō no kō to shi." *Shigaku zasshi* 100 (3): 36-61.

Haruna Hiroaki. 1993. "In ni tsuite: Heianki tennō, daijōtennō no shijū zaisan keisei." *Nihon rekishi* (538): 1-18.

Hashimoto Yoshihiko. 1976. "Sekkan seiji ron," in *Heian kizoku shakai no kenkyū*. Tokyo: Yoshikawa kōbunkan: 85-97.

Hayakawa Shōhachi. 1984. "Kodai tennōsei to daijōkan seiji," in *Kōza Nihonshi*, ed. Rekishigaku kenkyūkai/Nihonshi kenkyūkai. Vol. 2. Tokyo: Tokyo daigaku shuppankai: 1-42.

Hayashiya Tatsusaburō, ed. 1968-1976. *Kyōto no rekishi*. 6 vols. Tokyo: Gakugei shorin.

Hérail, Francine. 1968. *Fonctions et Fonctionnaires Japonais au début du XIème siècle*. 2 vols. Paris: Publications Orientalistes de France.

Hérail, Francine. 1987-1991. *Notes Journalières de Fujiwara no Michinaga, Ministre á la Cour de Heian (995-1018)*. Genève: Droz.

Hérail, Francine. 1995. *La Cour du Japon á l'Epoque de Heian: aux Xe et XIe siècles*. Paris: Hachette.

Hérail, Francine. 2001-2004. *Les Notes Journalieres de Fujiwara no Sukefusa: Traduction du Shunki*. Genève: Droz.

Hérail, Francine. 2006. *La Cour et L'administration du Japon a l'époque de Heian*. Genève: Droz.

Hiraoka Jōkai. 1981-1988. *Nihon jiinshi no kenkyū*. 2 vols. Tokyo:

Yoshikawa kōbunkan.

Hotate Michihisa. 1996. *Heian ōchō*. Tokyo: Iwanami shinsho.

Hurst, G. Cameron. 1976. *Insei*. New York: Columbia University Press.

Ichikawa Hisashi. 1989. *Kurōdo bu'nin*. Tokyo: Zokugunshoruijū kanseikai.

Ichikawa Hisashi. 1996. *Eimonfu bu'nin*. Tokyo: Zokugunshoruijū kanseikai.

Ichikawa Hisashi. 1992-93. *Konoefu bu'nin*. 2 vols. Tokyo: Zokugunshoruijū kanseikai.

Ihara Kesao. 1995. "Sekkan, insei, to tennō," in *Nihon chūsei no kokusei to kasei*. Tokyo: Azekura shobō: 191-205.

Inoue Kōji. 2004. *Geki bunin*. Tokyo: Zokugunshoruijū kanseikai.

Ishii Yoshinaga. 2002. *Kūya Shōnin no kenkyū*. Tokyo: Hōsōkan.

Iikura Harutake. 1982-1983. *Benkan bu'nin*. 3 vols. Tokyo: Zokugunshoruijū kanseikai.

Iwano Masao. 1999. *Japanese-English Buddhist Dictionary*. Tokyo: Daitō shuppansha.

Iyanaga Teizō. 1962. "Ninna ni nen no naien," in *Nihon kodaishi ronshū*, ed. Sakamoto Tarō Hakushi kanreki kinenkai. Tokyo: Yoshikawa kōbunkan: 502-563.

Izumiya Yasuo. 1997. *Kōfukuji*. Tokyo: Yoshikawa kōbunkan.

Kakehi Toshio. 1991. "Kodai ōken to ritsuryō kokka kikō no saihen: kurōdodokoro seiritsu no igi to zentei." *Nihon rekishi* (344): 1-26.

Kamens, Edward. 1990. *The Buddhist Poetry of the Great Kamo Priestess: Daisai'in Senshi and Hosshin Wakashū*. Ann Arbor: Center for Japanese Studies, University of Michigan.

Kamiya Masaaki. 1991. "Shishinden to sechie." *Kodai bunka* (43): 23-33.

Kamiya Masaaki. 1996. "Heian jidai no sesshō to gishiki," in *Nihon kodai no kokka to saigi*, ed. Hayashi Rokurō. Tokyo: Yūzankaku: 118-139.

Kamiya Masaaki. 1998. "Daijin daikyo no seiritsu." *Nihon rekishi* (597): 1-16.

Katō Tomoyasu. 2002. *Sekkan seiji to ōchō bunka*. Tokyo: Yoshikawa kōbunkan.

Kawajiri Akio. 2000. "Nihon kodai ni okeru gi." *Shigaku zasshi* 110 (3): 1-38.

Kawakita Agaru. 1979. "Kyūreki kara mita Fujiwara Morosuke ron." *Kodai bunka* 31 (7): 443-455.

Kawane Yoshiyasu. 2003. "Ritsuryō kokka no henshitsu to bunka no tenkan," in *Tenjin shinkō no seiritsu*. Tokyo: Hanawa shobō: 55-90.

Kiley, Cornelius. 1999. "Provincial Administration and Land Tenure in Early Heian," in *Cambridge History of Japan*, ed. D. H. Shively and W. H. McCullough. Vol. 2. Cambridge: Cambridge University Press: 236-340.

Kimoto Masayasu. 2000. *Kodai no dōro jijō*. Tokyo: Yoshikawa kōbunkan.

Kimura Shigemitsu. 1993. "Fujiwara Tadahira seiken no seiritsu katei," in *Chūsei seiritsuki no rekishizō*, ed. Jisseiki kenkyūkai. Tokyo: Tōkyōdō: 125-161.

Kōda Toshio. 1976. *Nenjūgyōji misōjimon chūkai*. Tokyo: Gunshoruijū kanseikai.

Kodaigaku kyōkai. 1969. *Engi Tenryaku jidai no kenkyū*. Tokyo: Yoshikawa kōbunkan.

Kokuritsu rekishi minzoku hakubutsukan, ed. 1997. *Nihon shōen shiryō*. 3 vols. Tokyo: Yoshikawa kōbunkan.

Kon Masahide. 1994. "Ōchō kokka chūō kikō no kōzō to tokushitsu: daijōkan to kurōdodokoro." *Hisutoria* (145):148-175.

Kon Masahide. 1997. "Sesshōsei seiritsu kō." *Shigaku zasshi* 160 (1): 42-63.

Kuramoto Kazuhiro. 2000. *Sekkan seiji to ōchō kizoku*. Tokyo: Yoshikawa kōbunkan.

LaFleur, William R. 1983. *The Karma of Words: Buddhism and the Literary Arts in Medieval Japan*. Berkeley: University of California Press.

Masuo Shin'ichirō. 1997. *Manyō kajin to Chūgoku shisō*. Tokyo: Yoshikawa kōbunkan.

Matsubara Hironobu. 1999. *Fujiwara no Sumitomo*. Tokyo: Yoshikawa kōbunkan.

McCullough, William and Helen McCullough. 1980. *Tales of Flowering Fortunes*. 2 vols. Stanford: Stanford University Press.

McMullin, Neil. 1989. "The Lotus Sutra and Politics in the Mid-Heian Period. " In *The Lotus Sutra in Japanese Culture*, ed. George and Willa Tanabe. Honolulu: University of Hawaii Press: 119-142.

Mezaki Tokue. 1969. "Uda Jōō no in to kokusei," in *Engi tenryaku jidai no kenkyū*, ed. Kodaigaku kyōkai. Tokyo: Yoshikawa kōbunkan: 89-122.

Mikawa Kei. 1994. "Heian jidai no seimu to sono henshitsu." *Kodai bunka* 46 (1): 26-36.

Miyazaki Yasumitsu. 1998-2006. *Kebiishi bu'nin*. 3 vols. Tokyo: Zokugunshoruijū kanseikai.

Miyazaki Yasumitsu. 1989-1999. *Kokushi bu'nin*. 6 vols. Tokyo: Zokugunshoruijū kanseikai.

Morita Tei. 1978. *Zuryō*. Tokyo: Kyōikusha.

Morita Tei. 2006. "Toward Regency Leadership at Court," in *Capital and Countryside in Japan, 300-1180: Japanese Historians Interpreted in English*, ed. Joan R. Piggott. Ithaca: Cornell East Asia Series: 209-226.

Mostow, Joshua S. 2004. *At the House of Gathered Leaves: Shorter Biographical and Autobiographical Narratives from Japanese Court Literature*. Honolulu: University of Hawaii Press.

Murai Shōsuke. 1995. "Ōdo ōmin shisō to kyūseiki no tenkan." *Shisō* (847): 23-45.

Murai Yasuhiko. 1995. *Yomigaeru Heiankyō*. Kyoto: Tankōsha.

Nagai Susumu. 1998. *Kanshi bu'nin*. Tokyo: Zokugunshoruijū kanseikai.

Nakamura Hajime. 1981. *Bukkyōgo daijiten*. Tokyo: Tōkyō shoseki.

Nakamura Hajime. 1989. *Iwanami bukkyō jiten*. Tokyo: Iwanami shoten.

Nitō Atsushi. 1990. "Kodai ni okeru ōken to kokka." *Rekishigaku kenkyū* (613): 33-44.

Nitō Atsushi. 1996. "Daijōtennōsei no tenkai." *Rekishigaku kenkyū* (681): 2-15.

Obinata Katsumi. 1993. "Jarai, noriyumi, yuba hajime," in *Kodai kokka to nenjūgyōji*. Tokyo: Yoshikawa kōbunkan: 7-39.

Obinata Katsumi. 1993a. "Gogatsu itsuka no sechi," in *Kodai kokka to nenjūgyōji*. Tokyo: Yoshikawa kōbunkan: 40-90.

Okada Shōji. 2004. "Uda-chō saishisei no seiritsu," in *Heian jidai no kokka to saishi*. Tokyo: Zokugunshoruijū kanseikai: 169-186.

Okamura Sachiko. 1993. "Onna joi ni kansuru kisoteki kōsatsu." *Nihon rekishi* (541): 20-34.

Okamura Sachiko. 1996. "Shikinomizōshi." *Nihon rekishi* (582): 1-17.

Okamura Sachiko. 1999. "Kansō no keifu." *Shigaku zasshi* 108 (12): 37-57.

Okamura Sachiko. 2003. "Heian zen, chūki ni okeru goin: tennō no shiyū, ruidai shizai ni kansuru ichi kōsatsu." *Shigaku zasshi* 112 (1): 37-59.

Ōsumi Kiyoharu. 1991. "Benkan no henshitsu to ritsuryō daijōkansei." *Shigaku zasshi* 100 (11): 1-42.

Ōtsu Tōru. 1996. "Sekkanki no kokka kōzō." *Kodai bunka* 48 (2): 36-45.

Piggott, Joan. 2003. "The Last Classical Female Sovereign: Kōken-Shōtoku," in *Women & Confucian Cultures in Premodern China, Korea and Japan* ed. Dorothy Ko, Ja-Hyun Haboush, and Joan Piggott. Berkeley & Los Angeles: University of California Press: 47-74.

Piggott, Joan R. 1997. *The Emergence of Japanese Kingship*. Stanford: Stanford University Press.

Piggott, Joan R. 2006. *Capital and Countryside in Japan, 300-1180.* Ithaca, New York: Cornell East Asian Series.

Piggott, Joan R. et al. 2006. *Dictionary of Sources of Classical Japan.* Paris: College de France.

Piggott, Joan R. 2007. "Court and Provinces under Regent Fujiwara no Tadahira," in *Heian Japan: Centers and Peripheries,* ed. M. Adolphson et al. Honolulu: University of Hawaii Press: 35-66.

Rabinovitch, Judith. 1986. *Shōmonki: The Story of Masakado's Rebellion.* Tokyo: Sophia University (Monumenta Nipponica).

Reischauer, Edwin O. 1955. *Ennin's Diary: The Record of a Pilgrimage to China in Search of the Law.* New York: Ronald Press Company.

Sasaki Muneo. 1999. "Sesshōsei, kanpakusei no seiritsu." *Nihon rekishi* (610): 1-18.

Sasaki Muneo. 2005. "The Court-centered Polity," in *Capital and Countryside in Japan, 300-1180,* ed. J. R. Piggott. Ithaca: Cornell East Asia Series: 227-44.

Satō Sōjun. 1977. "Fujiwara Tadahira seiken no keisei: Engi jūyonen shinsei wo chūshin ni," in *Heian zenki seijishi josetsu.* Tokyo: Tōkyō daigaku shuppankai: 295-319.

Shively, Donald H. and William H. McCullough, eds. 1999. *Cambridge History of Japan: Vol. 2, Heian.* Cambridge, England: Cambridge University Press.

Stevenson, Daniel B. 1986. "The Four Kinds of Samadhi in Early T'ien-t'ai Buddhism," in *Traditions of Meditation in Chinese Buddhism,* ed. P. N. Gregory. Honolulu: University of Hawaii Press: 45-97.

Takatori Masao. 1970. "Shidara no kami no jōkyō," in *Kyōto no rekishi,* ed. Hayashi Tatsusaburō. Vol. 1. Tokyo: Gakugei shorin: 419-424.

Takeuchi Rizō. 1954. "Sesshō, kanpaku." *Nihon rekishi* (69). Republished in *Takeuchi Rizō chosakushū.* 8 vols. Vol. 5. Tokyo: Kadokawa shoten: 76-88.

Takinami Sadako. 1982. "Nara jidai no jōō to kōin." *Shisō* (39): 56-71.

Takinami Sadako. 1986. "Sangiron no saikentō: kizoku gōgisei no seiritsu katei." *Shirin* (69): 43-81.

Takinami Sadako. 2000. "Ako no fungi." *Shisō* 58: 37-51.

Tamai Chikara. 1973. "Seiritsuki kurōdodokoro no seikaku ni tsuite: buninsha no kentō wo chūshin toshite." *Nagoya daigaku bungakubu kenkyū ronshū: shigaku* 59: 116-132.

Tamai Chikara. 2000. "Jū, Jūisseiki no Nihon, sekkan seiji," in *Heian jidai no kizoku to tennō.* Tokyo: Iwanami shoten: 3-70.

Tanabe, Willa Jane. 1984. "The Lotus Lectures: Hokke Hakkō in the Heian Period. " *Monumenta Nipponica* 39 (4): 393-408.

Tanabe, Willa Jane. 1988. *Paintings of the Lotus Sutra.* New York and Tokyo: Weatherhill.

Tokoro Isao. 1984. "Nenjūgyōji hisshō no seiritsu." *Nihon rekishi* (437): 1-20.

Tokoro Isao. 2002. *Sugawara Michizane no jitsuzō.* Kyoto: Rinsen shoten.

Tsuchida Naoshige. 1992a. "Sekkan seiji ni kansuru ni, san no gimon," in *Nara heian jidaishi kenkyū.* Tokyo: Yoshikawa kōbunkan: 297-332.

Tsuchida Naoshige. 1992b. "Shōkei ni tsuite," in *Nara heian jidaishi kenkyū.* Tokyo: Yoshikawa kōbunkan: 264-275.

Tsugei Yukio. 2001. "Sekkanki ni okeru kanji to shinkajō." *Kodai bunka* 53 (6): 1-16.

Tsunoda Bun'ei. 1969. "Taikōtaigō Yasuko," in *Murasaki Shikibu to sono jidai.* Tokyo: Kadokawa shoten: 295-377.

Tsunoda Bun'ei. 1984. "Higashi gojōtei," in *Ōchō bunka no shōsō (Chōsakushū 4).* Tokyo: Tōkyōdō: 185-187.

Tsunoda Bun'ei. 1994. *Heian jidaishi jiten.* 3 vols. Tokyo: Kadokawa shoten.

Tsunoda Bun'ei and Kodaigaku kyōkai/Kodaigaku kenkyūjo. 1994. *Heiankyō teiyō.* Tokyo: Kadokawa shoten.

Uraki Ziro trans. 1984. *Tale of the Cavern, Utsuho monogatari.* Tokyo: Shinozaki shorin.

Ury, Marian. 1999. "Chinese Learning and Intellectual life," in *Cambridge History of Japan: Heian.* Vol. 2. Cambridge: Cambridge University Press: 341-389.

von Verschuer, Charlotte. 2007. "Life of Commoners in the Provinces, The Owari no gebumi of 988," in *Heian Japan, Centers and Peripheries,* ed. Mikael Adolphson et al. Honolulu: University of Hawaii Press: 305-328.

Wetzler, Peter. 1977. "Yoshishige no Yasutane: Lineage, Learning, Office and Amida's Pure Land. " Ph.D. Diss. University of California at Berkeley.

Yamada Mitsuaki. 1996. "Kebiishi seiritsuki zengo no kyōchū keibi no jittai." *Nihonshi kenkyū* (406): 30-46.

Yamagiwa, Joseph K. 1966. *Ōkagami: A Japanese Historical Tale.* Rutland, Vermont and Tokyo, Japan: Charles E. Tuttle Company.

Yamaguchi Hideo. 1995a. "Bunken kara mita kodai bokuba no shiiku keitai." *Yamanashi kenshi kenkyū* (2): 27-48.

Yamaguchi Hideo. 1995b. "Heian jidai no kokuga to zaichi seiryoku: kyū, jū seiki no kokuga, kokufu." *Kokushigaku shinpojiumu: kodai Tōgoku no kokufu to keikan* (156): 91-102.

Yamashita Katsuaki. 1984. "Teishinkōki to reki ni tsuite." *Kodai bunkashi ronkō* (5): 19-25.

Yoneda Yūsuke. 2002. *Fujiwara sekkanke no tanjō*. Tokyo: Yoshikawa kōbunkan.

Yoshida Takashi. 1998. "Nara jidai no kekkon," in *Kekkon to josei (Nihon joseishi ronshū 4)*. Tokyo: Yoshikawa kōbunkan: 63-67.

Yoshida Takashi et al. 1995. "Kyū-jūseiki no Nihon: Heiankyō," in *Iwanami kōza: Nihon tsūshi, Kodai 4*. Tokyo: Iwanami shoten: 1-73.

Yoshikawa Shinji. 1988. "Ritsuryō daijōkansei to gōgisei." *Nihonshi kenkyū* (309): 27-42.

Yoshikawa Shinji. 1989. "Ritsuryō kanjinsei no saihen." *Nihonshi kenkyū* (320): 1-27.

Yoshikawa Shinji. 1990. "Ritsuryō kokka no nyokan, " in *Nihon josei seikatsushi*, ed. Josei sōgō kenkyūkai. Vol. 1. Tokyo: Tōkyō daigaku shuppankai: 105-142.

Yoshikawa Shinji. 1995. "Tennōke to Fujiwarake," in *Iwanami Nihon tsūshi*. Vol. 5. Tokyo: Iwanami shoten: 75-114.

Yoshikawa Shinji. 1998. "Sekkan seiji no tensei," in *Ritsuryō kanryōsei no kenkyū*. Tokyo: Hanawa shobō: 401-426.

Yoshioka Masayuki. 1993. "Heian jidai no seimu wo megutte," in *Shinshiten Nihon rekishi 3: Kodai*, ed. Yoshimura Takehiko. Tokyo: Shinjinbutsu ōraisha: 96–103.

CORNELL EAST ASIA SERIES

CORNELL
East Asia Series

Order online at www.einaudi.cornell.edu/eastasia/publications or contact Cornell University Press Services, P. O. Box 6525, 750 Cascadilla Street, Ithaca, NY 14851, USA. Tel toll-free: 1-800-666-2211 (USA or Canada), 1-607-277-2211 (International); Fax: 1-800-688-2877 (USA or Canada), 1-607-277-6292 (International); E-mail orders: orderbook@cupserv.org.